UP STICKS
by Tim Thomas

Copyright © 2016 Tim Thomas

ISBN - 13: 978-1540480620
ISBN - 10: 1540480623

My thanks go to Ali and Graham who encouraged (nagged) me to put pen to paper in the first place.
Also to celebrated author Holly Davis who helped me out with all the tricky stuff at the end.

Dedicated to all you would-be travellers out there. Go on, do it, go and have some fun, have some adventures, create some memories – you may regret it if you don't. Only maybe do it with a bit more forethought and planning than we did!

Contents

PREFACE

Home for us now, is a remote hilltop smallholding set in the foothills of the Cambrian Mountains in Mid Wales. This we share with several Arabian horses, rescue dogs and chickens and a cat called Arthur who makes his home in the hay barn.

We're off grid and so make our own electricity through a combination of a home built wind turbine, a small bank of solar panels and a back up diesel generator. We have our own beautiful mountain spring water, grow most of our own organic vegetables and have no television.

In the winter sometimes if we're lucky enough, we can be snowed in here for weeks on end, snug as bugs in rugs keeping warm around our two log burning stoves.

Needless to say, we don't like to leave our hilltop very often.

As we sit here in our rustic sunroom enjoying fresh coffee with home made scones, gazing out across the terrace and watching the horses idly grazing in the field below, the memories come flooding back to us.

We often remark on the similarities between this wonderful landscape and the ones we loved and explored as we travelled around Western Europe on our epic eight year road trip.

And so the inspiration for penning this account comes from living in this beautiful and tranquil setting in the now.

The tales however, come from back then, from our own very real life experiences which began after we sold our first home and all our belongings, together with our business and hit the road in a camper with our two lovely dogs.

We had no great plan other than to just follow the sun.

Leaving Wales

The year was 1988 and home for us back then was a tiny Welsh cottage nestled deep at the bottom of a valley next to an old stone bridge with a rushing stream beneath.

We lived in the end cottage of three, with joint access to the rear and common land next to the house where we parked our car. There was also access to a field literally right past our back door. A far from ideal arrangement but luckily, the other two cottages were holiday homes and so there was very rarely anyone there which made the whole set up bearable, for most of the year at least.

It was a steep sided valley and in the very depths of winter when the days were at their shortest, the sun didn't reach us at all and we would remain under a blanket of frost, sometimes for weeks on end. This was, for sun worshippers like ourselves quite frustrating and we longed for some warm sunshine.

We lived there with our two dogs, both boys, a black and white collie with a black patch on one eye called Nelson, no not Patch, and Caine, a black and tan collie cross retriever.

Nelson was intelligent and very grown up and no, he would not lower himself to chase after a stick and bring it back, what a ridiculous idea. He was quite happy though to tear around after Caine as *he* chased a ball or stick.

Caine on the other hand was game for anything and his life was dedicated to having fun and causing as much mischief as he could get away with.

We grew our own organic vegetables in the small garden which we'd painstakingly brought back to life after 30 years of total neglect and we planted a lovely rose hedge all around it.

We dug out a small pool fed by the stream with a slate bridge across it. I built stone steps leading down to the water so we could dangle our feet in and the dogs, well Caine anyway, could splash about in it on warm summer days.

Nelson did not go in water.

We lived there simply and happily for about 8 years and had built up a good window cleaning round in the local area which we worked together on every day, Suzi doing the bottom windows while I did the top ones.

The dogs always came with us every day so whenever we could, we would stop working to walk them on the beach or by a river, and having hedonistic tendencies we didn`t need much of an excuse to down tools and wander off somewhere.

We always said, half jokingly really, that if either of the neighbouring cottages went up for sale then we`d just have to sell up and move or go travelling as we couldn`t bear the idea of having neighbours that close to us. We didn't really want to move though; we were very happy living there and couldn't have afforded it anyway.

Suzi had always had a longing to travel but we had the dogs and you couldn`t take them abroad back then. Well you could take them out of course but you couldn`t bring them back in again without putting them through 6 months of quarantine.

This to us was unthinkable, so naturally we never went abroad, not even for a short time as we didn`t want to leave them. We wouldn`t have enjoyed a holiday much without 'the boys' anyway.

Then suddenly one day a 'For Sale' sign appeared in the front garden of the cottage next door, our hearts sank - now what.

We looked at each other in dismay – we were going to need time to give this some serious thought.

I reached for the kettle and as we stood outside shivering in the rain looking at the house and drinking tea, our future was decided.

We would sell up and go travelling, we didn't mind where, just as long as the sun was shining and the air was warm. We finished our tea, got straight into the car and went down to our local estate agent to put the cottage on the market.

We both agreed that if it sold it was fate, we were meant to go travelling, if not, well…. we would just have to wait and see.

As it turned out we didn't have to wait too long, we sold the cottage within 3 days for the full asking price, it was written in the stars, we were meant to do this. Not being able to come back with the dogs wasn't really an issue for us, we were going to follow the sun, work when we needed some money, explore, have adventures, swim naked in the Mediterranean, we just couldn't wait.

We quickly found a buyer for the window cleaning round, sold the car for a profit and gave all our furniture away. The remnants of our lives up until then fitted into three cardboard boxes which were stashed in the loft space of one of the outbuildings at my parent's farm.

We stayed there for the next few weeks as we searched for a camper, eventually settling for a VW with a lift up roof which we adapted to our liking and for full time living. Everyone thought we were mad for even contemplating such a hair brained scheme.

'You can't just up sticks like this, what happens if you don't like it?'

'You won't be able to come back while the dogs are still alive you know.'

'You can't all live in that thing.'

'What happens if you get ill?'

'What are you going to do when the money runs out, and it will you know!'

All this negativity was casually brushed aside as we busied ourselves with all the preparations, jumping through several hoops of red tape regarding the boys going abroad. This included rabies jabs, export certificate from the Animal Health Department and medicals 48 hours before departure. Ferry tickets booked, passports applied for, insurance and green card sorted and toilet made - oh yes I made us a toilet.

The regular camping type Porta potti wouldn`t fit in any of the cupboards so I took a 20 litre plastic jerry can, cut a hole in the top sort of toilet seat shaped, cut the top off another similar container which when pushed down over the other one acted as a lid. Unfortunately it wasn't completely water tight, or odour tight as we discovered some time later. It was functional though and it fitted nicely into one of our cupboards under the tiny round sink.

I fitted a new exhaust system which turned out to be a really awkward, fiddly job and which took a lot longer to fit than it should have. I was lying underneath struggling away with it and feeling everywhere for the hammer which I'd just been using but couldn't find it, so cursing, I dragged myself out from underneath to search for it but couldn't see it anywhere.

Just then I heard the dogs barking away at something down the field so I went off to investigate.

Caine was worrying at something on the ground, growling and chuntering and raking at it with his front paws, Nelson was running around him in circles barking his head off in delight. I had a feeling I knew what he'd got and went over to see what it was and yes, as I suspected, he had my hammer.

Nelson was quietly slinking away into the long grass as I approached as he knew Caine had done something wrong.

'I should have known, thanks Caine, that's very helpful.' I said in what I hoped was a stern voice, trying not to smile as he backed off and sat down.

He then did what he normally did when he thought he was in trouble (which was quite often). He sat up on his haunches and smiled ingratiatingly at me with his teeth rattling loudly, his paws either side of his face. It was really hard not to laugh when he did that, I picked up the hammer and showed it to him saying.

'This is not yours, it's not a toy for you to play with, we've been through this before haven't we, how many times.'

He carried on smiling and rattling his teeth only now his head was drooping down but his eyes were still looking up at me apologetically, very, very apologetically and I just caved in and laughed.

Instantly relieved and way beyond happy he went totally ballistic, running around me in circles barking ecstatically with his arse tucked in underneath him as Nelson suddenly broke cover and joined in the celebrations.

Despite several such interludes I was slowly getting through the jobs.

I fitted new brake shoes and wiper blades, two new tyres and got it MOT'd.

We also bought a small but very expensive air conditioning unit to go in the roof to help keep the boys cool which had it's own water supply and battery.

I added some shelves here and there and then every inch of space was filled with clothes, books, cooking utensils, a full set of enamel tinware, bedding etc. We bought two reclining sun chairs and a roll up table, which took up quite a bit of space, and also an awning to go on the side which just about fitted under the back seats.

The food cupboards were chocka too thanks to Suzi`s mum who seemed to think that perhaps they didn`t sell food abroad, I'd lost count of the number of tins of baked beans and boxes of tea bags I'd stowed away in various places. It was jam packed full by the time we'd finished and was well down on the springs thanks to all the extra weight.

The camper was orange and white and I painted a big smiley face on the front of it. It was a simple design, but it looked pretty good considering it was done freehand and with a brush. It made people smile whenever they saw it which was nice, well apart from my dad that is who was totally disgusted and stood there tut tutting and shaking his head disapprovingly the whole time I was doing it.

The number plate started with BLY so naturally we named it Billy. My dad thought this was a ridiculous name and that it should be called Captain Bligh.

'That`s a really naff name.' said Suze.

'Well you can't call it Billy, that`s just silly.' he replied.

'Billy`s not a silly name, it suits his happy face, Captain Bligh's silly.'

'Not as silly as Billy.'

'We`re not calling him Captain Bligh, he`s called Billy and that's that.'

'Bloody silly name if you ask me, and take that ridiculous face off the front before it dries or you'll never get it off without ruining the paintwork.'

'Dad, go away.' I said without looking up, and to be fair he did.

And so Billy was born, he looked happy and relaxed and ready for a great adventure - as were we.

It was a few weeks later, with engine fully fettled, fuel tank fully filled and tearful farewells fulfilled, that we headed for Dorset and Poole harbour for our crossing to Cherbourg. It took me a little while to get used to Billy's gearbox with it's strange long gearstick, and also the lack of any bonnet in front made us both feel a little vulnerable to begin with, but we soon got used to it.

It felt good though, to finally be on the road and heading for the great unknown as apart from one brief holiday each, neither of us had been abroad much. I'd certainly never driven on the right before which was something I was really looking forward to doing. We were booked on the midnight crossing and set off in good time so that we didn't have to rush. Better to be a couple of hours early than to risk missing the ferry.

Anyway it didn't really matter how long we had to wait there as essentially we were always 'at home' wherever we happened to be. If we were hungry we could cook ourselves some food, if we needed the toilet, it was right there in the cupboard. Tired? No problem, just pull the bed down and have a snooze. No need to hunt for a service station either, if we needed a cup of tea we could just pull over and put the kettle on, it was a great way to travel.

Trouble was looming though as a couple of hours into the journey Billy started coughing and spluttering and losing power. We shared an alarmed look - this we didn't need. He kept on going for a while but then as we were waiting at some traffic lights he conked out all together and simply refused to start again.

'Oh come on Billy please don't do this to us, not here, not now,' I groaned, 'there's a queue of traffic behind us and we've got a ferry to catch.'

'What's wrong with him?'

'No idea,' I mumbled in reply as I put the hazard lights on and tried again to start him without success.

I jumped out and went round to the back to where Billy kept his engine and had a quick look around for anything obvious that was wrong but it all looked ok to me. I waved the cars on that were impatiently waiting behind us and went back to Suzi.

'Tell you what, you steer and I'll push, there's a bit of a grass verge just up there, head for that.'

Billy was really heavy to push fully laden all by myself and it was slightly uphill as well, but bit by bit and with several stops to regain my breath we finally made the verge - well sort of anyway.

'That was nice of all those people walking by to come and help you wasn't it,' she said with just a hint of sarcasm.

'Huh! didn't need their help anyway,' I replied, puffing my chest out proudly when I'd recovered a bit.

'Aww, my hero,' she crooned and gave me a cuddle which made me feel much better, 'what now though?' she added.

'What now though? I'll tell you what now though, we'll do what all level headed right thinking people would do in such a crisis,' I said.

We looked at each other, smiled and as one we said.

'Put the kettle on!!'

And so it was, half pulled off the road, traffic thundering past the windows and with Billy leaning at a jaunty angle that I put the kettle on. It was a little tricky though making tea at that angle and with the roof down, I couldn't stand up straight and the kettle kept sliding off the cooker so I had to hold it in place until it boiled. I made the tea on the floor as the cups didn't slide about on the carpet and we enjoyed our first real 'on the road' brew in our lovely new tin mugs as we contemplated our next move.

'We'd be in big trouble if the police came along now, wouldn't we,' said Suzi from her place between the boys on the back seat.

'Not really,' I replied flippantly, perched on a box full of baked beans, 'we've got plenty of tea bags to go around.'

'Very funny,' she said almost choking on her tea, 'I meant it wouldn't look very good would it with us parked here like this, causing an obstruction and casually drinking tea.'

We both laughed, ok it wasn't an ideal start we agreed, but at least we were all together and we had everything we needed to survive - plenty of food and water, a bed to sleep in and our own toilet, what more could we need.

'Well a working Billy would be useful,' Suzi suggested.

'Hmm, I'll give him another try,' I said as I clambered into the driving seat and turned the key.

Billy roared into life like nothing had happened, we both cheered and clapped and I patted him on his dashboard saying.

'Yay! well done Billy, welcome back matey, feeling better now?'

'Aww maybe he just needed a break bless him, he has had a stressful few weeks after all,' said Suzi as she quickly stashed things away again.

I pulled back into the traffic and we continued on our journey, singing 'Back on the road again.'

♫ ♫ ♫ ♫ ♫

We made Poole harbour a few hours later without further incident and followed the signs to what we hoped was the right place to wait for the ferry. We were really early and the only ones there so I got out and walked about a bit to stretch my legs. I eventually came across an official looking person who confirmed that we were in the right place for our ferry so I returned to Billy, Nelson was in my seat as usual and he hopped in the back when he saw me coming. We had a couple of hours to kill so we had a bite to eat and tried unsuccessfully to get some sleep, the butterflies would not be stilled, we were just too excited.

Having our own toilet was proving invaluable at this time and not surprisingly it was filling up quite quickly. However, using it in such cramped conditions was taking a bit of getting used to. There was only about two square feet of available floor space and the toilet took up almost half of that. The lid, which was usually dripping with something unmentionable, had to be put down somewhere and took up most of the remaining space. Then with one foot on the floor and the other up on one of the many boxes of baked beans, it required some skill to get your bum in exactly the right place over the too small hole I'd made in the top of the worryingly tall and wobbly jerry can toilet. Also, because of the intimate surroundings it was, aromatically speaking quite a heady pastime and was performed as quickly as possible so we could get the doors open again.

Nelson did not approve of any of this and made his feelings known by jumping in the front, turning his back on us and staring out of the window until it was all over.

Gradually the place filled up with several rows of cars and campers and eventually we were moving towards the ferry. We were soon stopped by a stern looking official who looked at Billy's face without a change of expression as we approached him, that's not a good sign I thought.

'He looks happy,' chirped Suzi.

'Don't start,' said I as I wound down my window, I could hear Nelson grumbling quietly in the back, he obviously didn't like the look of him either and I turned to him, 'and you, shh.'

'Passports,' demanded the grumpy face at the window, I somehow resisted the temptation to say 'passports please' and handed them to him. He flicked through them quickly, clearly disappointed to find there was nothing inside them and as he handed them back he spotted the boys on the back seat.

'I hope you're not thinking of bringing those animals back into this country,' he said as he leant in through the window.

This was clearly too much of an intrusion for Nelson and he let rip. With fangs bared and breathing fire he leapt up onto the sink and stuck his head through the gap by my headrest, spitting and snarling right in the guys face. He stepped back quickly, ooh now there's some expression on his face I thought to myself happily. Caine had also joined in the chorus now and was giving his all from the space between our seats with his front feet on my legs. I had an angry dog in each ear and it felt really good to say.

'We're not coming back mate.'

'I'm not your mate, drive on,' he said through the din as he turned away.

'Tosser!' from the passenger seat.

He turned back and started to say something but thought better of approaching the window again and I drove off quickly leaving him standing there open mouthed and indignant. With my ears ringing I said.

'Susan will you behave yourself please!' we'd agreed not to draw attention to ourselves as we didn't want any complications getting the boys through customs which could get them impounded or something, 'can you just do as you're told for once in your life!' I added jokingly.

She threw her head back and laughed contemptuously at this ridiculous suggestion, then she looked round at the boys who had now regained their seats and were watching the man intently through the rear window.

'You should have told *them* that then shouldn't you hah hah, good boys' she said smiling, obviously pleased at the outcome,

'Miserable git, there`s no need to talk to them like that is there - "those animals" indeed!'

'I don't think they liked him very much did they.' I said, also pleased with their performance as well as their impeccable taste, 'ok then which way do we go?'

We were the first vehicle in the queue and I needed to concentrate on where I was going. I could just imagine me going the wrong way and having a long stream of cars following me onto a ferry bound for Norway or somewhere and causing utter chaos in the place.

There were official looking people scattered here and there, some of them were pointing in the direction they wanted me to go and others were just standing there staring at us blankly. I went in what I hoped was the right direction, waiting for some frantic arm waving or angry shouting, but it seemed I was doing ok as soon the ferry loomed into view and we could see the big open doors of the car deck.

We rattled up the ramp with our hearts in our mouths and entered the dark gloomy bowels of the ship; I suddenly realized I was shivering as I followed the waved instructions of the deckhands who were guiding us to our parking spot.

We sat quietly in the back, waiting until all the cars were on board as we planned to stay in Billy with the boys during the crossing. We'd received strict instructions about them, they weren`t allowed out of the vehicle at any time and we absolutely weren't allowed to stay in the vehicle in case of emergency.

'Should we ask someone if this is the right ferry d'you think?' asked Suzi.

'Why, does it matter?' I replied nonchalantly and she laughed saying.

'No not really, it doesn't really matter where we end up does it.'

We were enjoying this thought when suddenly there was a loud knock on the window which made us both jump and set the boys off again.

'Leave the vehicle now please,' called some official type person, 'you can`t stay down here once we are under way,' and he walked on, checking all the vehicles as he went.

We looked at each other and Suzi voiced what we were both thinking.

'Well we're not leaving them down here to drown on their own that's for sure; if the ferry's going to sink then at least we'll all go down together.'

'It's ok he's gone now and anyway it's not going to sink and nobody's going to drown.'

We were both quietly singing "we will all go down together" from Goodnight Saigon by Billy Joel as we closed all the curtains and waited for it to go quiet, suddenly noticing how cold it was. I was still shivering, though it wasn't just from the cold, it was more a mixture of nervous excitement and anticipation, with perhaps a dash of fear thrown in for good measure. That and not getting enough sleep of course as it was now midnight and way past my bed time.

Eventually we felt the ferry moving and as no one had come back to double check on us we relaxed in the darkness, put the kettle on, had something to eat and then tried to sleep.

We slept surprisingly well and were woken just before 5 a.m. by people coming back down to their cars. We were both really cold and aching all over from having slept curled up on the back seats. We quickly cleared everything away and clambered through into the front seats which were lovely and warm since the boys had slept in them.

I breathed a huge sigh of relief as Billy started first time and I patted him gently on his dashboard. Suzi put the heater on full blast which as it turned out was a total waste of time as it just blew cold air at us.

The huge bow doors started to open and the daylight flooded in, this was it - once we were off the ferry there was no going back.

Actually the point of no return had passed a long time ago when we had first announced our plans to our families but this felt more real somehow, more final.

We were bleary eyed but also buzzing with excitement as we drove out of the dark, frigid air of the car deck and out into the pale early morning sun. Suzi was clutching our passports in readiness as we rattled our way down the ramp and onto French soil, well French concrete actually, for the very first time, looking ahead for the customs officials who were going to ruin everything.

Well, we drove away from the ferry without seeing a soul, there were no officials anywhere to be seen, no orderly queue of traffic either, all the cars just fanned out, all heading in different directions and just disappeared, it was crazy.

We suddenly realized we were all by ourselves in the middle of a vast expanse of concrete and not having a clue how to get out; I brought Billy to a halt saying,

'Where have they all gone, did you see where they went?'

'No, they've all just disappeared,' replied Suzi, looking all around.

'Well where the hell are the exits then and how come everyone else found them? oh well this is a great start isn't it,' I groaned, 'how are we going to find our way around Europe when we can't even find our way out of a bloody ferry terminal?'

'Is that one over there?' said Suzi pointing towards what looked like the perimeter fence.

'Well let's find out shall we,' and we headed off. There was an exit gate there but it was locked so I followed the fence and eventually we came to another one which was also locked and so cursing, I pressed on. We followed the fence for so long we were very nearly back at the ferry by the time we found the way out, Suzi sighed and said.

'We must have gone straight past it as soon as we got off the ferry, how come neither of us saw it?'

'No idea, it's pretty obvious really though isn't it,' I said pointing to a massive blue sign with 'Sortie' on it, above the really wide exit gate with large personnel booths either side of it, 'and anyway if it's an exit gate, why the hell don't they put 'Exit' above it?' I added.

'Because we're in France now you plonker and Sortie is probably the French word for exit.'

'Ah yes, you could be right there.'

We both laughed and cheered as we approached it.

'Let's not celebrate too soon though, we're not out of here yet,' I said.

We fell silent as we drove up to the booths but we needn't have worried - there was no-one there. We just went straight through without stopping and before we knew it we were free again, out onto the road and heading for…. well we didn`t know where we were headed, apart from South, that was the exciting part of it.

Up Sticks

France

I drove slowly and carefully through the deserted streets of Cherbourg, partly because I was now driving on the wrong side of the road, and partly because we were busy looking at all the road signs which we didn't understand.

'Which road do we want?' I enquired of my co-driver.

'Erm, well I don't really know, how about this one here.' she said as she pointed to a spot in the atlas she was reading.

'Well I can`t see that from here now can I,' I said as I threw her a glance. 'what`s the road number, there are some more signs coming up.'

'Don't know, where *is* the number?' she replied.

'It`ll be on there somewhere, just look a bit further down, quick we're nearly on the signs.' I'd slowed right down to give her time, good job there was no traffic about that early.

'Oh hang on I've got it, well it could be either the..'

'Too late, there go the signs.'

'Ok what`s the name of the next town then?' she asked.

'How should I know, you're the one with the map, oh never mind just pick on a road that leads South, that would be downwards on the map my darling,' I ventured bravely, 'and I reckon you can probably put those passports away now.' I added as I noticed she was still holding them.

'I know which way South is thank you very much smartarse.' came the reply.

'Look there`s a sign for Martinvest, that sounds interesting let`s head for that.' I said as I swung sharply across two lanes and took a left.

Instinctively I went on what was now the wrong side but up until fairly recently had been the correct side of an island at the junction. This placed us nicely on the wrong side of the road going against the flow of traffic, if there had been any that is. I really hoped there wouldn't be any as well because now there was a raised section in the middle of the road and so for the next two or three hundred yards, or should that now be metres, we were stuck on the wrong side of the road.

I was frantically looking around for signs of that John Darmes fellow we'd been warned about, when thankfully the middle bit ended and I swerved back to the other side. We both heaved a huge sigh of relief, laughed, and started breathing again as we must have been subconsciously holding our breaths the whole time.

'Phew, please don't do *that* again Tim.' uttered my co driver - well at least that was the gist of what she said anyway!

'Well that was fun wasn't it,' I said not really meaning it, 'you really can put those passports away now you know.'

At this point however, the thought did cross my mind that a certain someone could have practiced her map reading in the weeks before we left. Fortunately for me though and given my most recent misdemeanour the thought died before it reached my lips. I just smirked quietly to myself instead.

We somehow managed to get out of Cherbourg in one piece and headed south in a bit of a daze and in total awe at our new and unfamiliar surroundings.

There was a bewildering mixture of emotions welling up inside us with the enormity of what we were doing just beginning to sink in. There was a really strong, positive sense of freedom and liberation slamming up against a negative wall of entrapment which was the knowledge of not being able to return if we needed to.

Also, we were now technically homeless and with no source of income, how long would the money last? Where were we going? Would we be able to find work when we needed it?

There were those at home who were just waiting for us to come running back with our tails between our legs when the money ran out. We couldn't go back we knew that, but that really wasn't a problem for us, we didn't want to go back.

Anyway, I had set ourselves a goal that if we did eventually return it would be with our heads held high and with more money than we'd left with.

We settled on heading for Granville in the end, or G G Granville as it soon became known thanks to a certain Mr. Barker. We drove through the wakening town and pulled into a sort of lay by on the far side to have our first breakfast in Billy on foreign soil.

This consisted of one of the many quiches Suzi's mum had made for us, together with just some of the fresh salad she'd insisted on filling our food cupboards up with at the last minute. We were never going to eat it all before it went off as the fridge wasn't working very well, but we were determined not to waste any.

It did save us having to go food shopping on our first few days though, which I supposed was the object of the operation in the first place.

We didn't get much further on that first day as we were tired from not getting enough sleep and with all the excitement of the leaving and everything. We stopped at a small campsite which we came across a little bit later on, near the town of Pontaubault. It was really quiet there with just one or two tents and us.

We were shown where to go by a very nice lady who spoke no English at all, but we understood what she meant, thanks to all the arm waving and hand gestures. We parked in a nice little spot surrounded by trees, laid a blanket out on the grass and fell asleep in the sunshine.

We spent the rest of the day relaxing, writing diaries and phoning home from the campsite phone booth which was something we were struggling with. Luckily for us another very nice non English speaking French woman came along and offered to help with the numbers and the coins needed to call the UK.

We bought our first genuine French baguettes from the little shop they had on the site, we did have a phrase book but our brains were a bit fuzzy so I just pointed to the baguettes and held up two fingers. I had no idea how much they were so I just gave the woman a note and waited to see how much change I got, hoping she wasn't going to diddle me.

I re-stocked our water supply and also had a good look at Billy's engine to try and see what the problem had been earlier. I couldn't find anything wrong anywhere so it remained a mystery.

We had Quiche and salad again that evening and so did the boys, followed by a nice lazy stroll along the banks of the nearby river Sélune.

Later on I emptied the toilet down the designated emptying spout next to the toilet block and then refreshed it with a good slosh of the blue chemical stuff that breaks everything down and keeps it smelling sweet.

We went to bed early that night as we wanted to be bright eyed and bushy tailed for the next days journey, wherever that was going to take us.

The bed folded down lengthwise and so rather than getting in from the side, we had to get used to getting in from the top, or bottom depending on which end we had the pillows. This was determined by whichever way Billy was sloping; we'd already discovered that sleeping with our feet higher than our heads meant a headache in the morning.

The back seat easily folded down flat to make the bed but this simple process turned out to be quite an undertaking as there was a huge pile of stuff stashed away behind it and also on the floor in front of it. It took quite a while to move everything - some of it went in the front down in the foot wells, some went on the dashboard, some up in the roof, anywhere there was space really but we had to keep the front seats clear as the boys slept on them.

We realized that night that a lot of this clobber wasn't going to be around for very long - we simply couldn't go through this rigmarole every night.

It was going to be even worse when it was raining as the boys and one of us had to go outside while the other performed this ritual as there just wasn't enough room for more than one during the upheaval.

We slept well that night, woke early and went for a nice long walk along the river again before returning for a breakfast of yesterdays baguette toasted, coffee and croissants, which we warmed up under the grill.

Afterwards as Suzi washed up in the tiny round sink, getting more than a bit ratty with the now seriously malfunctioning foot pump, I started going through the lengthy and tedious process of putting the bed back and replacing everything where it had been.

When we were eventually ready to go, we both went across to the office to pay the bill and the very nice lady who owned the site told us the amount was 26 francs. We were very proud of ourselves for having understood what she'd said and I ferreted around in my pocket for the money. I counted it out on the table in my very best French until I'd amassed the required 26 francs in various coins.

She then said something which went completely over our heads and she pushed the coins back to me smiling. I got the distinct impression something wasn't quite right here. I counted the coins again, and again it came to 26.

'She did say twenty six didn't she?' I asked of Suzi, seeking reassurance.

'Yes I'm sure she did.' she replied, equally puzzled.

I pushed the coins back across the counter to the French side.

'Non! Non! Vingt six *Francs*.' she repeated narrowing her eyes at us but still smiling and she even wrote it down on a piece of paper so the silly English people would understand. She took some notes from the till and counted them out for us.

'Allor! Vingt six *Francs*,' she repeated again, holding them up in front of us, snapping them open noisily.

'Yes, we are right look,' I said 'It is twenty si….ohhh hang on no it isn't,' I began with an embarrassed smile, 'she wants twenty six francs and we're trying to give her twenty six centimes. That's like giving her twenty six pence instead of two pounds sixty, not quite the same thing at all is it.'

'Hey what d'you mean we, you're in charge of the money, don't bring me into it.'

Luckily Madame campsite was now laughing away, happy that we finally understood. We scuttled hastily out of the office and headed back to Billy for some real money.

'Oh my god Tim, you complete and utter plonker, how embarrassing is that.'

'I'm not at all embarrassed.' I lied.

'Well you should be, I can't believe you sometimes, what an idiot!'

'Ok ok, don't go on about it it's an easy mistake to make, nobody died did they, blimey.'

'Well I'm not taking the money back after that,' she said adamantly, 'it's your cock up, you sort it out.'

'Well neither am I then so there, anyway you'd probably have done exactly the same thing as me!'

I shan't write the response to that, but in the end we both took the correct money over. We had a good old laugh about it with the madame and also her husband who had now joined her after obviously having been informed of the incident, before leaving the place forever.

From there we headed west along the coast a short way and came upon Le Mont Saint Michel. A small island just off the coast with a medieval looking town on it which can be walked to when the tide is out. It looked really interesting and we'd have loved to have had a look around it, but when we got there the car park was full of buses and cars and campers with people milling around everywhere.

If we'd wanted to get to the island we would have had to join the long queue of people who were on their way over to it and fight against the tide of people coming back from it. Instead, we got back into Billy and fled. Maybe another time we said, knowing full well we'd probably never come back this way again.

꠹ ꠹ ꠹ ꠹ ꠹

From there we headed in the general direction of Rennes, for no particular reason really other than it was southwards.

We had to avoid the Peage roads at all costs as being on a really tight budget we had to make the money last as long as possible. We were told they could be quite expensive so every time we saw a sign saying Peage we panicked a bit and turned off, or just stopped so I could study the map to make sure we didn't end up on one.

Notice I said 'I' studied the map there?

We were loving the French roads, long straight and smooth, they seemed so easy to drive on despite me still getting used to being on the right hand side.

A lot of the French drivers seemed to be in the habit of flashing their headlights just as they're beginning to overtake which was a little unsettling to begin with, either that or they blow their horns which was really quite annoying.

It's quite good fun though going round a roundabout the wrong way, takes me back to when I was a crazy biker and did that sort of thing for a laugh on the M4 one dark night but that's another story.

Also sometimes, you can just go straight onto a roundabout without stopping and the traffic on it has to give you priority and stop to let you on. This is fine until you get halfway round one yourself and then forget that you now also have to stop to let the other traffic on.

This was clearly fraught for the uninitiated, but after several close calls accompanied by blaring horns, rude gestures and shouted obscenities which thankfully we didn't understand I quickly got the hang of it.

Of course there were road signs before the roundabouts explaining boring things like priorities etc, but we didn't understand them and quite honestly couldn't have cared less anyway. We were learning from experience which was a lot more fun than wasting time trying to figure out what the signs meant.

We also learnt that the French drivers seemed to be taking into account the fact that we were driving a foreign vehicle. It was as if they were expecting the foreign imbecile to do something stupid, which I have to say at this early stage of our travels was pretty frequent.

Also it gave me a lovely warm glow inside to see the drivers waving their arms about and shouting their heads off at us as they took avoiding action. They obviously craved the release it gave them and so I looked upon it as providing an invaluable form of therapy for them.

We were in awe at the seemingly endless rows of huge Plane trees all along the roadside and the cooling canopies they created high above us. Alongside the road there would often be a tree lined canal of calm green water spanned by numerous single arched stone bridges. Every so often on a whim, I would turn off just to drive over one of them, stopping halfway across for us to admire the beauty of the peaceful green waterways as they meandered lazily through the French landscape.

Some of the bridges seemed too small to allow canal boats through and if there was no traffic wanting to cross the bridge, we'd stay there until a boat or barge came along. It was fun just to watch it pass beneath and to exchange a 'Bon Jour' or two with whoever was on board.

We would usually rejoin the main road afterwards, but sometimes we'd carry on over the bridge and just go wherever the road led us.

Where we were going we had no idea as the atlas seemed to spend most of it's time in a heap on the floor in the back, having been chucked there by my indignant and incompetent navigator.

'Pffft! stupid bloody book,' she'd say 'It's all upside down look - we're following this road here aren't we? going this way.' she continued as she stabbed her finger at the page 'It'd make much more sense for the road to be going away from me, look if I hold it upside down then it all makes sense, the roads in front of me then just like the real one and I can follow where we're going, much more sensible.'

'OK then, just keep it upside down if you find it easier.' I replied trying to hide a smirk, anything for a happy co driver I thought.

'Yeah but now I can't read the road numbers can I, they're all upside down! stupid bloody book.' she said again.

'A book can't be stupid now can it.'

'This one can, it's just illogical and stupid!' and with a deft flick of the wrist the atlas sailed through the air and landed in the back. There was a loud bang as it ricocheted off a cupboard accompanied by the sound of tearing paper, much to the consternation of the boys on the back seat.

'Yep that'll make it more readable the next time we need it.' I laughed.

'There won't be a next time, oh wow Tim look at that old building over there by the canal, doesn't it look gorgeous with those tall thin trees around it!' the atlas incident instantly forgotten as we gazed in wonder at the scene passing us by slowly.

'What trees are they?' she asked.

'Don't know.'

'Well why don't you know, I thought you knew everything.'

'No that sounds more like you my sweet.'

'Piss off!' this with a smile as she punched me on the arm.

I cried out, feigning injury and ended up going off the road and onto the bumpy verge, sending clouds of dust up all around us. I quickly regained the road but with Billy now full of dry choking dust which covered everything inside.

'Hey what did those signs say at that crossroads?' came a voice through the dusty haze.

'Which signs, what crossroads? didn't see any, anyway you're supposed to be the navigator,' I replied coughing and spluttering, desperately trying to see where I was going, 'quick, pass the water bottle!'

26

'There were signs back there, we need to turn around and go back.' she said, passing me the bottle.

'Nope, too late, we're not going back.' I said as I gulped down some water.

'Not going back, why not?'

'Never go back, it's in the past, live for the moment, onward and upward!' I said punching the air.

'OK, let's see where we end up then, are we lost again?' she asked, smiling expectantly.

'Yup, reckon we are,' I replied, 'ok after three then, one, two, three.' and we both started singing our own version of Bonnie Tyler's song.

> 'We are lost in France,
> Though our journey's just beginning.
> We are lost in France,
> It's a song we're always singing.
> We are lost, in France, in love.'

And then we turned to each laughing and air kissed, 'mwahh, mwahh!' as we trundled merrily along with absolutely no idea where we were going, but always we hoped in a generally southwards direction.

♥♥♥♥♥

It was late morning and we were a few kilometers north of Rennes, passing through the town of Liffre when we saw a small market.

We were finding it hard to pass a market with their stalls laden with fresh fruit and vegetables and an endless variety of different mushrooms which we were loving experimenting with.

I turned off down a narrow street and came upon the square where I found a nice parking spot under a shady tree. I also spotted a water tap underneath a small statue in the centre, great we could fill up here before leaving. It was nice and cool in Billy with the windows open, we knew they would never jump out so we left the boys there and wandered off to the market. We told them we'd bring them a baguette each if they promised to look after Billy while we were gone.

They agreed.

It was only a small market and we bought some lovely black cherries, a couple of melons and two flutes, which were loaves, the same shape as a baguette but bigger and softer - they seemed to stay fresher longer too.

We came across one stall which had wooden caskets filled to the brim with different coloured olives, some with garlic, others with herbs, lemon and peppers, they looked really delicious. Up until now, neither of us had liked olives at all, my Granny had always loved them and she used to try and get us to eat them, they were stuffed ones in a jar and tasted quite disgusting.

We were going to pass them by but the sights and smells that were assaulting our senses were just too much for us and we just had to buy some, eventually settling for a small tub of whole green ones with herbs.

We got back to Billy and whilst Suzi put things away, I filled a jerry can up with water from the tap hoping it was drinkable, topped Billy's tank up and refilled the can again before heading off once more. We drove for a while until we found a nice picnic site and I pulled in, parking Billy with his side door facing the sun.

Whilst the boys were outside munching away happily on their wages, we sat down in the side doorway and spread our picnic out on the floor. We tucked in to the deliciously fresh bread, wrinkly dried up quiche, soggy limp salad, a pot of coffee and the olives.

With the coffee poured and sipped, the knob off the loaf eagerly fought over and scoffed by the eventual winner - me, it was time to try the olives. We both took a bite at the same time and turned to each other in wonderment.

'Oh my god these are beautiful!' Suzi exclaimed in joy.

'Wow, delicious,' I agreed 'they're nothing like the ones granny has in her jars are they?' I said as I stuffed another one in, 'this little tub's not going to go far is it.'

'No, we should have bought a bigger one shouldn't we,' came the reply from a mouth stuffed with bread and olives. She looked like a cute little hamster with bulgy cheeks. 'Shall we go back and get some more?'

'No there's no going back,' I reminded her as I sucked the last of the flesh from a stone, 'anyway it's too far to go back, we'll just have to wait till we see another market.'

'We'd better save a couple for later then,' she said as she fiddled and faffed about trying to get the 'stupid' plastic lid back on the tub.

From then on we were hooked, but couldn't work out why we'd suddenly developed a taste for them, was it because they were fresh maybe? or did it have something to do with us being in France, we were puzzled.

As well as being delicious to eat, we discovered the really fun part about eating olives that day.

When we'd finished one we'd take great delight in spitting the stones at each other, it was great fun but the down side was there were olive stones all over the place and we'd be forever treading on them in our bare feet.

It was also fun to spit them at the boys too because they loved crunching on them and they'd sit there expectantly waiting for the next one, of which there were many. It was a step up for us as we already enjoyed spitting grape pips at each other.

I have to say at this point that it wasn't me who started all this disgusting, childish behaviour, it was my charming wife. She thought it was really hilarious to see me with a grape pip stuck on my forehead and in the beginning I did try to discourage it. Unfortunately for me my whining only seemed to encourage her and I'd end up plastered in the damn things while she rolled about laughing, so in the end I gave in and from then on battle lines were drawn and it just became normal behaviour.

We continued our journey, trundling along happily through the countryside, enjoying the warm breeze and the lovely scenery when all of a sudden the hedges and trees were replaced by drab town houses and a cobbled road. We must have passed a sign but neither of us had seen one - some French towns and villages just seem to spring up out of nowhere.

We entered this small, unidentified town around midday and drove slowly through its sleepy streets, remarking on all the closed shutters on the windows and how run down and un-painted all the houses looked.

Eventually we came upon a cobbled square, completely enclosed by tall pastel coloured houses with closed shutters of faded greens and blues with the occasional tiny wrought iron balcony. In the centre there was a low circular stone wall surrounding a single tree, its spreading, leaf laden branches creating shade all around it where I imagined the local people would sit.

On the side of one of the buildings there were stone steps leading up to a doorway with an old bicycle resting against them. There wasn't a soul to be seen so I parked Billy in the shade underneath the tree and we decided to have lunch.

I left Suzi preparing the lunch while I took the boys over to a tap I'd seen in the corner. I filled my cupped hands with water and they both drank from them together. Once they'd had their fill they both had pees against the bike and then trotted off back to Billy to lie underneath him where there was a nice cool breeze.

We sat on the wall under the tree in the shade next to Billy and enjoyed a simple lunch of baguette with some cheese, fresh tomatoes, the last slice of quiche and the remaining two olives.

'Ooh coffees ready,' I said when I heard it gurgling and spitting away in Billy. I got up and brought the pot out on to the wall and poured us a cup each, it was delicious. It was the first we'd had from our new coffee maker which we'd bought the day before in a tiny shop in a small unknown town in the middle of nowhere, next to some river or other.

We were intrigued by the complete silence we were enjoying in the centre of a town and we sat there for some time, basking in the tranquility and taking the opportunity to write some letters to friends and family.

Slowly the town stirred, there were voices coming from somewhere but we saw no-one. An old Citroen van came rattling into the square, disappearing again down a narrow alleyway, a green shutter opened with a squeak and a bang,

We reckoned the shops would probably be open again now so we left the boys in Billy and strolled off down the narrow streets in search of a boulangerie. We soon found one down one of the narrow streets being guided by the aroma of freshly baked bread. We bought two baguettes as they had no flutes, one for us and one for the boys.

Some time later we headed out of town fully stocked once more with bread and water, not looking at any of the road signs just heading towards the sun which we hoped would eventually lead us to the Med.

That was our only plan really, getting to and swimming in the Med, that and finding somewhere warm to spend the winter months which would probably be Benidorm or somewhere around there, we hadn't really thought that far ahead.

We found ourselves heading south west towards the Atlantic coast where we dropped down to sea level and came upon the harbour town of Mortagne Sur Gironde.

As the road led us down into the town there was a lovely panoramic view over the rooftops of the houses with their wavy red tiles of varying hues and contrasting angles. In the distance long rows of masts showed us where the harbour was so we headed there.

I parked Billy on the grass right by the harbours edge and we sat for a while relaxing and taking in the peaceful scene, there was no-one to be seen anywhere. After a while we took the boys for a walk around the deserted harbour, then along the river and down to the sea which turned out not to be the sea at all but the very muddy estuary of the Gironde river.

Still, the boys enjoyed themselves wallowing and splashing about getting plastered in mud and we had to get them swimming off the slipway in the harbour when we got back to wash all the mud off.

It was so peaceful we decided to spend the night there and we sat on the floor in the side door with our feet dangling out, enjoying watching the sun slowly setting, casting its dying rays on the surrounding houses and the yachts as they lay quietly at their moorings.

Early the next morning, we went to the Boulangerie for two fresh flutes as the baguettes we'd bought the day before had gone all hard really quickly. We were finding it a bit hit and miss to get good baguettes, some were really nice but others were really horrible, still the boys always enjoyed them so nothing was wasted.

I found a tap along the quayside so I filled up with water just in case we didn't find another one for a while and then we set off again.

We were determined to reach the Mediterranean.

We were approaching Bordeaux at morning rush hour - we tried to go around it but ended up slap bang in the middle of the town centre, amongst all the usual chaos we'd so far encountered in large French towns.

As was customary we found ourselves in the wrong lane, hemmed in by all the traffic, seeing the signs we needed to follow but ending up being ushered in completely the wrong direction. It was futile to indicate my intention to change lanes as the French drivers were having none of it and just blew their horns angrily at me if I dared to start to move across.

So once again I just gave up and went with the flow of traffic, which eventually came to a standstill again at a huge, busy junction which I overshot slightly.

Unfortunately we were the first in the queue which always made me a little nervous as I liked to have a car to follow at times like this to make sure I kept to the right lane on the other side of the junction.

Given my position, I was straining to see the lights when eventually the cross traffic stopped and the lights went green so

I took off towards the other side with my eyes fixed firmly on our exit.

Suddenly four lanes of traffic came at us from the right, some swerving around us, others screeching to a halt, horns blaring and drivers shouting angrily at the foreign imbecile who was now parked slap bang in the middle of the junction.

Now what was I going to do? it was too late to go back so I thought, sod it, 'When in France,' I leant out of the window and started yelling back at the top of my voice and making aggressive gestures with my arm just like they were doing. I didn't wait to see their reaction; I just revved up and roared off to the sanctuary of the other side hoping that there were no police around.

I still had steam coming out of my ears as we sped along, going much too fast when I glanced across at Suzi expecting trouble, but she was curled up on her seat in hysterics.

'What's so funny?' I asked, my anger already melting away.

'You, you plonker,' she giggled in reply, 'having a tantrum when it was all your fault.'

'It wasn't my fault,' I protested, 'the lights were on green, *they* must have gone on red, anyway I wasn't having a tantrum, I was just being French.'

'Oh right, so all of those cars went on red did they? How come we were the only ones to go from our side then?'

No idea,' I said shrugging, laughing along with her now, 'I saw green lights ok?'

'Well they must have been theirs then, the ones above us were still on red,' she said pointing upwards.

'Well I couldn't see them up there could I? I mean, what is the bloody point of having traffic lights up in the sky where no-one can see them!'

'I saw them.'

'Well yes, but then you're a short arse, you see things from a different angle to me,' I joked.

'Cheeky git, just keep you're eyes open in future,' she countered, laughing away 'anyway, if you'd stopped in the right place you'd have been able to see the lights.'

'Oh blah di blah di blah,' I chimed, 'oh no look out, more lights coming up, now pay attention will you.'

Anyway, after some considerable time we eventually found a way out and ended up heading inland. We kept seeing signs for Bergerac which wasn't really in the right direction, but we liked the sound of it for some reason, so we decided to go there anyway.

Along the way we passed people in lay-by's selling fruit from a stall or a van, they looked delicious all laid out in the sunshine - the fruit that is, not the people - but by the time we'd spotted them we were upon them and speeding by.

'Look!' exclaimed Suzi pointing at them as we sailed on by 'three melons for ten francs, how much is that?'

'A quid,' I replied.

'Wow that's good go back, we must get some.'

'No, we're not going back, we'll stop at the next one, there's bound to be another one soon.'

Sure enough, a few kilometers down the road, we drove past another one.

'Why didn't you stop?' she demanded.

'Didn't see it in time,' I replied trying not to laugh, there was a big sigh from the passenger side and we carried on.

'Well we're stopping at the next one even if we have to turn around,' she said adamantly, 'Look there's another sign, so there must be one coming up, slow down a bit and keep your eyes open.'

We rounded a bend and sure enough there it was.

'There it is, pull over,' she said urgently, pointing and leaning forward excitedly.

'Ooh no, wrong side of the road, we'll wait for one on this side,' I was laughing to myself now as I loved winding her up, 'well come on I mean it could be really dangerous to cross over, what with all the traffic and everything. And then we'd be on the wrong side of the road when we pulled out and have to cross back over again, no sorry not doing it, far too risky.'

'Hmm, yes I suppose it would be dangerous, especially with your driving.' she said, giving me one of her looks.

We continued in silence for a few more kilometres until we saw another sign.

'Right, here comes another one, and it's on this side of the road as well so no more excuses,' she said as she leaned across and flicked the indicator on, 'I know what you're up to you know' she said.

'I'm not up to anything my darling and you've just put the left hand indicator on you *twit*!' I replied as I flicked it over to the right one and pulled into the lay-by with the sound of an angrily honking horn behind us ringing in our ears.

Suzi got out and went over to the stall but she came straight back looking glum saying.

'They've sold out of melons, can you believe it!' she said sadly, 'I blame you.'

'Of course you do, well get some Cherries or something then.'

'We've got cherries, I wanted melons.' she said pouting and smiling at the same time.

'The next one might have some, come on get in.'

She got back in and we roared off in search of the next one and I was really hoping there would be a next one. It was some time before we saw another one and we were beginning to give up hope when I spotted it at the last minute, it was on our side of the road as well, good.

I pulled off the road just in time, but forgot how fast I was going and as bad luck would have it the lay-by turned out to be really bumpy and full of pot holes.

Billy hit the first bump with a whump and then took off, landed with a sickening crash, took off again and crashed back down. Everything was flying around in the back - books, cups, plates, dogs, all going everywhere. Cupboard doors flew open spewing their contents out all over the place and I also heard some strange noises coming from the region of the passenger seat.

I was hard on the brakes at this point too and the wheels were locking up on the gravel, spraying chippings everywhere and making an almighty din. We disappeared in a thick cloud of dry, choking dust with Billy eventually coming to a standstill at an odd angle.

As the dust slowly cleared, the melon stall re-appeared through the gloom revealing an ashen faced woman holding two melons in front of her, staring open mouthed at us from no more than six feet away.

We looked at each other with wide eyes and slowly exhaled as we turned to look at the carnage in the back just as the boys were clambering back on to their seats. Then we slowly turned back to see the melon lady still standing there holding her melons and staring at us, mouthing something. Almost in a whisper Suzi said.

'Let's try the next one shall we?'

'Good idea, not sure I liked the look of her melons anyway.'

We both burst out laughing as I carefully reversed away from her stall and pulled back onto the road while Suzi gave the woman a lovely big smile and a wave as we departed.

Still tittering away and with all hopes of buying melons abandoned, I turned off at the next opportunity and drove down a narrow road until we found a nice big lay by where I pulled in and stopped.

I wanted to get underneath Billy to see if there was any damage after that little episode and we also needed to put everything back in the cupboards again.

I had a good look around underneath but thankfully everything seemed to be ok. Suzi had just finished tidying up by the time I'd finished and it seemed the only casualty was the coffee pot, which now had a broken handle.

We decided to stop there for lunch and then afterwards, we carried on along the same little road, not having a clue where it was taking us so once again we found ourselves completely lost. We knew though, judging by the position of the sun that we were probably still heading inland, in the general direction of Bergerac, which wasn't directly southwards but it would do for now.

We were pootling along the narrow, bendy minor roads when we met a car coming the other way and instinct took over, I naturally pulled over to the left so we could pass each other.

This I quickly realised was a stupid thing to do as it really threw the other driver, who now had to pull over on to his left, which of course went against all *his* instincts. Luckily, the occupants seemed to have a good sense of humour and we all had a bit of a laugh as we inched past each other with me slapping myself on the forehead feigning stupidity.

'You don't have to *pretend* to be stupid you know,' sighed Suzi, shaking her head sadly.

'Thanks honey you're too kind.' I replied smiling as we drove on again.

☺ ☺ ☺ ☺ ☺

We went through the tiny village of Fraise with its tall steepled church and then started climbing. We passed a small picnic site but there were quite a few cars there and too many people for our liking so we went on past, rounded a sharp bend and pulled off the road onto a nice, wide grassy verge a bit further on.

We all clambered out to stretch our legs and to walk about for a bit. The picnic area we'd just passed was not far below us, down through the trees and we decided that this would be a better place to stop for a tea and toilet break.

I needed the loo but not for a pee, no this was more serious and I thought, to save filling our toilet up I would just nip down the bank a short way and fulfill my needs down there.

I announced my intentions and took the little shovel and a loo roll with me and clambered on down. It was a lot steeper than it looked as well as quite loose underfoot and I had a bit of a job to stay on my feet – wearing flip flops wasn't helping much either.

I found a suitable patch of soft earth and dug a hole with one hand whilst clinging onto a tree for support with the other. I could see the people at the picnic area not far below me now but told myself it would be ok as long as I kept nice and quiet and anyway, people very rarely look upwards. I was only wearing shorts which made it much easier but just as I dropped my shorts to my ankles, both the dogs came bounding down the slope towards me barking their heads off and spraying soil and stones everywhere.

'Oh no, shut up you two for gods sake.' I hissed in a panic and shot a glance down at the picnickers – oh bugger, they'd spotted me! Foolishly, I used the hand that I was holding on with to fend them off which of course immediately threw me off balance.

Suddenly the earth moved and I lost my footing, I dropped the loo roll as well which then took off down the slope, bouncing its way merrily downhill unraveling itself as it went.

A flailing left hand made a futile grab for the tree again but missed by a mile and despite some frantic windmill-like arm waving and weird balance seeking body movements, I just couldn't stop myself. I staggered off down through the trees at an alarming rate of knots, hurtling downwards on a wave of soil and gravel.

I desperately tried to stay on my feet but my shorts were still around my ankles and I couldn't open my legs wide enough to regain any balance or to stop my descent – I was clearly doomed.

No amount of maniacal arm waving or panicky little penguin steps were going to save me and inevitably a few agonizing seconds later my feet went from under me and I fell flat on my face. I rolled over and over down through the undergrowth, my shorts clad legs waving stupidly about in the air above me as two rabid dogs barked their heads off in sheer delight at the unfolding spectacle.

I ended up sliding head first downhill on my back on the wave of the small avalanche I'd created and came to an abrupt and painful halt as I slammed into a tree stump. The boys carried on down the slope, chasing the loo roll all the way down which was leaving a nice bright white line leading all the way back to me like a marker, just in case someone down there still hadn't spotted me.

I quickly pulled my shorts up as I cast a furtive glance down at the now open mouthed, staring picnickers who were not so very far below me any more.

I left the boys to it and with as much dignity as I could muster - there wasn't much left at this point I can tell you - I got back on my feet and received a lovely round of applause from my delighted audience.

And so with the sound of their laughter echoing in my ears, I retrieved the shovel and scrambled my way slipping and sliding back up the steep slope. The dogs had got to the top already and were now both waiting for me, Nelson had a big happy grin on his face and Caine had what was left of the loo roll in his mouth.

I emerged from the trees panting for breath, and limped slowly back to Billy, the pain only now beginning to kick in.

'Did you manage ok?' enquired Suzi.

'Yep no problem at all,' I replied in what I hoped was a casual manner, thinking maybe I could get away without having to explain myself - I really should have known better.

'Hey your knees bleeding, and your back, ooh that looks sore, did you fall over or something, what were the boys barking at?'

'Erm... oh I dunno, nothing much probably, you know what they're like, I just need to go to the loo,' I said as I tried to wrestle the remnants of the squashed and soggy loo roll from Caine's mouth.

'What, but I thought you went.... oh no,' she laughed, 'what's happened, what have you done this time, come on tell Suzi all about it and why are you only wearing one flip flop?'

'Ohh, ok then,' I sighed heavily, 'but only if you promise not to laugh.'

'Of course I won't laugh my darling,' she said in gleeful anticipation, she might as well have been rubbing her hands together, 'I would never do such a thing.'

Well of course she laughed didn't she, she laughed for the rest of the day and she was still tittering away to herself when we went to bed.

I slept on my front that night!

We were awake at first light and I desperately tried to avoid eye contact with a certain someone as I knew what the outcome would be. My worst fears were soon realized as the very first time we looked at each other she burst out laughing and annoyingly, so did I. So that was the end of any sympathy which may have been coming my way, despite my traumatic experience and the serious nature of my injuries.

We enjoyed a lovely long stroll through the woods with the boys before having a breakfast of coffee and toast outside on the grass next to Billy. Then, in the warmth of the early morning sun Suzi changed the dressings on my wounds – all seven of them - as we pored over our long suffering atlas trying to decide where to go next. We set off soon afterwards, deciding to carry on towards Bergerac.

We could hear the distant sound of church bells as we drove along the narrow country roads, passing through quaint little villages with their old sandstone coloured, red roofed houses. Scattered about in the fields were old black wooden barns and I imagined Steve McQueen popping out from behind one of them on his motorbike, but he never did.

If we came to a main road I quickly got off it again at the first opportunity and we'd be back on small roads again, seeing France as the natives saw it and not from the window of a car speeding along the motorway.

We were never sure if the locals liked seeing us in their villages, but we were enjoying seeing them and liked to stop at the local shops, or to get some water whenever we saw a tap.

We soon discovered that nearly every village and town had a water tap somewhere if you just knew where to find it, something we were getting pretty good at now.

We reached Bergerac where once again we found ourselves going the wrong way in a busy town centre. We somehow ended up going down narrow cobbled backstreets turning right, then left, then another left and so on, eventually ending up at a river, which we later discovered was the Dordogne.

We followed it for a while along a poorly surfaced road until we came to a dead end. Right at the end there was a narrow track which led us down towards the river and on to the shoreline where we parked under the trees next to a sign which read 'Camping Interdit'.

We stayed for a few hours and enjoyed a lovely long walk with the boys along the shore. Later on we strolled through the town before returning to Billy for lunch and a snooze in the sunshine, lying on the lovely warm, soft, shingle beach.

We set off again some time later and soon realized we must be in an apple growing region given that all we'd seen for the last several kilometers had been apple trees.

I could resist it no longer and pulled off the road, parking on the verge.

'What are you doing?' Suzi asked, knowing full well what I was up to.

'I'm going to pick some apples,' I replied nonchalantly.

'What, you can't do that, someone might see you.'

'There's no-one around to see me though is there,' I said, looking all around, 'do you see anyone? no nor me.'

'There was a car back there somewhere,' she replied worriedly, 'anyway you can't just take them that's stealing, what about the poor farmer?' she pleaded.

'He won't miss a couple now will he, and anyway, that car was way back there so they can't see us can they.'

I hopped out of Billy, closing the door quietly and went into the trees a short distance. I had a quick look around for any obvious signs of a farmer, selected two beautiful looking dark green specimens and picked them.

I returned to the edge of the trees, leant casually against one of them and took a bite, savouring the juicy mouthful of freshness whilst enjoying the fact that Suzi was becoming increasingly agitated in Billy, beckoning for me to hurry the hell up. This appealed to my impish sense of humour and I made a big show of lounging around there, enjoying the fruits of my labour while she was frantically looking this way and that and generally looking worried.

'Come on Tim, hurry up will you for God's sake,' she hissed.

'Mmmm yum yum!' I said in a big loud squelchy voice, 'this is delicious.'

Just then Caine clambered onto her lap, stuck his head out of the window and gave a single loud bark as if to say.

'Come on!'

'Ok ok I'm coming, be quiet will you!'

I walked quickly back to Billy to find a very relieved Suzi and a happy Caine.

Nelson just wasn't interested and he was dozing with his head lolling over the back seat. I handed Suzi the other apple which she immediately sank her teeth into.

'Oh wow, that's absolutely gorgeous,' she crooned with streams of apple juice running down her chin, 'did you only get the two then? you should take a bag next time and get a whole load.'

'I can't take a whole bag full now can I, that would just be wrong and anyway what about the poor farmer?' I enquired with just a hint of sarcasm, as I started Billy up and pulled back onto the road.

'Pah! there must be millions of apples in there, he's not going to miss a few now is he?'

'You're a bad influence on me you are,' I said and we both shared a smile as I threw my core at her. She grabbed it, and turned to give it to Nelson who munched on it happily; he and Caine always had our apple cores.

44

This scrumping behaviour became a routine part of our life as we passed through the French countryside, there were apples, peaches and baby sweetcorn, all ripe for the picking, it was fun and it was also saving us money.

I would pull Billy off the road as close to whatever crop it was we came across, then I'd nip into the field and pick the fruit and pass them through the window to Suzi who would quickly stash them out of sight in case we were spotted.

'I'll pick, you stash,' I said as I dropped half a dozen baby sweetcorn in through the window, 'ooh, me Pick, you Stash, those can be our scrumping names, what d'you think?'

'Ha ha, I like it, Pick and Stash.' and she laughed happily as we drove off from the scene of the crime in a cloud of dust, laughing and joking about our outrageous exploits, just like a modern day Bonnie and Clyde.

☺ ☺ ☺ ☺ ☺

Our dreams of swimming naked in the Mediterranean under a scorching sun were cruelly shattered when we finally arrived on the South coast. We were greeted by a howling gale with rain pelting down from a dark menacing sky - not what we'd had in mind at all.

The road led us down through the hills to the seaside town of Narbonne Plage where we found a car park with access onto the beach. The sand looked nice and firm so I took Billy through and parked a short way from the entrance.

We stayed in Billy until there was a break in the rain and then we all went for a long walk across the beach, well wrapped up against the wind. We'd waited a long time for this, a lovely stroll along a Mediterranean shoreline with the boys and we were damn well going to enjoy it.

Well we damn well didn't, it was horrible.

On the way out, the wind was battering us from behind and we were being blown about all over the place but on the way back it was even worse. The howling wind was now coming straight into our faces and we had to fight our way back through driving, stinging sand and now also the rain which had returned with a vengeance.

To top it all off it had now started with thunder and lightning and by the time we got back we were wet through and absolutely freezing. We quickly shut ourselves away inside and because of the wind, the roof had to stay down so we couldn't stand up.

With the front seats occupied by two soggy, stinky dogs we struggled in the remaining space to change out of our wet clothes. Bent almost double, I put the kettle on and made a nice warming cup of tea and then we had baked beans with left over baguette while the storm raged around us.

Some time later during a break in the rain we took another walk along the shoreline and gathered armfuls of driftwood to make a camp fire with.

I rigged up a makeshift windbreak from some sticks and towels and despite the biting wind and driving sand, we managed to cook some potatoes and all sorts of vegetables wrapped up in tin foil on the fire.

They were delicious and really enjoyable although a bit crunchy!.

Later, as Suzi was sitting in the side doorway in a thick wooly jumper busily writing in her diary, I decided to take a stroll around to see if I could fulfill my manly hunter - gatherer role and find some water as we were getting quite low.

I had a good look around but the only water I could find was in the outdoor showers that were on the beach by the boulevard. I didn't fancy driving around looking for a tap so I went back to Billy to fetch the jerry cans. It shouldn't be too difficult to get water from a shower head should it, I mean how hard could it be?

As it turned out it was pretty bloody hard and I very quickly realized that it was a really stupid idea.

It proved to be quite a tricky operation holding the ten litre container high up above my head right up against the shower head with one hand, whilst using the other hand to keep pressing the tap which annoyingly kept going off every few seconds.

Gradually, as the container slowly - very slowly filled with water, it became heavier and heavier and as my arm got tired it would slip off the shower head every so often and I would get a regular soaking of cold water.

As it was still blowing a gale and I was cold to begin with anyway, getting soaking wet didn't help raise my core temperature or improve my mood any.

Nevertheless, I was determined to master this technique as surely I could provide water for my family without making a complete tit of myself in front of all the people who I'd just noticed were sitting in their cars on the windswept boulevard.

Finally after what seemed like an eternity, both jerry cans were full, I picked them both up and staggered back across the beach soaked to the skin and freezing cold.

Once back at Billy I fell to my knees exhausted, my arms were killing me and I was panting for breath after struggling through the soft sand with my heavy burden. I was quite proud of myself to have found water that close, feeling that the sacrifice I'd made to obtain it had been worth it and I felt sure my mate would be impressed with my efforts.

I should have known better really - she promptly burst out laughing when she saw the state of me.

I was a little put out to say the least given the extreme conditions I'd just endured, not to mention the spectacle I'd made of myself.

I very carefully and patiently explained my ordeal to a now almost hysterical wife who was rolling around on the sand by this time. I also made it quite clear that if I hadn't manned up to the task then god knows where we would have found water.

She managed to control her hysteria long enough to say.

'Why didn't you just use that tap over there you plonker.' and she pointed to a little wall with a tap on it a mere thirty yards, sorry metres away. 'It would have been a lot simpler.'

I stared stupidly at the damn tap for a few seconds, hands on hips, turned back to Suzi and before I could say anything we both burst out laughing.

'Well why the hell didn't you tell me that in the first place.' I whined as a dewdrop fell from my nose.

'Because I've only just spotted it and anyway you just wandered off without saying a word, typical of you that is, how was I supposed to know what you were up to?'

'Well,…me walking off carrying two empty water containers might have given you a bit of a clue don't you think?'

'I didn't notice, I was so engrossed in my diary, sorry darling.' she said, still tittering away.

'Oh yeah a likely story, just pass me a towel will you I'm bloody freezing.'

☺ ☺ ☺ ☺ ☺

We spent that night right there on the beach, being rocked gently to sleep by the wind and woke early the next morning to a clear blue sky and a rising sun. After a lovely long walk along the beach we had coffee and croissants for breakfast and then drove a few kilometers inland to Narbonne town to do some shopping at the out of town Supermarche.

Once we'd finished there we drove into the town, parking in a tree lined car park alongside the canal. We went to a bank to cash a Eurocheque and then we all sat on the grassy bank in the sunshine, watching the boats go by and munching happily on fresh bread and olives.

We'd discovered there was no need to pay on the car park as we were a foreign vehicle and we wouldn't get fined. We'd had this patiently explained to us by a dog loving, non English speaking Frenchman who had stopped to talk to us. We hadn't understood a word he'd said but we got what he meant thanks to a very good miming act on his part.

Because of our lack of French we usually started a conversation with a shopkeeper by asking them in our best French, if they spoke any English. Inevitably, they would always shake their head, shrug their shoulders and say no. By now though we were at least able to ask for the basics like bread and croissants but not much else.

When we arrived at the South coast we thought they were bound to know at least a little English due to it being a touristy area, but we still got the same response.

I thought by going into a camping shop and asking for the loo blue stuff we'd have some success but again, no English. I said the word for blue and did various mimes and sound effects associated with using a toilet, but still the woman behind the counter refused to understand.

By this time my darling wife was killing herself laughing, at my expense as usual although the shopkeeper didn't seem in the least bit amused.

Later that same day we were speaking to a young Australian couple we'd met. They also had a Vee Dub except theirs wasn't called Billy it was called Mabel - silly name if you ask me but there you go.

Anyway, we were telling them about our lack of success with non English speaking French people who also refused to understand their own language when being spoken by an English person.

He had breath that smelt really strongly of garlic and he tilted his head to one side at an acute angle when in conversation, or convo as he called it, how could *that* be comfortable. His head was so far over it was nearly touching his shoulder and as he spoke to Suzi I found myself fighting the urge to do the same as him to see what it was like.

He spent a long time in convo with Suzi, completely ignoring me - as has been the case with a lot of men over the years - and as usual, I glazed over.

I found my head involuntarily beginning to tilt to one side just like his and I had to force it back up again quickly when he did eventually turn to me, hoping he hadn't noticed.

Luckily I got away with it several times, but as it turned out his girlfriend had been watching me do it and she certainly had noticed, I could tell. I desperately wanted to say something to her but my mouth just wouldn't open, which with hindsight was probably for the best.

I just comforted myself with the thought that I probably wasn't the first bloke to mimic her boyfriend's strange affliction.

Anyway I'm digressing, he told us - or rather he told Suzi even though it was me who had addressed him in the first place - to try something next time we went into a shop....

So the next day we went back to the same camping store to try again.

As we entered the shop our hearts sank when we saw that the same stern, non English speaking woman was behind the counter, we approached her tentatively and I said.

'Parlez vous Anglais?'

She of course replied no and I even found myself shaking my head and saying no with her. I noticed Suzi turning quickly away at this point and then, remembering what our Australian friend had told us the day before I said in my best Dame Edna voice.

'Do you speak Australian?'

To which she replied in almost perfect English.

'Yes, I speak a little Australian.'

Swiftly, and with raised eyebrows I turned to Suzi.

'Ooh look Suze she speaks .....' but she was sliding down the front of the counter with her hands over her mouth, trying unsuccessfully to control her hysterics.

I did try to keep a straight face, I really did.

I got halfway through my next sentence when the muffled snorts coming from down by my feet became too much for me and I just had to let go, I just couldn't help it. The stony face staring back at me from behind the counter wasn't helping either.

The other shoppers were a little bemused by this spectacle but most of them ended up laughing along with us as they watched me pick my limp, helpless wife up off the floor, even though they didn't know what they were laughing at.

The only one who still wasn't laughing by this time was Madame miserables behind the counter who just didn't get it, which only made things worse and we had to help each other out of the shop.

We made the sanctuary of the street where I said.

'There must be another shop that sells....' and we both erupted in fits of laughter again as we staggered off down the street.

I never did finish that sentence.

We stayed there on the beach at Narbonne for some time – it was nice and quiet, convenient for the shops and oh yes, there was a tap practically right next to us for water!

Another reason for staying there was that we were waiting for some letters to arrive from home. We'd been to the post Office a few days before to get the address for 'Post Restante' which we gave to friends and family back home so they could write to us.

We went to the Post Office every day to check, but each day there was nothing for us which was a bit disappointing - we were keen for news from home and we also wanted to move on.

Still there were worse places to be held up at and anyway, the weather was slowly improving and warming up so we were quite happy to stay here for a while longer. It was before the holiday season had started and we lazed around on the almost deserted beach for most of the day, cooking our food over a small camp fire in the evenings.

Each morning we walked into the town for fresh bread and to check for post, then later we all went for long walks along the shoreline collecting firewood as we went. When we had ice creams we all had one each as the boys loved them too. We held theirs for them as we were eating ours which always amused the passers by.

Every few days we'd leave the coast and drive a few miles back into the hills to do some washing and also to find somewhere to empty the toilet. We found a lovely place just down off the road amongst some trees, close to a small gurgling stream and I parked Billy alongside with the side door facing it.

Whist Suzi was preparing some lunch, I got the sun chairs out from behind the back seats and made up the roll up table which was already broken. We had lunch there by the stream, in the shade of the canopy made from one of our bed sheets which I'd strung up from Billy to a nearby tree.

After a long lazy lunch, Suzi took some clothes to the stream and did some washing while I wandered off into the trees a bit with the toilet and the fold up spade. It was a good place to empty the loo as the ground was soft and I could dig a nice deep hole to tip it into.

It could be a bit tricky to empty sometimes though, especially if there wasn't enough water in it as the contents would then be a bit thick and stodgy. There would often be a big gooey lump left that just slopped up and down as I tipped it, refusing to come out of the hole. This would require adding some more water to it to thin it down, another good reason for stopping by a stream.

Also I'd stopped putting that blue chemical stuff in as we considered it an unnecessary expense as well as being bad for the environment. Consequently if it was left for more than two or three days before emptying, it would start to stink a bit which made the emptying process a little flavoursome to say the least. I'd very quickly learned to keep my mouth shut tight during the emptying process as it was prone to splashback - I'd already had one mouthful of it and it wasn't very pleasant.

Once emptied, rinsed out and hole filled in again, I went back to the stream to swill all the little drops of foul smelling brown liquid from my arms and legs, filled the toilet about a third full of fresh water and put it back in it's cupboard.

Job done and I wiped the sweat from my forehead with the back of my hand only to find that my sweat had somehow turned brown and my hand now smelt disgusting – eeww!

I sauntered off back to the stream, stripped all my clothes off and had an all over sluice in the cold water, rinsed my shorts and t- shirt and walked naked back to Billy.

'There's no point in just using water, you need soap to get rid of that stink.' said Suzi as she hung various items of freshly washed clothes all over Billy to dry.

'Nah, it's ok I'm clean now and the smells gone.' I replied.

'Oh no it hasn't, I can smell you from here!'

'Well I can't smell anything.' I said sniffing my arm.

'There's something wrong with your nose then,' she retorted handing me a bar of soap, 'go and have a proper wash, you smell disgusting.'

'I can't use that in the stream now can I, it might poison the fish.' I protested lamely.

'Oh for god's sake!' she said, 'just stay there then.'

She went to the stream with the washing up bowl, filled it and then climbed onto a rock.

'Come and stand here,' she said, 'so I can pour this over you, I'll pour you wash.'

And that's how we had our first outdoor shower together as after I'd finished mine, I returned the favour and poured the water for Suzi whilst she showered. She kept on winging about how cold it was all the time which was understandable really as it *was* mountain stream water after all.

We didn't bother drying ourselves; we just lay on the ground and let the sun dry us.

It was then I came up with a plan to paint one of our water containers black so that it would warm up in the sun and we could have warm showers.

The air conditioning unit, which I had painstakingly installed in Billy's roof to keep the boys cool, turned out to be a complete and utter waste of time and money. It was ridiculously ineffective against the heat, even on full blast there was no cool air coming from it.

It had four small reservoirs of water which was pumped up to the unit from a five litre plastic jerry can under the sink. I was constantly having to top this up from our valuable water supply as it just kept evaporating too quickly in the heat.

The pump was powered by Billy's second battery which given how often the pump was going on and off had soon gone flat. We didn't have a way of charging it up again other than when Billy was running, which lately hadn't been that often so it just stayed flat. I had to keep his main battery fully charged or we wouldn't be able to start him.

I decided I would use this jerry can for our solar shower heater which nicely freed up a cupboard for some of our excess stuff that had no home and on our next trip to the Supermarche in Narbonne, I bought a paintbrush and some matt black paint.

Also I used the pump to replace the faulty one at the sink, which all in all was a happy outcome and the air conditioning unit which wasn't, was left as an expensive talking point.

Anyway, we'd found the best way to keep Billy cool was to keep all the curtains closed and the windows open which created a nice through breeze.

Eventually the post arrived – we had to pay for each letter we got, but as there were only three it wasn't going to break the bank.

There were two from Suzi's family and a packet from my mum which obviously cost us more, we didn't mind really as we were excited to see what was in it.

I opened it quickly when we got back to Billy.

Inside the packet there was an edition of the local newspaper and about thirty letters which all turned out to be circulars that were addressed to me at home and which she'd thought fit to forward to me for some unknown reason. We both just sat there staring at them numbly, not really believing what we were seeing. I looked through them again in search of a letter from her but there really wasn't one to be found.

What made it worse was the fact that we'd just paid to have a load of circulars posted to me. I was speechless, not to mention the fact that we'd waited here for nearly two weeks just for this. We'd been keen to move on for some time but also longed for some contact from family back home and now this, not even a letter.

I scooped them all up and stormed off in high dudgeon to the nearest rubbish bin and threw them in with a disgusted flourish - which is what should have happened to them in the first place mother!

We took a different route back from Narbonne one day and came across a lake a couple of kilometers from Narbonne Plage called Etang de Metaille. It was only a small lake and totally surrounded by a large flat sandy beach.

It was early afternoon when we arrived there and quite busy so I parked Billy in the first nice spot I could find, close to the hedge. We'd explore tomorrow and find a quieter place to camp, maybe over the other side where there were fewer cars parked.

It was obviously a popular haunt for windsurfers as there were quite a few of them racing back and forth across the lake. We watched them while we had something to eat and then afterwards I painted the jerry can with the black paint, filled it with water and left it in the sun to dry whilst we took the boys for a walk and a swim.

The lake was nice and warm, so we both went in for a splash about, everyone else had gone by this time and we were the only ones left apart from one camper over on the other side.

When we got back, the paint was dry and the water had warmed slightly so we both stripped off and had showers by Billy to wash the salt off. I poured the water over Suzi and then over myself as she's too short to hold it over my head and there was nothing for her to stand on.

There was still some warmth left in the sun so we strolled naked by the shore with the boys until we were nice and dry again, then played with the bat and ball game we'd just bought. The ball was like a squash ball and the bats were round and flat, like table tennis bats only twice the size. We'd hit the ball back and forth to each other seeing how long we could go before one of us missed it.

Caine always stood in the middle watching the ball and when one of us missed it he'd run off after it, bring it back and have a good old chew on it before letting us have it back so we could carry on. It was really handy having a ball boy but it came at a price. The ball would be covered in his slobber and when we hit it again there would be a soggy splat and we'd get a shower of saliva and sand, great, thanks Caine!

Nelson just watched from the sidelines, he was far too aloof to chase after a ball and bring it back.

The wind got up in the night and Billy started rocking so I clambered out of bed to bring the roof down, trying really hard not to tread on Suzi's head as I extricated myself.

Then a bit later on I had to get out of bed again and go outside to stuff a towel in the grille on the side of Billy as it was making a horrible noise and keeping us awake.

We decided to stay where we were for the time being as it didn't seem as busy as the previous day. It was still really windy though and soon the lake was covered with windsurfers again. Luckily they were all down the other end except for the odd stray one so it was fairly quiet where we were, apart from a few cars and a couple of campers.

We had a nice relaxing day there, swimming, sunbathing and writing letters and diaries. I left our new solar shower in the sun up against Billy's wheel and went snorkeling with Caine - well I was snorkeling he wasn't, he was just swimming along with me.

The lake wasn't very deep and I was swimming along the bottom amongst the tall wavering grass like plants, watching the small fish darting about. We soon found ourselves on the opposite side and we had a walk about to see if it was a good place to move to.

It was quieter over here and the beach was much bigger as well as being nice and firm so no worries of getting bogged down. I walked some distance from the lake and clambered up a steep bank and onto a rough track which ran along the top. On the other side there was a massive beach and in the far distance, the sea. The breakers were quite big because of the onshore wind and there were cars parked all along the shore.

It looked like it would be a good place to camp, once the wind died down.

We got back to the lake, swam back across and then packed a few things away and drove slowly around the lake to the other side, parking near the water's edge.

It was a lovely evening despite the wind so we sat outside, watching the sun slowly setting and sharing a bottle of Malibu. Afterwards we played the bat and ball game which got out of hand due to a certain someone cheating and I ended up putting her over my shoulder and walking into the lake, to the delight of the remaining windsurfers.

The solar shower proved to be a big success, it had heated up really well and we both enjoyed hot showers that evening, in fact the water was so hot I had to add cold to it!

It was a clear night, the wind was dying and the moon was rising just as we were going to bed.

Sometime later I was rudely awakened.

'Wake up Tim, come on, we're in the lake!' came a panicky voice in the moonlight.

'What, how can we be in the lake, have we moved?'

'No but the lake has, look outside.'

I looked out through the window and gazed upon a scene of utter tranquility, we were completely surrounded by flat calm moonlit water.

I opened the side door to see the water almost up to the sills, another inch or two and it would be coming in.

'Oh shit, we're sinking.' I joked.

'Oh shut up will you, this is no time for jokes, do something!'

I stepped out into the water and waded around Billy in knee deep water. Caine jumped out with me, it was almost deep enough for him to be able to swim in but not quite, still he was thrilled to bits to be having a splash about at this time of night.

Billy looked quite beautiful, surreal almost, marooned in the middle of a lake in the moonlight. I just had to take a picture of the scene so I went back and got my camera.

'You're not serious, Tim for god's sake, we've got to move come *on*!'

'I'll be back in a jiffy, don't go anywhere will you.' I laughed as I splashed off again.

Meanwhile Caine was having the time of his life, charging around in sheer delight, half swimming and half bounding through the water - oh this was just *too* much fun!

I took a few hasty pictures, not really expecting them to come out then we got back into Billy.

Nelson was horrified that Caine was allowed inside in his dripping wet condition and promptly leapt up onto our bed for cover just as he started to shake. Nothing was spared a soaking in that confined space though and he still got a lovely fine shower as did our bed, even the roof was dripping. He fled right to the back in disgust and started cleaning himself whilst Caine just stood there still dripping wet with a big happy smile on his face.

There was a tense moment as I went to start Billy but thankfully he came to life instantly.

So far so good I thought as I reversed slowly away. I didn't want to risk going forwards in case the sand was too soft and when I'd gone a good distance back, I went forward and swung round. I wasn't going to chance going back round the lake the way we'd come as it was a long way and we might get bogged down.

Instead I headed for the nearest bit of dry land I could think of which was the track I'd found earlier on top of that bank.

There was a loud silence in Billy as I drove really slowly through the water. It was so tempting to just race to safety but I didn't want to risk swamping the engine.

Eventually we came to the steep bank I'd climbed earlier - it looked a lot steeper now! I didn't want to stop in case we got bogged down and we had no idea how high the water was going to rise either so I just kept on going.

I headed for what looked like a good place to go up and just hoped for the best. There was only going to be one go at this, if it all went wrong we would be in the fertilizer good and proper.

When we got to the bottom of the bank I put the pedal to the metal and just went for it.

Nelson was ok he was still on the bed, Caine had squeezed his soggy self up between us with a foot on each of our seats and was looking out through the front thoroughly enjoying the ride. I daren't slow down now, we were rocketing upwards into the night sky on a trajectory to the full moon when suddenly we came crashing down on the track at the top, we'd made it, we were safe.

'Wow, well done Billy.' I said and we both patted him on his dashboard gratefully.

On the other side, the sea had come in as far as the bottom of the track and there was a carpet of little white breakers as far as the eye could see. We were now on the only bit of dry land left anywhere and it was lucky we hadn't moved round to the beach earlier - we wouldn't have escaped that little lot so easily.

I drove slowly along the bumpy track until we came to a road, parking up on a sandy car parking area at the beach entrance.

'I thought you said the Med wasn't supposed to be tidal.' said Suzi accusingly.

'Well it is a little bit but I wasn't expecting this much,' I replied, 'It's a very flat beach though I suppose, and it is a full moon as well, plus there's been a strong onshore wind blowing for the last few days. All the water must have been blown up this end of the Med, I bet the tides gone out in Africa!'

☺ ☺ ☺ ☺ ☺

We stayed on that car park for the next few days, walking into Gruissan every morning for fresh bread and odds and ends. The sea slowly retreated, exposing the huge beach again and as the sand dried, cars started to return, driving further along it each day.

When I thought it was safe enough for Billy to go on there we went off to do some shopping and to fill up with water from 'my tap' at Narbonne Plage and then when we got back we drove along the beach. There were quite a few cars on there by this time so we went a lot further along where it was quieter. The sand was nice and firm so no chance of getting stuck and I parked Billy with his side door facing the sea.

Everyone we'd seen so far was naked, so we assumed it was a naturist beach which suited us just fine. We eagerly stripped off and took the boys for a nice long walk along the shoreline before returning to Billy and setting up camp. The sun chairs were in a bit of a sorry state now, both were ripped and kept spewing their stuffing out all over the place. Plus a couple of the springs had broken and one of the plastic arms had a big crack in it which kept pinching our arms.

As for the roll up table, well that was in an even worse state and frankly didn't have long left, something I was quite pleased about as it took up a lot of space in Billy. I was getting really fed up of moving it from the back to the front every night to make the bed, then to the back again in the morning. It was quite a cumbersome thing to get in and out and a bit of a faff to put up and take down, and so consequently it wasn't used very often. It was also on the receiving end of some fairly rough treatment, which was probably a contributing factor to its early demise.

We spent the rest of that day there just soaking up the glorious sunshine and having endless dips in the sea.

And so at last one of our dreams was now fulfilled - we were swimming naked in the Mediterranean. It had been well worth the wait, it was a truly wonderful, liberating feeling and something we could now tick off our 'to do' list.

We're both avid people watchers and being on a naturist beach just made things all the more interesting for us. One particular woman who I have to say, had a stunning body, came along and laid her towel just a few feet directly in front of us and stood over it doing stretch exercises. She had the whole beach to choose from but *oh* no, she had to come and plonk herself down right in front of us. Still, I suppose she was quite understandably proud of her beautiful body and wanted to show herself off to us.

Now normally we would have been more than a bit miffed by this intrusion, but she was facing the sea with her back to us and I at least was thoroughly enjoying the performance.

Well at least I was until she spread her legs wide and bent forward to reveal a tampon string dangling down between her legs.

This changed my mood somewhat and I was reminded of the feed bags on the farm as a kid, the ones with the string along the top and the written instruction 'pull cord to open.'

I shared this thought with Suzi after we'd exchanged amused glances and we had to stifle our childish giggles.

We may not have done such a good job of that as she picked up her towel and walked off a couple of minutes later.

We just loved being naked on the beach but for some reason we felt the need to put a t-shirt on whenever we sat down for something to eat. Just a t-shirt nothing else, don't know why, it just felt right - bare bottoms we were quite happy with.

Our feet were toughening up too, in the beginning we couldn't walk across the hot sand without having something on our feet but now we could.

We didn't want to risk sleeping on the beach that night just in case the sea came back and got us so we stayed there until bedtime, enjoying the empty beach in the moonlight and then retreated to the safety of the car park at the entrance for the night.

In the morning after walking to the shops for some bread and croissants, we returned to roughly the same spot on the naturist beach and set up camp again. We had the beach all to ourselves for a while and enjoyed a lovely long walk along the deserted shoreline. When the thought of coffee and croissants became too much to resist, we headed back.

Later that morning a very nice looking middle aged French couple came and parked near us. They had very posh new looking sun loungers, not like ours - a parasol, ooh now that's a good idea, we had seen them in the shops but were reluctant to spend money on one - and also a cool box.

We eyed that cool box enviously - a good idea but of course first you need something cool to put in it and as our fridge wasn't working we didn't have anything remotely cool so there didn't seem much point really.

Wearing only sunglasses, the woman stood and allowed her husband to apply sun tan oil - no not like that, more gently please - to her entire body before gracefully laying herself out on a fluffy white towel on her lounger. She then picked up a book, relaxed back like a queen and gave her husband instructions to position perfectly, the pristine yellow and pink parasol so as to provide shade for her head, whilst allowing the rest of her body to be caressed by the sun.

He then slapped some oil on his front and plonked himself in his chair which did not have a fluffy white towel on.

They both sat quietly reading until late morning when she leant forward and opened the cool box. We watched discreetly as she rummaged around in there for a bit and then produced half of an obviously chilled, moist melon.

Both the dogs I noticed, had their ears pricked up and were also watching intently, drooling and fidgeting, edging forward, they looked about ready to pounce.

She was totally oblivious to the four pairs of eyes that were focused on her from not so very far away. At least I hoped she was as she had sunglasses on and it was hard to see where she was looking.

'Ooh, I bet that's just come straight from an ice cold fridge.' whispered Suzi, eyeing the melon as she took a swig of warm water from a bottle.

'Mmm, yes and I reckon that box is full of ice blocks as well.' I added, licking my lips, not at all envious.

We continued watching as she spooned a couple of mouthfuls of crisp, cold melon out with what looked like a very shiny silver spoon and then promptly dropped the rest of it into their rubbish bag.

Our faces dropped, we turned to each other and shared an aghast look. To say we were horrified at this waste of good, not to mention *cold* food would be an understatement.

Caine looked round at me with a startled expression on his face.

'No Caine, you stay there,' I said quietly to him knowing full well what was on his mind, he cursed and turned back to look at her, licking his chops expectantly.

I very nearly went over and asked her if we could have it but decided to give her the benefit of the doubt, just in case it was off or something. She then slowly and almost seductively - well I thought so anyway - dabbed at some sticky melon drops on her front with a small white towel moistened with some chilled bottled water from the cool box, then she relaxed back and continued reading.

She did the same thing a little later on - another cold moist melon, a few mouthfuls then in the bin it went. I would have been really annoyed with her if she wasn't so damned lovely to look at. I was caught in limbo between admiration for the loveliness of her beautifully tanned, lightly oiled, exquisitely formed naked outer body and the disgust I was feeling for the ugliness of her inner self which allowed such a waste of good food, and *cold* food at that!

Caine however was in no such quandary, he just wanted the melons!

ᙅᙓ ᙅᙓ ᙅᙓ

That night we decided to risk staying on the beach but I drove Billy right away from the shoreline and parked at the top of the beach next to the bank which the track was on. The sand was a bit softer but I'd seen cars parked here during the day so reckoned it must be ok to drive on.

We woke just after sunrise the next morning and were relieved to find that the sea hadn't moved and we were still on dry land. We tumbled out of bed and ran straight down to the water and had a swim and a walk before anyone else arrived. It was idyllic strolling naked along the water's edge on what felt like 'our beach,' watching the sun rise and enjoying the early morning warmth before returning to Billy for breakfast without seeing a soul.

A bit later on we decided to move back down to the sea for the day and so we all hopped in. But then just as I was turning him around, Billy sank deep into the sand and simply refused to come out again no matter what I did.

I got out to have a look and his back end was well and truly down in the sand - we were clearly going nowhere.

I started digging sand away from the wheels with my hands and when there was a good bit of room in front of them I got back in and tried again, we went forward about a foot and then got stuck again. He was even lower in the sand now, if we were stuck before, we were really stuck this time and he was down so deep the wheels had practically disappeared.

(Sigh) - ok then, we'll just have to do this the hard way - time to put plan B into action.

I gave instructions to my assistant and we both wandered off and collected as many stones and rocks as we could find. I found a sturdy plank of wood about six feet long which I knew would come in very handy. I dug a hole under Billy, got the jack out and mounted it on a rock in the bottom of the hole to stop it sinking and then started jacking Billy up. It was really awkward having the jack down in the hole as the winding handle was at a difficult angle making it almost impossible to turn it.

It took a painfully long time and now sand was getting into the jack as well which really wasn't good for it but eventually I'd raised Billy up as far as he could go. Next, I filled the hole under the wheel with stones and twigs and bits of wood and laid the plank on top of them before lowering Billy back down onto the plank – ok, halfway there.

I carried out the same labourious process on the other side except there was no plank for this side so I had to make do with just stones.

Eventually it was done, Billy was level again and at ground level so I tried again. He went forward ok but as soon as he was off the plank he sank, as did our hearts.

(Sigh) - well ok it worked once so it should work a second time, I would just have to do it all over again – we had all day after all.

It was hot work so I decided to walk down to the sea to cool off; I also needed to wash off all the wet sticky sand which had found its way into all sorts of uncomfortable places after scrabbling around on my belly for the last hour or so.

Caine was more than happy with this arrangement as he loved the water and was a really strong swimmer. He followed me straight into the water and we swam out to sea for a good few minutes before turning back towards the shore, which now looked an awfully long way away. It seemed to take longer to get back and I wondered how far he could actually swim before needing a rest but he never faltered, he was loving it.

On the way back up the beach and purely by coincidence - I wasn't looking for her at all honest - I happened to pass by the melon queen reading beneath her parasol. I couldn't help thinking how nice and refreshing it would be to bury my face into her juicy melons right now.

I pushed such thoughts aside and walked on by.

Caine on the other hand had no such scruples; he had his head buried deep in their rubbish bag, tail wagging away happily. I called him away and eventually he reappeared with half a melon in his mouth. I mumbled an apology and then he proudly carried his prize all the way back to Billy where I wrestled it from him in the vague hope of having it for lunch.

Sadly though, as well as where she'd taken the soft centre bit out, it was full of his teeth marks and plastered in slobber and sand from having been dropped during our wrestling match. I quickly abandoned all hope of a rescue, broke it in half and gave the boys a piece each and they both trotted off happily into the shade next to Billy and tucked in.

In the meantime Suzi had collected some more stones and bits of wood in readiness for round two.

Judging from the sand, I would have to repeat the same laborious process at least another two or three times before we reached solid ground again so I got stuck in. We didn't have enough stones so first I had to dig up the now deeply buried ones from the first attempt, then jack Billy up again, fill the hole under the wheel and then lower him back down on to the stones and the plank.

The day was warming up quickly now and I had a good sweat going which of course the sand loved to cling to.

Eventually though we were ready for another go at freedom, again with the same result, a few feet forward, off the end of the plank then down again. Another swim was called for so I strolled off down the beach with Caine and we both ran into the sea together and swam out, only not so far this time. We went around a posh yacht which was anchored there before returning to the shore and the long walk back to Billy.

It was well past lunchtime by the time Billy was finally liberated, leaving a trail of devastation across the sand. I wanted to keep the plank in case there was a next time but we had nowhere to keep it, so it was with some regret and also a tinge of sadness that I drove away from the scene leaving it lying there - it felt like a betrayal.

We'd come to know each other so well over the past few hours and it really deserved better, especially after helping us out of a hole so to speak.

'Poor old Frank.' I muttered as we headed off down the beach.

'Who's Frank?'

'That plank of wood, Frank the plank, I feel really bad just abandoning him there like that.'

'Aww never mind, there are plenty more planks in the sea, you'll see,' she said patting my leg reassuringly, 'someone will find him and give him a good home don't you worry.'

֍ ֍ ֍ ֍ ֍

The next time we went to the shops we succumbed and bought a parasol and a cool box which took a sizeable chunk out of our weekly budget. This meant we would have to go without a few things, but we felt it was a necessary expense as we all needed some shade to sit under from time to time.

Also if we could keep some things at least a little cool-*ish*, we could then buy more when we went shopping which would mean less travelling and therefore less money spent on petrol.

The parasol was a great buy, it was very pretty in broad red and blue stripes which clashed perfectly with the bright orange of Billy. When it was up it provided a lovely big area of shade, big enough for the both of us to relax under in our rapidly declining reclining chairs. There was also enough space for the boys and they seemed to prefer it to being underneath Billy as they had a much better view of their surroundings.

The coolbox though was not such a good buy.

As I said, we had no way of making ice, or even anything remotely cool so I came up with a clever plan. I reckoned that if we filled it with the things we wanted to keep cool, then bought a couple of things which were already cold and put them in as well, they would keep everything else cool as well.

So with this in mind, we drove to the shops and bought a litre bottle of chilled spring water and as a treat, two bottles of ice cold beer. Then we rushed back to Billy and stuffed them in the box and quickly closed the lid. Not only would they keep the food cool but we would also be able to enjoy a nice cold beer at lunchtime.

Well lunchtime came and we opened the box excitedly only to find that the beers were warm, the water was warm and everything else in there was warm as well. It was going to take a lot more cold drinks to cool it down which would mean driving to the shops at least once a day, using valuable petrol just to keep buying drinks which we didn't need. I had seen bags of ice in the shops but that would still mean a trip to the shops every day.

I could have walked to the shops but it was a good couple of miles and the ice would have melted by the time I got back.

Then I had a brainwave, the sea's quite cool I thought, I could swim out with an empty bottle, dive down as far as I could go where the waters cold, fill the bottle up and voila - one cold bottle of water - how hard could it be.

Well, diving down twenty feet or so into the murky frigid depths, holding your breath long enough to take the top off and waiting for the bottle to glug itself full was no easy task I can tell you. An empty two litre bottle takes some holding on to at that depth and it was only after several aborted attempts that I managed to hold on to it long enough to fill it.

It was really cold down there and as I emerged for the final time, coughing and spluttering and gasping for air, I comforted myself with the thought that if the bottle was as cold as I was then we could be in business. I swam back to the shore with my teeth chattering where a concerned Caine was lying in wait for me in the shallows.

Without warning he pounced, grabbed the bottle from my hand and ran off with it, shaking it vigorously as he went. He charged back up the beach to Billy mouthing the punctured bottle and spraying cold water everywhere. There were shrieks and shouts as people scattered in all directions, the biggest one coming from Suzi as he ran straight up to her and had a good old shake, bottle still in mouth.

I noticed the melon queen was dabbing at herself with her towel, her husband was smiling but *she* wasn't and I thought it best to stay in the water for a while until the heat died down.

Needless to say that particular idea was shelved and the coolbox became a storage box, a table and a seat.

We stayed on that beach for the next few wonderful weeks with the melon queen parking next to us every day. Her Caine encounters obviously hadn't put her off that much then. Suzi had become a little bored with her by this time - I for some reason hadn't!

Eventually though, the wanderlust overcame us again and we headed south - Spain was calling - the heat beckoning to us.

We went gladly.

A short way down the coast we drove through the town of Leucate where the road followed the edges of a large inland sea lake covered in windsurfers. The lake was on our right and off to the left just a couple of hundred metres away was the sea. We went over a bridge looking for a left turn to try and get near the beach, but typically took the wrong exit at one of the many roundabouts. We carried on a bit further and then turned off onto a sandy track which luckily was really packed down hard so there was no chance of getting stuck. We drove around for a bit and eventually parked Billy near the water's edge at a little inlet with a small beach.

We all got out and had a walk about, exploring our new surroundings, it was idyllic, there was no-one around anywhere.

I reckoned there must be access to the sea somewhere as we could see several yachts moored just across the water near to some villas. I went for a swim and was surprised at how cold the water was compared to up the coast a few kilometers, then we spent the rest of the day by Billy, relaxing, reading, swimming and playing bat and ball.

The odd car came and went but no-one came near us and we had the little beach all to ourselves, it was great. We spent a very peaceful night there and early next morning before breakfast I went for a quick swim. I charged into the water, dived under and oh my god what a shock, it was freezing! It was so cold the shock made my eyes vibrate - it was really weird and I didn't stay in very long!

A small yacht was moored in the inlet close to the beach which must have arrived during the night sometime. It made such a tranquil scene lying there quietly, basking in the warm glow of the early morning sun surrounded by the millpond calm water – well apart from the waves I'd just made that is!

We had breakfast outside and then we played bat and ball, we were determined to break our non stop record of 135. As we were playing, a man from the yacht paddled ashore in a tatty old hand painted inflatable dinghy, he looked weather beaten, tired and bedraggled and came over to us saying.

'Hallo, you are English yes? I am from Belgium, my name is Pierre.'

We all shook hands as he continued, yawning and stretching.

'I sail from Antibes yesterday, always I come here to this place and park my ship, is always quiet, is very nice no?'

We agreed it was.

'I arrive in the night very tired, I do not tie my ship up so good I think, I fall asleep very quickly, I am happy to still be here now!' he said laughing.

'I hear big splash just now and I wake up thinking "What the fuck is this big noise, is something falling off my ship?" but then I sleep again. Later I wake up and I hear tat tat tat and I think I go crazy in my sleep, tat tat tat, oh my god what is this tat tat tat all the time. Now, I think for sure there is problem with my ship.'

He was gesticulating with his hands and arms, shrugging his shoulders, scratching his head and laughing as he prattled on.

'Then I get up from my bed and look out and see these crazy English people on the beach playing tennis with their dogs and I see the tat tat tat is the ball and then I know everything is ok with my ship. I have only two hours sleep, I must tie the ropes again and *then*,' he paused and raised his finger in the air, 'more sleep, I will come back, this is ok yes?'

Before we could say anything, he walked off to tie his mooring ropes properly then got back in his dinghy and paddled back to his little yacht.

'I think we woke him up,' I said, putting the bats and ball away.

'I know, poor bugger, he must be shattered.'

'Tat tat tat, that's good I like that, that's exactly what it sounds like, sorry Caine game over until later ok?'

I went snorkeling a bit later on along the shoreline. Nelson stayed with Suzi as usual whilst Caine came with me, swimming alongside; it was fun to watch his hairy legs paddling away underwater as he swam along.

Along the way I came across a black, sleeveless t-shirt crumpled up on the sand which someone must have left behind by accident. It looked quite new and had palm trees with 'White Island' written on it - I tried it on when I got back later and it fitted perfectly. I wore it for the rest of the day, and the next day and the next, in fact I wore it practically every day from then on until it eventually wore out.

For reasons known only to her, Suzi called it my 'Black Island' T shirt and in the end so did I.

Much later that day, Pierre resurfaced and we idly watched him for a while as he worked on his boat, tidying the sails up, washing things and fiddling with ropes.

'Invite him over for coffee Tim,' Suzi said, 'it's the least we can do after waking him up like that.'

I took the broken coffee pot and went down to the water's edge and called to him, holding up the pot.

'Pierre, come over for coffee,' I shouted.

'Ah yes - please,' he called back smiling, 'very nice, I come in five minutes ok?'

Some half an hour later he paddled ashore in his multi-coloured, multi-patched dinghy. He was dressed in a faded blue t-shirt, very skimpy red trunks, flip flops and carrying a very old and tired looking rucksack. He also had an old bike with him which had been lashed onto the cabin roof and he fiddled around with it for a while before coming over to us.

'My ship is like crazy,' he began, waving his arms in the air, 'so many things to do from yesterday, now is better again. I come long way in last two days, I love your dogs they are very beautiful,' he said as he got down on his knees to fuss them, 'I see immediately you are from England when I see the number and the steering wheel on the wrong side,' he said pointing in Billy.

'Well actually we're from Wal.....' I began.

'I like very much England, I go there many times before but never in my ship,' he continued as he sat down in the side doorway, tipping his faded red cap back on his head.

'You make holiday in France, is pretty country no? but strange people I think,' he said, screwing his face up and shrugging his shoulders again, 'Belgium people much nicer,' and he roared with laughter. 'I stay here for a few days and then I take my ship to Spain, I go there before.'

'Oh, we're on our way to...' I began again.

'Yes, from here I go to Cadaques, you go there? you *should* go there, is very beautiful you know,' he continued as he slurped away at his coffee, 'Last time I go there, there were many ships like mine all parked in the bay, is a very beautiful bay, but they only put one anchor down. I always put down two anchors - why? because in this place one anchor will not keep you there if the Tramontana blows. I say to myself, "why they no put down two anchors," is crazy no? If big wind comes in the night when they sleep, bam!' he slapped his hands together, 'they have big problems I think. This day I can see from the air there is a big wind coming soon and I say to them to put down two anchors but they say no, is ok with one. They are crazy and of course Pierre is right, a big wind comes from the land in the night, blowing down the mountain. When in the morning I look out, I am the only ship left, all of them are blown out to sea in the night, I can not see them anymore and I laugh at them. They use their ships for only two weeks in one year, they know nothing and they will not listen to me. Is crazy - why they no listen to me?' he demanded, looking puzzled and he shrugged yet again.

'If wind blows from the sea that night they would all be fucking dead by now, their ships all smashed up on the rocks, crazy crazy bastards.' he said shaking his head vigorously in disbelief.

We both sat quietly, amused by his ramblings and he continued.

'Today I go to the Intermarche for buy some things,' he said holding up his rucksack, 'I like very much this coffee, what is the name please?'

I didn't bother attempting a reply and sure enough he wasn't waiting for one.

'I buy some today I think, and also some wine and bread, I make a list look,' he said as he brandished a crumpled piece of paper at us, 'but first I must make good my bike, I have problems with the gears, I think maybe the sea go inside and make trouble, maybe I walk today.'

'We're going to the Intermarche soon,' I said, 'you're welcome to come with us if you don't mind sharing the back seat with the dogs that is.'

'Ah yes thank you this is not a problem for me, I love your dogs, if they are happy with me, I am happy with them,' he laughed as he fussed them both enthusiastically; even Nelson was sitting by him allowing himself to be stroked which was unusual.

We packed everything away and drove to the Intermarche with Pierre sharing the back seat with the boys. Nelson begrudgingly moved over to let him sit down and then stared out of the window in disgust, occasionally throwing him the odd scowl – having to share his seat was just one step too far.

Caine on the other hand greeted him happily and leant against him the whole way, much to Pierre's delight.

As we were walking around the supermarket Pierre was talking away loudly, non stop as usual and it was only then that we realised just *how* skimpy his trunks actually were. This combined with the fact that they'd obviously seen many years of active service meant they'd become really loose and baggy. The front was hanging down so far that most of his pubes were on display and it seemed only a matter of time before his hairy balls escaped out through the sides. When he bent over the freezer compartments the rear view was hilarious.

His t-shirt was too short as well and there was a large expanse of belly on display which only made his nether regions all the more visible. We were quite amused by his appearance and his couldn't care less attitude, it made an otherwise boring shopping expedition really good fun as we watched the reactions of the other shoppers.

Just as I was about to pay, Pierre pushed forward insisting he paid for our groceries as payment for giving him a lift to the shop.

The cashier held her hand out for his money and as he leant forward to pay, somehow his trunks got caught on something pulling them down and all his bits plopped out onto the stainless steel counter. The poor cashier withdrew her hand a bit sharpish as Pierre jabbered away continuously to her the whole time, casually rearranging himself as he waited for his change.

She wasn't bothered in the least though and I was thinking had that been in the UK, she'd probably have been really shocked and offended or called the police or something.

☺ ☺ ☺ ☺ ☺

On the way back he came forward and crouched on the floor between the front seats so he could talk to us better. He was telling us there were some good places to go 'shopping' when he suddenly shouted excitedly.

'Here Tim, turn here, we go up here!'

It dawned on us then that when he said 'shopping' what he really meant was scrumping! I slammed the brakes on and turned onto a bumpy dirt track sending a lovely big cloud of dust up all around us as if to mark our arrival - not something Pick and Stash would normally do on a scrumping run!

I was nervously following the track when I received further shouted instructions from the back.

'Stop here Tim this is ok, we go shopping now,' he threw the sliding door open and he and the boys jumped out before I'd even stopped.

I looked back in dismay at the huge cloud of dust we'd created as he sloped off into the rows of vines. He wasn't even looking around for a farmer or anything he just went off and started picking, talking noisily to us the whole time.

I got the uneasy feeling that we were being led astray at this point and as I nervously picked a couple of bunches of under ripe grapes, I looked up and saw a long low building overlooking the vineyard we were in. There a row of windows in one part of it and I could just make out people standing there looking in our direction, It was then that I saw the word 'GENDARMERIE' painted on the side of the building in large black letters, how could we not have noticed that before?

'Oh shit, you have got be kidding,' I groaned quietly to Suzi, 'look, that's a bloody police station over there and they're watching us too, Pierre come on that's a police station.'

'Pah!, no need for worry Tim,' he replied, waving my concerns aside with a hand gesture, 'they think we are the farmers maybe.' he said nonchalantly as he stuffed his rucksack with more grapes.

I looked back and to my horror saw Billy sitting in the middle of the vineyard, standing out like a beacon of bright orange and white amongst a vast sea of green. All we needed to do now was to put a banner up saying "Scrumping in progress" and it would be perfect. No, we do not look like farmers I was thinking to myself as I heard the sound of a car starting up somewhere in the distance.

'Oh shit!' I said again as I pointed at Billy, 'that's a dead giveaway that is - come on you two we're going!' and I walked quickly back to Billy.

I started him up and turned around quickly whilst the others piled in through the side door spilling their spoils all over the place as I sped off back down the bumpy, dusty track raising another dust cloud for anyone that hadn't already seen us. Luckily it was only a short way back to the road where we were soon flying along enjoying the warm breeze and a good laugh at our exploits. I was keeping a worried eye on the rear view mirror when Pierre suddenly pushed forward between us, pointing animatedly.

'Turn here Tim, here!'

Against my better judgment, I slammed the brakes on again and we skidded onto another dirt track.

'What's up here then Pierre?' Suzi enquired.

With an eccentric shrug of the shoulders he laughed and said.

'I don't know, but I hope no police!'

This track was much longer and rougher than the other one and we wound our way slowly uphill, I was hoping we didn't have to make a quick getaway this time. The track came to an end near some fruit trees and when we got out I saw a blue Renault 4 police car driving slowly along the road below us. It looked like we'd given them the slip, at least for the time being and I for one wasn't in a rush to leave for a while.

The thought crossed my mind at this point that I might paint Billy green, just for times like these; ooh then he'd have a surname as well!

I was pleased to see there was no sign of a gendarmerie this time and we got some lovely ripe peaches and a carrier bag full of almonds before we left. I climbed the trees and dropped the almonds down to Suzi who tried to catch them in the bag which proved to be a waste of time as she was hopeless at it.

She hardly caught any and I ended up just throwing them at her instead - it was great fun, well me and Pierre thought so anyway.

When we got back, we spent a long time shelling the almonds as they have two shells, a softer outer one which we could get off with our hands and then a hard inner one, which we had to break using a couple of stones from the beach. There was a knack to doing this without squashing the nut inside but we got the hang of it after a while.

Considering the carrier bag was full to bursting, the amount of nuts we had at the end wasn't that much and the bag of empty shells looked as full as it did before we started.

Needless to say we never went 'shopping' around there again.

☺ ☺ ☺ ☺ ☺

Pierre invited us onto his yacht for drinks that night and he came over in his little dinghy and ferried us across.

His 'ship' was even smaller than it looked from the shore; it was about 6 metres long and badly in need of some paint and varnish. We clambered aboard and sat in the tiny cockpit with our knees all touching. He opened one of the seat lockers and a breath stopping smell escaped from within. It was a heady mixture of stale sea water, damp mouldy old rope, sails and god knows what else.

'This is my wine cellar' he announced proudly as he produced a bottle from deep amongst some coils of old rope, 'You like wine? I have some Moscatel left from when I make visit in Spain once before. I keep for such an evening is very nice very sweet, you will like I think.'

He poured some from the half empty bottle into tatty old plastic beakers for us. He was right, it *was* very sweet and syrupy but really nice, I said,

'Does your ship have an engine Pierre?'

'Yes of course' he replied gesturing for me to stand up so he could open the locker I was sitting on. I should have held my breath as the same toxic fumes assaulted my nostrils when he opened it.

'Here is my engine,' he said proudly as he patted a tiny rusty old outboard motor which was wedged firmly between more coils of smelly old rope and what looked like rolled up sails.

'Erm…does it work?'

'Yes for sure it works…..sometimes!' and he threw back his head and roared with laughter at his joke, 'anyway Pierre does not need an engine, Pierre is a sailor his ship has sails,'

He drained his beaker and pointed to the top of the mast saying.

'Tomorrow I must climb up there and make good my lights, sometimes I have lights other times not, I think the sea has been there like in my bike, always the sea makes trouble for me.'

It's no wonder the sea gets into your bike I thought, it was lashed down with bits of old rope on the cabin roof and it wasn't even covered with anything.

'You want go inside?' he asked, gesturing towards the cabin.

We went down below to see his living space, if space is the right word as there wasn't much of it. He stayed up in the cockpit as there simply wasn't room for three of us down there.

There was no headroom either and I had to crouch down all the time – it was like being in Billy with the roof down. It got uncomfortable after a while so I sat down. Two tiny windows provided what little light there was down there and it was *very* lived in and absolutely crammed with stuff; there was no room for us to move around whatsoever.

All over the walls there were pictures and postcards from his travels and his bed was in the tiny pointy shaped cabin in the bows which wouldn't have been long enough for me to sleep in.

I saw no radio and no navigation desk either; there wasn't enough space for one anyway. When I asked him about them he waved the thought aside flamboyantly with both hands.

'Pah! Pierre does not need those things, I follow the land wherever I go is easy for me,' he held up a road atlas similar to ours, only even more dog eared if that was possible and some of the pages spilled onto the floor.

He scooped them up roughly saying.

'This is my chart, is simple no? I am here now,' he said pointing, 'and in one week I will be here, in Santa Margarita,' he continued as he sorted the loose pages out eventually finding the one with the right place on.

'I have very special place, only I go there, everybody else? hah! too scared to take their ships in, I am the only one there, is very beautiful.'

'No compass or radio?' I asked.

He just shrugged and said, 'What for I need a radio?'

'Well, to let people like the coastguard know where you are and where you're going,' I replied.

'Pah! is none of their fucking business where I'm going!' he retorted making some strange hand gestures for emphasis. 'Pierre goes where he wants to when he wants to is not necessary to tell anyone, never I speak with coastguard. If I want to speak with someone I use a telephone.'

'What do you do at night then when it's dark with no compass?

'Is very easy, at night I drive by the stars and always there are lights on the land so I see how close to the rocks I am. When the lights become too big, I go away again from the land. I know how big the lights should be, this way I never crash, also is very beautiful to be on the sea with only the stars, I like it very much - and now, we drink a beer yes?'

His head disappeared from the entrance and we watched as he leaned over the side of the boat and pulled on a rope.

'Come to Pierre my little beauties,' he crooned as a holdall full of beer bottles emerged from the depths, 'how you like my fridge eh? here you have one please.'

He opened them and handed us one each, it was really cold and a nice treat. It was certainly better than our fridge and I wasn't surprised they were cold remembering how cold the water had been the other morning.

There was a splash and then a curse.

'Oh merde!' he groaned, 'I lose my bottle opener into the water; I must swim down and find it tomorrow.'

☺ ☺ ☺ ☺ ☺

The next morning we were sitting outside on our faded torn and taped up sun loungers, enjoying breakfast on our broken and taped up roll up table. I was just pouring the coffee when there was a huge splash from over by Pierre's boat, Suzi turned to me and said.

'What was that, has he fallen in?'

'Dunno, maybe.' I replied, casually stirring my coffee as a concerned Caine ran down to the waterline to investigate.

'He could be in trouble Tim.'

'Yeah, he could be.' I agreed, relaxing back with my coffee, Caine was now swimming out to Pierre's ship.

'Go and see if he's ok.'

'You must be joking, the water's too cold and anyway Caine's gone to rescue him.' I said smirking, he loved rescuing people and he'd 'rescued' me a few times before. It was only in view of the incredulousness of the look I was receiving that I said.

'Look just give him a minute, he's probably gone down for that bottle opener that went overboard last night.'

Sure enough, a few seconds later he popped up again right next to Caine, holding the opener in the air triumphantly.

'I have it, I have my opener!' he shouted and we gave him a nice round of applause. Caine was swimming around him in circles and I shouted to Pierre.

'He's come to rescue you, grab hold of his tail!'

He grabbed hold and Caine turned for the shore pulling him along until they reached the shallows, Pierre was laughing his head off.

'Oh my god, I fucking love this dog!' and he sank to his knees and hugged him, 'thank you thank you thank you, is incredible, you save my life for sure you fucking beautiful dog!'

He rolled over on the sand with tears in his eyes and Caine jumped on him in delight. They had an impromptu wrestling match whilst Nelson just ran around them barking as usual and I put the coffee pot back on.

'Why you no play tat tat today?' he asked when he'd regained his composure.

'We didn't want to wake you,' I replied, 'and we're going off to buy some bread in a minute.'

'No no no, is not necessary,' he said wagging his finger at us, 'you can buy bread from the village over there, I go there many times before,' he said pointing across the water to all the villas, 'is a naturist village clothes are not necessary over there, you are ok with this?'

We agreed that we were, and pointing at his dinghy he said.

'You can take my *small* ship, but the dogs must stay here they are not allowed in the village, I will look after them.'

'Thanks Pierre, I can't swim though,' said Suzi as she looked worryingly at the sorry state of the dinghy, 'what happens if it goes down, can we take the pump?'

'Is ok it won't go down so quickly, also is not good idea to take the pump someone maybe steal it, no no is ok is inflatable, is not possible for sinking.' he smiled, slapping the side reassuringly.

Hmm this one could I thought to myself and reluctantly Suzi agreed to the arrangement.

We got into the dinghy and started paddling out across the channel, only now realizing just how many patches there actually were on it. The reason for all the paint now became worryingly clear, it was there to bung the leaks up and to help hold the patches on.

It was a tiny dinghy and we had to sit one each side with a foot trailing in the water as we paddled. It seemed quite soft and I noticed a trail of bubbles coming up from underneath. As we were now halfway across the channel I decided it maybe wasn't the best time to mention it so I just carried on paddling and we reached the other side safely. I left the dinghy floating in the shallows and tied it to a stone, we stripped off and wearing only money belts, walked into the village.

It was a lovely clean little village made up of new red roofed pastel coloured villas each with their own small gardens full of beautiful flowers and exotic shrubs. We strolled along a lovely flower lined avenue of shady palm trees which led us down to the beach, and as it wasn't too crowded we decided to go for a swim

Actually I went for a swim leaving Suzi sitting on the sand, complaining the water was too cold which it was and I didn't stay in too long. Afterwards we walked back into the village in search of a boulangerie, eventually finding one with a dishearteningly long queue outside. We reluctantly joined the slow moving line of naked people which snaked its way across the freshly cut grass.

Now I've never been able to stand perfectly still for very long and as usual I was fidgeting away, looking around and talking to Suzi. I must have leant forward a bit towards the woman in front of me and I felt my willy nudge her backside.

She turned and I quickly blurted an apology, waiting for the slap which happily didn't come and I involuntarily stepped back - only to press my bum into the willy of the man standing behind me. I jumped forward mumbling another apology and connected with the woman in front again who turned around more sharply this time. In an effort to prove my innocence I went to put my hands out of the way behind my back but thankfully managed to stop myself in time before things got out of hand – so to speak. As I forced a ridiculous smile and yet another apology she looked down and then smiled to herself before turning to face front again.

I looked down - why did she smile?

Wifey meanwhile, was standing to one side watching this pantomime unfolding, rolling her eyes, sighing and shaking her head sadly at me. I stood completely still after that with the annoying sound of her tittering in my ear.

'That'll teach you not to fidget.' she whispered.

'Shut up.' I whispered back.

Eventually we made it into the shop without any further embarrassment. There was a low counter and a naked man serving the bread who had the biggest willy I've ever seen in my life, and I'd seen quite a few lately.

He had a lovely all over tan and it looked just like a baguette hanging there. In fact if he'd laid it out on the counter I might have accidently grabbed it and tried to walk off with it.

I felt a dig in the ribs.

'Stop staring Tim for god's sake, it's really rude,' hissed Suzi as he turned away to get our two baguettes.

'I'm not staring,' I lied, struggling to look him in the eye as he wrapped our bread up and gave me my change.

'Anyway you can talk, I wasn't the only one staring.' I said as we left the shop, noticing the dreamy look in her eyes.

'Allright I may have glanced at it once or twice but you made it so obvious you plonker, he saw you looking you know.'

'Well he must be used to that by now.' I grumbled.

We both decided then that doing naked shopping wasn't really for us. On the beaches and around Billy it was fine but apart from that, not really our scene.

When we got back to the dinghy I noticed it looked a lot softer than it did on the way over. I pushed us off from the bank and hopped aboard and yes, it was *definitely* a lot softer now but I didn't say anything.

Progress was slower now as I was holding the baguettes in one hand trying to keep them dry and paddling with the other.

Our weight on the sides was pushing the remaining air out even quicker and pretty soon our bums were under water. By the time we'd got halfway back the dinghy was full of water and had started to fold up underneath us.

'Oh shit Tim, we're sinking!' said Suzi throwing me an alarmed, accusing look.

'No we're not don't worry,' I said reassuringly, 'is inflatable, is not possible for sinking! - just keep paddling, we'll make it.'

We sank lower and lower with every passing second, the water was now up to our waists and the dinghy had folded up completely, squashing us in the middle. As a result we were getting nowhere fast, despite some frantic paddling on our part.

The worst part about it all was that the water was really cold down where our feet and legs now were. A fact which was quite colourfully pointed out to me several times by my long suffering wife who understandably was distinctly unimpressed with the way things were turning out.

My obvious delight in the situation wasn't helping her mood much either.

'Ok so it *is* possible for sinking after all,' I joked.

'Oh shut up Tim, I'm going to kill that bloody Belgian when I get back!' she fumed.

That 'bloody Belgian' was watching from the shore with a big grin on his face!

We eventually abandoned ship a good way off the beach with cursing and spluttering in one ear and a now guffawing Pierre who was clearly loving the spectacle in the other.

Caine was also aware of our plight and was on his way out to rescue us, he knew Suzi couldn't swim very well so he went over to her side and offered her his tail. She got hold of it with one hand but was too scared to let go of what was left of the dinghy with the other so Caine ended up towing her and a dinghy full of water back to shore.

I swam alongside keeping a good eye on them, still holding the baguettes above the water.

It was slow progress for him towing all that weight but he wouldn't give up until he'd reached the shore where we were greeted by an almost hysterical thigh slapping Belgian.

'This dog needs a fucking medal for sure.' he said as a very wet but very happy Caine stood up and planted his paws on his chest.

'I thought you said we wouldn't sink,' demanded Suzi irately as we were walking out of the water.

Pierre was too busy laughing to answer and then Caine, full of himself after saving suzi's life suddenly made a lunge for the baguettes. He was too quick for me and managed to snatch them both from my hand before I knew what was going on and then promptly went completely crackerdog, running around us in circles like a lunatic. Nelson meanwhile just bided his time and then pounced, relieving Caine of one of them and then they both trotted off very pleased with themselves and got stuck in.

'But is not sinking look, she floats' said Pierre still laughing and pointing to the practically submerged dinghy which now there was no one in it had unfolded itself and looked more like a dinghy again. I dragged it out and tipped it up to empty all the water out.

'Thanks Tim, you were a big help weren't you!' she snapped, though laughing as well now, 'you were more concerned for the bloody baguettes than for me, I could have drowned.'

'No no no,' laughed Pierre, waving his finger in the air, 'is not possible for drowning, Caine, he was rescuing you and also I am watching from the land.

'Huh, you'd probably have rescued your bloody boat first knowing you, and what a waste of time the whole thing was anyway, we still haven't got any bread for today – I nearly died for nothing.'

'Hah hah, but this is so funny no? I took picture just now of my boat like this,' he said laughing, making a V shape with his two hands.

'Oh yeah, really funny,' she said, drying herself off as Pierre pumped the dinghy back up and went back to his ship still chuckling away to himself.

A few minutes passed and the next time we looked up he was climbing up his mast like a monkey. He had a safety harness on and when he got to the top he clipped it onto something and spent the next half hour up there, presumably mending his dodgy navigation lights.

ꩠ ꩠ ꩠ ꩠ ꩠ

The next day he asked us if we would take him shopping to his 'special shop' as he needed some things for his boat. I eyed him suspiciously but he just laughed and assured me there would be no police this time so 'no need for worry'. After coffee we all piled into Billy and I drove inland for a few kilometers following his shouted instructions from the back - he couldn't come forward as Caine was lying across his legs pinning him to the seat.

Nelson didn't approve of such behaviour and had his head turned away, staring out of the window.

Soon enough we ended up on an unsurfaced track in the middle of nowhere where eventually we came to a wide entrance with a big sign which we couldn't understand.

'Here Tim here, turn in here,' he said excitedly, 'hah, now Pierre goes shopping.'

It soon became clear where we were.

'It's a bloody rubbish dump,' I said and we were all laughing away as I drove slowly around the place. I was on the lookout for an angry owner or a rabid dog or two but the place was deserted.

'Is incredible you know Tim I find some very nice things here, these rich people on their beautiful ships they are crazy,' he said tapping his head with his finger as he looked out of the window excitedly, 'They use their ships for only one time, maybe two times in the summer and then they throw their things away, they are crazy no? They have too much money I think, ok stop, stop here Tim this is good now I go shopping.'

I stopped as ordered and we all got out, Pierre rushed straight across to the nearest pile and started sifting through it and a few seconds later there was a shout,

'Hey look at this,' he shouted holding up a length of blue rope, 'what is wrong with this rope huh? nothing is wrong is like new, I take it for my ship, hah! look at this, oh my god you guys look at this, I find *real* treasure today!'

He was squealing with delight and almost falling over in excitement as he stood precariously on top of the pile. He held up a deflated inflatable dinghy, it was a bit bigger than the one he had already and it looked in pretty good shape too, although it did have several patches on it.

'Crazy rich bastards why they no fix this, I fix it for sure is very simple I will show you later, crazy crazy peoples,' he chuntered on and on like this the whole time as he ferreted through the pile, eventually ending up with quite a haul.

He'd found a very nice set of paddles for the dinghy, as well as two not as nice but perfectly functional fenders to 'protect his ship', several more lengths of rope, an assortment of timber, a diving mask and also a red baseball cap which he was now proudly wearing after casually discarding his other one.

We saw no-one the whole time we were there and when we got back we unloaded everything into his dinghy and he took it all over to his ship leaving the 'new' dinghy behind. He hung his new fenders over the side with all the others before coming back with his pump and inflated it. The only leak was from a patch which was coming off and he set about fixing it straightaway.

'Look Tim,' he began, pointing at the patch, 'everyone, they put one patch on the outside like this and think is good job, I say no no no!' finger waving in the air, 'is no good like this, always you must put two, I show you my way you will like I think.'

He took the patch off, cut a slit in the rubber to make the hole bigger and sprinkled some white powder inside. He then took a piece of rubber cut from another dinghy, which presumably he'd found on a rubbish tip somewhere and cut it into a suitably sized piece. Next he slapped some glue on it and inserted it inside the hole he'd just made, pressing it down firmly.

Then he made a bigger patch and stuck it on the outside, covered it with a piece of wood then put a big rock on it and left it for a couple of hours.

Later on he removed the rock and the wood, opened a very old tin of blue paint and poured it all around the patch to keep the edges down then pumped the dinghy up and refloated it. Caine immediately jumped into it and sat there with a big grin on his face.

'Oh my god I fucking love this dog,' he said laughing, 'hey what do you think Tim?' he asked of his patchwork, 'is beautiful job no? always I do this, never I have leaks in my boat,' he said laughing.

I was just going to mention the fact that we'd nearly died in his other 'beautifully' patched up boat when we saw a large yacht of about 12 metres or so approaching the beach.

'Oh my god look at this crazy bastard where does he think he's going? he is too big, he will hit the ground for sure or my ship, oh merde no not my ship!'

He quickly pulled Caine and the dinghy to one side and started jumping up and down waving at them to stop.

'Stop stop the beach is too steep, is too shallow for you!' he shouted, making an obvious gesture to the captain and waving his finger in the air.

All this sound seafaring advice went completely unheeded as the yacht glided at some speed straight towards us. It hit the steep beach with a sickening crunch accompanied by the muffled sounds of breaking crockery and screams from down below.

The Captain, and I use that term very loosely didn't even bat an eyelid. He just slammed it noisily into reverse and opened the throttle churning all the sand up and then shot off backwards without even looking behind him.

Now he was heading straight for Pierre's yacht.

'No no no you crazy rich bastard not my ship not my ship, you break my ship I fucking kill you!' he yelled at the top of his voice as he jumped up and down frantically, fit to burst.

We looked on helplessly, holding our breaths and waiting for the inevitable impact as they continued backwards. Seconds later there was a loud hollow thump as they hit the side of his little yacht sending it rocking and reeling at its mooring ropes.

Luckily it was only a glancing blow with the impact being softened by the vast array of fenders and old tyres Pierre had hanging over the side.

The yacht then continued out into the channel where it was noisily slammed into forward gear before disappearing around the corner, the captain never looked our way once the whole time.

'Ai ai ai you crazy crazy bastard!' he said incredulously, 'you see what I mean Tim, these rich bastards with their big ships which they cannot drive, if they break them they can buy another one,'

He held both hands out towards his little yacht which was still protesting at the violent intrusion, mast swaying like a pendulum.

'But she is my house no? I have only the one, this is why I leave as many things on the outside as possible just in case some crazy rich bastard tries to sink me. It happens before so now always I do this wherever I park, I think she is ok though no? merde, merde, merde!, I need to sit down now please,'

With a bright red face and close to tears he collapsed heavily into one of our sun loungers which belched out another handful of stuffing.

'Think I'd better put the kettle on,' I said.

Slowly, his colour returned to normal and over tea he gave us the names of a few places which we 'must be visiting' as we told him we were heading towards Spain. We planned to move on the next day and he told us where his ship would be 'parked' in a couple of weeks time.

'Is very beautiful place, I am the only ship here you will see my mast,' he said nodding reassuringly at us as he drew a cross in our atlas, 'there is boatyard at this place with many ships, you will find work there I think, always people are painting their ships, you can do this yes?

This sounded good to us as our money was disappearing at an alarming rate.

A couple of years previously we'd built a fiberglass dinghy in our dining room and also renovated an old wooden clinker built lifeboat so this was something we could both do to earn some money.

We all passed a moonlit evening around the campfire right by the water's edge as his little ship waited quietly in the shadows, none the worse for its ordeal. We sang silly songs and polished off Pierre's prized bottle of Moscatel whilst he regaled us with tales of his seafaring adventures long into the night.

We said our drunken goodbyes in the early hours and then he fell into his new dinghy and paddled off back to his ship.

ꐱ ꐱ ꐱ ꐱ ꐱ

Despite our late night we were still awake just after sunrise - we had breakfast, packed things away quietly and with a wave to Pierre's ship, we were off.

We wanted to keep to the coast road after leaving Leucate but somehow went wrong in Canet Plage and ended up heading towards Perpignan. This was something we really didn't want so I turned off the main road at the first opportunity and went across country, passing through some really beautiful scenery.

We went through a place called Cabestany before coming to Villeneuve-de-la Raho where according to the atlas there was a lake which we soon found. I pulled into a car park right by the water but there were too many people so we found a track and drove around the lake. The track took us across the middle of it and we parked halfway across with the water on both sides of us.

We all jumped out and ran down to the water, I threw a stick in for Caine while Nelson stayed on the beach waiting for him to come out so he could take it off him. Caine was happy with this little arrangement most of the time as he enjoyed swimming out for the next one. Occasionally though if he really liked a particular stick or if he was ready for a lie down and a chew, he would make his feelings known in no uncertain terms and Nelson would back off and just run around in circles barking at him.

There were hazy blue mountains in the far distance, were they the Pyrenees? I reckoned they were and this filled us with excitement and anticipation as it meant that we were getting closer to Spain. We spent the rest of that day there - it was an idyllic spot to spend the night and then we moved on just after daybreak the next morning.

We set off without having any breakfast and headed straight for the Pyrenees, they were the biggest mountains we'd ever seen and we wanted to get as close to them as possible - drive up and over them if we could.

We came to Laroque-des-Alberes, a beautiful old town right in the foothills of the Pyrenees with a small castle on a hill which we drove up to and had a walk around. We'd bought some baguettes and croissants down in the town and had our breakfast sitting on an old stone wall overlooking all the rooftops.

We couldn't find a road leading into the mountains from there so we turned towards the coast again - I wanted to drive the coast road into Spain anyway. On the map it looked as though it could be quite spectacular as it was right on the edge, with the sea one side and the mountains on the other.

We found some water in the next town - it was an old fashioned tap with a long handle which we had to pump to get the water out. The place was called Sorede, another quaint old town and we could have walked around these places for hours but we also wanted to keep travelling. From there we headed towards Argeles-sur-Mer along a nice quiet road with very little traffic and with the mountains rising up to our right.

It was hot by this time and we had all the windows open enjoying the warm breeze. The road opened out and it became straight for as far as we could see - I couldn't resist it and I put my foot down despite the protestations from my co driver. Pretty soon we were belting along approaching seventy with all the tinware rattling about in the cupboards and the curtains flapping about crazily.

We were singing "Y Viva Espana" at the tops of our voices when suddenly there was an almighty bang from the back somewhere which frightened the living daylights out of all of us. Billy suddenly started weaving and careering all over the road but luckily I managed to keep control and slowed down gradually - Suzi turned to look in the back.

'Oh my god the roofs blown up!' she exclaimed.

'Blown up, what d'you mean blown up?' I asked as I brought Billy to a standstill, 'I didn't know we were carrying explosives.'

'Oh shut up Tim stop being stupid,' she retorted giving me a filthy look into the bargain, 'it's been blown up by the wind, that's what the bang was look.'

I turned and sure enough, Billy's roof was fully erected. Going at that speed with the windows open must have made it shoot up suddenly.

'I told you you shouldn't have been going that fast didn't I,' she began.

'I wasn't going *that* fast,' I protested, 'anyway that shouldn't have happened should it, must be a design flaw,' I offered.

'Design flaw my arse you forgot to fasten it down before we set off didn't you, look,' she said pointing to the obviously unfastened clips which normally held the roof down.

'Ah yes it looks like you forgot to fasten it down,' I ventured lamely.

'Oh very funny - you always do the roof, it could have blown right off you idiot!'

'Yeah well it didn't did it ok? there's no damage is there, look It still works,' I said reassuringly as I lowered it and raised it again.

It did seem a lot heavier than before though and I noticed that one of the struts at the back was cracked and bent. Also one of the clips didn't quite reach anymore but I decided not to mention these minor details for the time being. As a distraction I looked out of the window and opened the sliding door saying.

'This looks like a nice spot to stop for our second breakfast, I'll empty the loo whilst we're here as well.'

I pulled Billy off the road, dug a hole and emptied the loo – carefully - and then we all went for a stroll across some dry dusty scrubland before returning for more fresh croissants and coffee. As I was lowering the roof before setting off again there was a loud bang as the cracked strut gave way and the roof came crashing down, jamming my hand in the mechanism and giving me a hefty teeth-jarring blow on the head into the bargain.

I squealed in agony and somehow managed to push the roof up again using my free hand and sore head whilst at the same time trying to free my other hand from the tangle of criss cross framework and struts. Unfortunately for me Suzi poked her head in the door and caught me wincing and cursing quietly to myself.

'What was that bang?'

'Hmmm? oh nothing it just slipped that's all, carry on, nothing to see here,' I began as I wrapped my hanky round my hand to stem the flow of blood, knowing full well I wasn't going to get away with this one.

I was right, she took one look at the blood soaked hanky and the wonky roof and sighed.

'No it didn't just slip, it's broken isn't it?'

'My hand? no no, it's fine,' I said, tightening the hanky, 'just a flesh wound, no need to worry.'

'Not your hand you fool the roof, it's broken isn't it.'

'Erm… well I think possibly, just a little bit,' I replied as I heaved it back up again. 'My hands fine by the way, thanks for your concern,' I continued, spilling blood all over everything in the process. The roof was a lot heavier now and it wouldn't stay up properly by itself which was no good, we couldn't live in Billy if we couldn't stand up in him.

'I think Billy has developed erectile dysfunction,' I said staring at the sagging roof, 'It's going to take more than a pill to fix this, I reckon he'll need an operation!'

We both had a good laugh about it and the kettle was brought into action as I waited for the bleeding to slow down. We sat down in the side doorway sipping our tea as we pondered the situation.

How could I fix it, I had no tools to fix the broken strut with and a new one would be too expensive, even if we could find one. I spent some considerable time wracking my brain over this latest dilemma when Caine bounded up to us with a stick in his mouth wanting one of us to throw it for him. I had a cup of tea in one hand and the other one was hurting too much.

'Oh not now please Caine, I'm really not in the mood,' I said between slurps of tea.

Suzi took the stick from him and brandishing it at me she said.

'Why don't you shove this up there?'

'Aww come on now there's no need for that,' I moaned, 'I'm suffering enough already.'

'Ha ha very funny, no you plonker why don't you shove this stick up in the roof to hold it up,' she said brightly.

'Oh my god you're a genius, I love you,' I shouted and planted a big smackeroony on her forehead.

I leapt up and with my working hand, jammed the stick in the roof and hey presto it was perfect, simple but effective.

With the pain in my head and hand almost gone, I sat back down to finish my tea to find a very confused dog staring at me wondering where the hell his stick had gone to.

☺ ☺ ☺ ☺ ☺

My hand was still bleeding a bit so with a sticky, bloody steering wheel we set off again - with the roof firmly secured this time - and headed for the coast.

We noticed a change in the number plates of some of the cars we passed, they were quite different from the now familiar French ones we'd become used to.

'We can't be far from Spain now,' I said.

'I wonder if we'll see Pierre again.'

'I hope so,' I replied, 'he said he'd take us out sailing, I'm really looking forward to that.'

'Me too that sounds lovely, as long as we don't go too far out.'

'I don't think he goes too far away from the land.' I said smiling, remembering some of his stories.

We never quite reached Argeles sur Mer because we went wrong somewhere and ended up on a major road which thankfully wasn't a peage.

'Hey look it's only 20 Kilometres to Cerbere, which I think is the last town in France, we need to get off this big road, I want to do the coast road.'

'How far is 20 Kilometres then?'

'About twelve miles,' I said, 'we're nearly there, I hope there's a turn off soon.'

Luckily there was, and a lovely twisty road took us down into the old harbour town of Collioure. We passed slowly through the narrow cobbled streets, hemmed in by tall pastel coloured houses and I had to carefully squeeze Billy passed parked cars and dodge aimlessly wandering flat capped old men.

We emerged into the morning sunshine again and onto a beautifully cobbled seafront near an old stone tower and I parked Billy near an archway in the old town wall. There were cafes with their rows of tables and brightly coloured chairs outside right by the beach with an old fort like building at the far end. It was still fairly early and most of the cafes were not yet open, alone on a wooden bench sat a woman eating an ice cream.

'Ooh I want to do that.' I said pointing to her.

'What, you want to lick her ice-cream?'

'No you *twit*, I want to sit on a bench and eat ice-cream like she's doing.'

'Yeah and me let's stop and do it then, Spain can wait for a bit.'

It was so peaceful there even the sea was silent, only the occasional seagull was to be heard, that and the distant scraping of chairs as café owners readied for business. I bought four ice creams then found a bench right by the sand and we all ate in silence, it was as if we didn't want to break the spell of the place.

The ice-cream eating woman was still on her bench and she was now smiling at the boys as she watched them enjoying theirs.

The spell was eventually broken by a drinks lorry noisily rattling along on the cobbles, how did *that* get down those narrow streets?

It was now the middle of July, it was hot here in this corner of France and it was going to be even hotter in Spain. I was just wondering how the boys were going to cope with it when Suzi turned to me and said.

'I hope it's not going to be too hot for the boys in Spain.' a blob of ice cream stuck on the end of her nose.

'They should be fine,' I said as I licked it off, 'as long as we can park near water so they can cool off.'

'It'd be nice to get some work at that boatyard wouldn't it?'

'It would but we're not that desperate yet, we can last a few more weeks before the money runs out.'

She turned to me in horror.

'What! a few weeks, is that all?'

Then she saw the silly smirk I had on my face.

'Oh very funny, you're a real comedian aren't you.'

'I know, what can I say, it's a gift.'

'More like a curse you mean.' she said smiling and punched me on the leg. I was glad I'd finished my ice cream by then otherwise it could have been a far messier outcome. I stood up.

'Right then, beautiful though this place is we need to move out, come along children - next stop Spain!'

Up Sticks

Up Sticks

Spain

'Hey what are you doing, I thought you said next stop Spain,' said Suzi as I brought Billy to a halt by a low stone wall along the Sea front in the picturesque French seaside town of Cerbere.

'I know I did but how can we not stop here,' I protested, 'it's beautiful.'

'Yes it is but we're not allowed to park here, look there are yellow lines.'

'Oh who cares, we're foreigners we can get away with anything, anyway where are they going to send the ticket, we're homeless remember!'

She laughed and said.

'Where are you going now?'

'I saw a tap underneath that statue back there, I'm going to fill up with water while we've got the chance,' I replied as I clambered through into the back. 'You can't be too careful you know we might get stranded in the mountains for days on end and die a slow and horrible waterless death.'

'Oh stop being such a plonker and be quick about it will you before the police turn up.'

I took a jerry can over to the tap which unfortunately turned out to be out of order so I returned to Billy empty handed, well apart from the can that is. We sat for a while on the hot stone wall right next to Billy with the side door open, both dogs were sitting in the doorway doing what we were doing, just looking around and watching the world go by.

Our reverie was shattered when a blue Renault Four pulled up next to Billy and two Gendarmes got out.

I got an 'I told you we shouldn't have parked here you idiot,' kind of look as they walked slowly round to our side and stood there looking down at us.

We exchanged 'Bonjours' with them and then one of them said something to us in French - well why wouldn't he?

He could see we didn't understand him so he pointed to the yellow lines on the road, then to Billy and waggled his finger in the air. Ah yes, that's French for *'no no no'* - our sea faring friend Pierre had taught us that much.

We got the message and as we got up to go they both went up to the dogs and fussed them - most French people seemed to like dogs. Caine was of course overjoyed as he loved making new friends, Nelson just endured it all, keeping his eyes fixed firmly on us like he always did at such times as if to say, 'I'm letting them do this to me but I'm really not interested in them, only you.'

We said our 'au revoirs' to the nice policemen, got back into Billy and pootled off again.

The coast road up and over the Pyrenees was turning out to be every bit as beautiful and spectacular as we'd hoped - the views were breathtaking. Every time there was a lay-by we stopped and just stared out to sea or sometimes we'd get out and sit on the cliff tops, breathing in the fresh sea air and gazing down at the waves breaking onto the rocks far below us.

We weren't going to get very far today at this rate, not that it really mattered though, there wasn't anywhere we needed to be apart from where we were.

There was a lovely view back across the bay as the winding, twisty road took us ever upwards. I pulled off the road at a big lay by and drove as close to the edge as I could….. wait for it.

'Tim for god's sake, do you have to do that?' exclaimed Suzi grabbing hold of the door and pressing her foot down hard on her imaginary brake pedal, 'You know I don't like being this close to the edge.'

'Oh yeah sorry I forgot about that, what a lovely view though, look at that house all on its own right on the edge of the cliff, wouldn't you just love to live there?'

'No!'

'Fair enough.'

We set off again.

We climbed steadily and eventually reached the Spanish border, there was a German car in front of us and they were waved through passport control without stopping. I went to follow them but there was a shout from the guard in the booth and another guard stepped out in front of Billy and stopped us.

He approached the passenger window probably expecting to speak to the driver and gave us a good look up and down, there was growling coming from the back seat - not now boys please, he's got a gun.

'Buenos dias, passaportes por favor' he said putting his hand in the window.

Well I knew that wasn't going to be tolerated and in less than a heartbeat Nelson appeared between us, front feet up on Suzi's seat growling and glaring at the guard who wisely took a step back.

He was very protective towards his Suzi, if a stranger ever happened to get too close to her he'd immediately put himself between them, head slightly turned away but with his eyes fixed firmly on them saying 'go on then pal, I dare you.'

Suzi handed him our as yet, still unstamped passports over with a big cheeky smile and he flicked through them quickly before handing them back. He was very careful not to put his hand back in the window.

'You make holidays in Spain?' he enquired.

'Yes, long holidays,'

'Gracias, enjoy,' he said smiling as he stepped back gesturing me to drive on.

I started to go but then stopped and called to him.

'Why stop us but not the car in front?' I asked in English, hoping he would understand.

He did and he smiled.

'They do like this with passaportes,' he said holding imaginary passports up.

'Ahh like this?' laughed Suzi holding our passports up in his face.

'Si si, like this is good, is important I see passaportes.'

We were all laughing now, Nelson had relaxed a bit and the growling had stopped.

Caine couldn't resist the laughter - he muscled his way through between the seats squashing poor old Nelson in the process and clambered up onto Suzi's lap. He stuck his head and front legs out of the window chuntering away happily, demanding some attention from the guard who tentatively put his hand out and stroked his head.

When he realized he wasn't going to get eaten he relaxed and fussed him properly, much to Caine's delight who nearly fell out of the window in his excitement over this latest conquest.

Nelson had retired to the back seat, disgusted once more with Caine's effusiveness and I had to drive off with him still hanging out of the window or we'd have been there all day.

We descended into the lovely harbour town of Portbou and followed a road along the water's edge. We were hoping it would take us around the coast but it only led us to a marina and unfortunately a dead end so we had to go all the way back again.

The road after Portbou was sensational, slow and twisty with breathtaking panoramic views over the sea - we passed a sign to a place called Colera.

'Colera? not sure I like the sound of that are you?'

'Hmm, yes let's give it a miss,' I agreed - we laughed and sailed on past.

Another lay by on another sharp bend right on the edge of the cliffs, another stop to take in the views - we were loving it.

Eventually though we were down at sea level again in the wide sweeping bay of Platja Grifeu where we stopped on the seafront .

'Wow that's got to be the best road I've ever driven on,' I said.

'I know, those views were amazing weren't they, shame it's all over.'

'Tell you what, let's do it again shall we?' I said as I turned Billy round and set off in a Francewards direction.

'Don't be ridiculous Tim this is just silly,' laughed Suzi, 'and what a waste of petrol, anyway I thought you said we never go back.'

'Well in the case of such awe inspiring natural beauty I'm prepared to make an exception to that rule.'

'You just don't have the strength of your own convictions do you my darling.'

'Oh shut up,' I replied and we both laughed as I changed down and rounded a bend, trying to watch the road and admire the view at the same time.

'Hey, this is even better, I'm closer to the edge this time, wow what a view!' I said as I gazed down at the sea far below us.

'Look just watch the road will you, anyway how far are you going?'

'I always go all the way baby.'

'Woo hoo that's my man, no seriously though we're not going over the border again are we?'

'Of course, why not, I'm sure Caine would love to see his new friend again.'

He was once again sharing Suzi's seat with his head and front legs hanging out of the window enjoying the breeze as we approached the checkpoint once more. Suzi held our passports out at arms length and there was a bemused look on the guard's face as we drove slowly through - to him it must have looked like Caine was holding the passports.

I immediately swung Billy round and we ended up on the other side of the booths. Suzi was still waving our passports about in the air laughing her head off whilst Caine barked a greeting at his new friend who broke out into a big smile and waved us back into Spain.

We didn't stop anywhere this time, I just drove really slowly so we could admire the view again.

We were approaching sea level again and I'd devised myself a new game, I was trying to see if I could let Billy drive himself round the bends without me having to use any brakes. Most of the time it was working out pretty well providing there was no oncoming traffic and I could cut the corners and use all of the road. On some of the tighter bends though we were just going far too fast, the tyres were squealing loudly on the hot tarmac and Billy was soon filled with the smell of burning rubber. Some of the cupboards had been sick but I still hadn't used the brakes - hold tight in the back boys!

I received a disapproving look and a resigned shake of the head from my so-called navigator who had both her feet wedged firmly up against the dashboard.

I'd just successfully navigated a particularly tricky bend when I spotted someone collecting water at the side of the road.

Ok then game over and I slammed the brakes on, swerved sharply and skidded noisily to a halt in the shade of some overhanging trees.

This time I got a 'was that *really* necessary you idiot?' look for my troubles.

'Water' I said by way of explanation as Suzi turned to look in the back at the dogs who were busy replacing themselves on the back seat again.

'I know boys your dad's a twat isn't he.'

Ignoring the insults and leaving Suzi to put things back in their cupboards, I took a jerry can over to where the man was filling his bottle up from a pipe coming out of a stone wall. He said something to me which I didn't understand and pointed to a sign which I did understand, it read 'No Potable'.

Then he took a drink from the bottle he'd just filled up and laughed before disappearing into the hedge. Well ok I thought, if he can drink it then so can we, it looked clear enough.

By this time the boys had jumped out as well, Nelson had a quick pee and a drink from the drain and then jumped back in again. Caine came over to the pipe, delighted to see the flowing water and he stuck his head under it with teeth bared and lapped at the water whilst I patiently waited for him to finish.

Eventually he stood back smacking his dripping chops so I went to fill up, straightaway he dived under it again and started drinking giving me a sideways look, tail wagging happily.

He stopped, but then as soon as I moved forward he started again.

'Oh yes Caine very funny, come on you've had your fun it's my turn now, you can't drink all of it y'know.'

He had other ideas but I wrestled him out of the way and then filled up the can. We decided to do some washing whilst we were there in the shade, we could dry it later when we found somewhere to stop for the night.

Caine then went back to the water pipe and just stood underneath it allowing the water to run all over his back, then he lay down on the wet ground and watched us doing the washing with a contented smile on his face.

Some time later we left the relative coolness of the water pipe and set off again. A few hundred metres further along we spotted a couple of campers parked on some rough ground below the road, it looked like a nice spot to camp so I slowed down to look for a way in.

At the last second I saw a rough track hidden between some trees and a half built house. I swung across the road and despite the fact I was going quite slowly, it was still too fast for the condition of the track. I saw the first massive pot hole a little too late, slammed the brakes on and we lurched to a very dusty halt at the bottom of the hole. There were the usual crashing noises coming from the back and the cushion the boys were sitting on shot forward onto the floor leaving them sliding around on the wooden seat.

Thankfully Billy climbed out of the hole unharmed and I gingerly picked our way down the rest of the track and onto the rough ground where the campers were. One was a German and the other a Swiss and we drove around a bit looking for somewhere nice to park which wasn't too close to them.

We found a lovely spot right down by the rocks just a few feet from the sea and I parked Billy with his side door facing the water. We now had our very own rocky Mediterranean seafront terrace, it was perfect.

The water looked crystal clear so me and Caine decided to go for a snorkel and a swim whilst Suzi sat in the sun and wrote letters. We climbed down the rocks and I jumped in, Caine jumped straight in after me and followed me everywhere.

It was about twenty feet deep and I could see the bottom quite clearly, I just had to get down there. I let all the air out of my lungs and slowly sank until I was sitting on the sandy bottom.

It was a beautifully sunlit aqua blue underwater world down there and so peaceful, there wasn't a sound - and with a view that seemed to go on forever. Little fish darted here and there, flashing in the sunlight, occasional clumps of bright green weeds moved idly in the currents.

I looked up to see Caine's undercarriage gliding gracefully through the water, long hair flowing and legs paddling away. I didn't want to leave that surreal tranquil scene but I needed some oxygen so I stood up and kicked off the bottom, aiming for Caine. I came up just behind him to hear him crying and looking all around, when he saw me he turned and came straight at me making a strange chuntery whiney noise.

Poor old Caine he was beside himself, he'd been desperately worried about me being underwater for so long. He turned and I grabbed hold of his tail so that he could 'rescue' me, and he towed me to safety.

We clambered out and he ran straight over to Suzi and Nelson without shaking and pounced on them both excitedly, thoroughly drenching them in the process, ha ha, lovely.

Nelson was of course disgusted and retreated quickly to a safe place underneath Billy and started cleaning himself.

Caine hadn't finished yet though and he ran around Suzi in sheer delight soaking everything in sight before eventually deciding to have a good old shake just to make sure she was as wet as we were.

She wasn't impressed at all and tried her best to protect the letters she'd been writing but they never stood a chance really and anyway, when I told her how concerned he'd been about me and how he'd 'rescued' me again, she immediately forgave him. We were then left sitting in the middle of a very large wet patch of rock, steam gently rising into the air as Caine sat there still dripping wet and panting heavily with his long tongue hanging out of the side of his mouth.

It was such a beautiful, peaceful spot we decided to stay there for the night. Okay, if we looked behind us it was a just building site with piles of rubble and rubbish scattered everywhere amongst the scrubby dust covered bushes, but on our side we had the beautiful Mediterranean literally right on our doorstep.

We set up our sorry looking furniture on our new waterfront terrace whilst Caine played with a dog which had come over from the German camper. It was a Saluki and of course he had no chance of keeping up with it so he soon gave up trying. He just stood there waiting as it ran off at top speed and then came back, buzzed him and then charged off again. He was a little bemused and not at all sure how to go about playing with someone you couldn't catch.

Eventually though the dog tired a bit and slowed down enough so they could play properly together, either that or he just felt sorry for Caine.

We heard a whistle and then the dog shot off back to it's own van.

A long lazy afternoon was spent lounging around on the rocks with frequent plunges to cool off. There was no-one working on the building site and nobody bothered us at all, only the dog who came over every now and again to taunt Caine.

We slept with the side door open that night with the sound and the smell of the sea filling our senses. The last thing we saw before sleeping was Nelson lying on the rocks just outside Billy, on guard duty as usual and fully alert. The first thing we saw when we woke up was him in exactly the same place, same position and still fully alert.

He'd lived with us for almost ten years now and we'd never once seen him sleeping.

♥ ♥ ♥ ♥ ♥

It was early with the sun rising over a flat calm, weak blue sea and it was already warm.

As Suzi fed the boys their breakfast I prepared ours - a pot of fresh coffee and re-heated three day old croissants. We didn't have an oven so they were warmed up under the grill which was a little fraught as they often got a bit burned, but they still tasted delicious.

Using our biggest hard backed book as a tray, which was barely big enough for everything and with a couple of towels for us to sit on wedged under my arm I very carefully made my way down the rocks to where Suzi was now sitting, dangling her feet in the water - it was such a beautiful place to have breakfast.

Both the boys were watching us intently, eagerly waiting for their croissants despite the fact that they'd already had their breakfasts.

Nelson was watching discreetly and politely from a distance but not Caine - dripping wet from his first swim of the day he was right there next to us, staring intently and fidgeting. When he thought it was high time he got his, he sat up on his haunches with his front paws tucked under his chin with a 'please feed me I'm starving.' expression on his face.

Needless to say this little trick always worked and he ate his croissant on my nice clean towel which he'd craftily worked his soggy bum on to, leaving crumbs and slobber all over it - Nelson came over and took his back to Billy.

As the morning went on, cars and campers began turning up and we soon had people either side of us. The silence was shattered, the spell was broken, it was time to move on.

We packed everything away after lunch and drove back to the water pipe to fill up again before heading South once more.

It was late afternoon by the time we reached Platja Grifeu again, just in time to find a bank and cash a Eurocheque for some Pesetas.

The rest of the day was spent parked on the seafront by the marina with various articles of washing draped on a low wall and all over Billy, it dried in no time. Nobody objected to us being there so we stayed there for the night and set off early next morning.

We turned off for Cadaques, following the long and winding road down the hillside which of course prompted the inevitably badly sung sing along song. Some time later we reached the very beautiful but very crowded old harbour town with sadly absolutely nowhere to park.

'This is where Pierre told us that story about all the yachts being blown out to sea one night remember?' I said as I worked my way slowly through the traffic, searching without success for somewhere to park.

'Yes, all except him because he'd put two anchors down.'

'That's right - why they no leesten to heem, they are crazy crazy bastards no?' I joked, and we laughed as we followed the seafront round onto a very narrow, cobbled road. There were houses on one side and a drop into the water on the other with no barrier to stop us going straight over the edge. This of course was making my co driver just a little bit nervous as she was really close to the edge on her side.

'Lovely view,' I said teasingly.

'Yeah very nice, just watch where you're going will you,' said Suzi looking straight ahead.

'Oh look that's Pierre's yacht,' I said pointing - she half looked and then turned back straightaway.

'No it isn't just stop it will you and watch where you're going,' she said grabbing hold of the wheel.

'Hey don't do that we'll hit those crates you lunatic!' I shouted and made an exaggerated swerve around them which took us perilously close to the edge.

'Tim for god's sake pack it in will you it's not funny!'

'Well stop interfering with the driver then, just relax and enjoy the view,' I said laughing.

Silence.

Boats of every kind filled the entire bay and on the far side the white washed houses crowded the waterfront falling over each other in their quest to be nearest to the water.

The road led us around the point to a small beach, it was less crowded but still there was nowhere to park so we carried on until we came to another one. Right at the end of the seafront there was a small shingle beach with hardly anyone on it and with room to park so we stopped for a while.

We all got out and went down to the water so Caine could have a swim and a cooling lie down whilst Nelson minced about in the shallows getting his toes wet, waiting to pounce on him when he came out.

We lingered there for a little while sitting next to Billy on the hot stone wall just watching the world go by while the boys made friends with a local dog down on the shore line.

'Well that was Cadaques then,' I said.

'Yep, shame we couldn't see much of it.'

'Maybe we'll come back sometime when it's not so crowded.'

'Hmmm, maybe,' I said.

We looked at each other and shook our heads.

'Nah, that's never going to happen is it,' said Suzi smiling.

'Nope,'
We were both laughing as we stood up to go.

We carried on along the same road out of Cadaques which climbed up between the houses, eventually taking us out onto the open hills.

The road surface deteriorated quickly until it became just a dirt track and Billy was soon filled with dry choking dust. It was great fun to drive on though and my inner rally driver took over the controls - I changed down a gear coming out of a corner and put the hammer down. The engine was screaming away accompanied by the all too familiar crashing sounds coming from the back and on top of all that there was an almighty din from the clatter of all the stones being thrown up against Billy's underside.

'Hey mind Billy's tummy you idiot, you could hurt him!' shouted Suzi over the noise. She was hanging on for dear life with her feet braced up against the dashboard again, trying in vain to wave some of the dust away from her face. 'You know if you slowed down a bit it wouldn't be quite so dusty in here.' she managed between coughs.'

'Yeah I know, but it wouldn't be half as much fun would it,' I shouted back as I threw Billy into another tight turn with reckless abandon.

Despite my best efforts however, I very quickly realized that a fully laden VW camper is simply not a rally car and poor old Billy was protesting as I tried unsuccessfully to get his back end to drift out on the corners.

'Hold tight boys!'

They both leaned into a corner, Nelson was enduring it through gritted teeth, 'Oh god, here he goes again.' Whereas Caine was smiling, 'Yay this is great fun Tim, go faster!'

Luckily I managed to banish my inner rally driver before tragedy struck and relative calm ensued once more. I had a quick look in the back - that's ok, we could tidy up later!

The road wasn't in the atlas so once again we had no idea where we were going or where we'd end up. We took a left for no other reason that it seemed like it would lead us back to the sea again and who knows, we might find a lovely little hidden cove at the end.

There was no hidden cove, we just came to a dead end literally right on the very edge of the cliffs with only just enough room to park Billy. There was a dizzying drop of about 100metres straight down onto the rocks below and with my stomach doing somersaults, I manoeuvred Billy carefully - very carefully, parking him so that his side door was facing the sea with the edge of the cliff being a mere ten feet away.

'You can open your eyes now,' I said laughing as I switched the engine off.

'Oh god I hate that - oh wow what a view!!'

We all got out and Caine went straight over to the edge and looked down at the sea, probably wondering how the hell he was going to be able to go for a swim.

'Now that's what I call a sea view,' I said.

'Caine come away from the edge, Tim tell him.'

'It's ok he won't fall over, he may be daft but he's not stupid,' I said, hoping I was right.

As we were hungry we decided to stop there for lunch and also empty the toilet. It was really stinking at this point as it hadn't been emptied for a good few days and was in urgent need of a clean out. I went and emptied it in the shallow hole I'd managed to dig, wow what a stink!

I still needed to rinse it out and refill it and I was reluctant to use our valuable drinking water as I would need quite a lot for this job. Then I had a brainwave - I could climb down to the sea and fetch some water.

'Or we could just wait until we found a tap,' came the sensible suggestion.

'Yeah but where's the fun in that,' I replied as I reached for a jerry can.

I took the can and a length of rope which Pierre had gifted to me and went over to the edge and looked down. 'Hmm, that's a long way down Tim' I said to myself, but it looked do-able.

'Be careful,' came the unnecessary advice from nowhere near the edge.

I carefully began my descent, it was a bit tricky only having one hand to hang on with and it turned out to be a bit steeper than it looked but I was doing ok. Luckily there were little ledges here and there which were just about big enough for my feet. I was almost halfway down when I heard a noise above me and a pebble hit me on the head, I looked up and there was Caine working his way down head first after me.

'Oh no Caine you can't.... go back,' I said, more to myself really.

He couldn't turn around and go back up even if he'd wanted to, which he obviously didn't. How dare I try and sneak off without him!

This dog knows no fear I thought, he was practically vertical as he dropped from one ledge to another, how is that possible without overbalancing? If he slipped and fell now he would land on me and knock me off my perch and we'd both be gonners.

Luckily though he didn't, and he slowly inched his way down until he was right in my arms with his face pressed into mine.

'Hey you, don't push!'

'Hi Tim I'm here, wow this is fun isn't it, are we going down for a swim?'

He looked really comical close up, his ears were dangling down across his face and all his skin had flopped forward so his eyes had all but disappeared. He now had nowhere to go but he wasn't bothered in the least, he was just thrilled to have reached me and to be having another adventure. He chuntered happily and licked my face, waiting patiently as I decided what to do next.

Well there was no way he could turn around and go back up and as I was, well as *we* were now nearly halfway down I decided to carry on. I was familiar with Caine's climbing abilities but this was taking things to a whole new level. I *was* however just a little more concerned than he was about our current predicament as I had no free hand to help him, not that he needed it.

He waited whilst I took a couple of steps down and then he would drop down a step, leaving his back legs on the one above, he was very finely balanced. It seemed to take ages but he was very relaxed about our situation and didn't panic or slip once.

We descended virtually as one all the way to the bottom - I was already thinking about the best way to get back up again.

When we reached the pebbly beach he jumped off and went completely crackerdog, running around madly with his arse tucked under and then charged straight into the sea. I found a stick and threw it as far as I could for him, he powered out through the waves, grabbed the stick and then he surfed his way back to the beach.

I waded out a bit and filled the jerry can with water and carried it back up the beach. When I reached the bottom of the cliff I looked up, if it had been a long way down then it was going to be an even longer climb back up.

I tried to get Caine to go up first but no, he wanted *me* to go first so after tying the rope to the can and leaving it at the bottom, I started the long climb back up again. When I'd climbed up a few steps Caine began his ascent and was soon right at my feet, looking up at me, 'Alright Tim?'

I smiled at him, so far so good I thought, this might actually work.

When I reached a good sized ledge I stopped and pulled the jerry can up and it bounced and banged its way up the rocks until it was just below Caine and sitting on its own ledge. He waited patiently, poised almost vertically but again, perfectly balanced.

I climbed up again slowly with Caine right at my heels until I reached another ledge and pulled the can up behind us again. The trouble was, every time I looked down to check on Caine or to pull the can up my head would start swimming - whose daft idea was this anyway!

This process was painstakingly repeated over and over again - I was trying hard not to look down as we got higher in case I lost my nerve, or my balance, or my mind or something - Caine wasn't worried in the least. 'It's ok Tim don't worry, you're doing fine, just keep going, I'm right behind you.'

After what seemed like an eternity we both made it to the top without loss of life and Caine immediately charged off to Billy to tell the others of his latest adventure.

If there ever was a next time I promised myself I would go for the 'sensible option'.

It was such a beautiful spot we decided to stay there for the rest of the day on the edge of the cliffs with the deep blue

Mediterranean below us and not a soul around. I got our broken table out and managed to set it up, it was now held together with string and gaffa tape and was more than a bit wobbly, but it was still functional - just.

The chairs by this time had practically no stuffing left in them, two of the broken arm rests were taped up to stop them pinching our arms and most of the springs had gone. Needless to say they weren't very comfortable any more and it required some skill to actually sit on them without falling through!

Sometime during the afternoon the wind picked up, the sea darkened and became quite angry looking. The table and chairs got picked up by the wind and just took off into the distance, tumbling their way merrily across the clifftops.

'We'd better move from here Tim it's getting dangerous.'

'No we'll be fine don't worry,' I said as we trudged off after them 'It's an onshore wind so we won't get blown over the edge.'

The table was now in a *really* sorry state and in need of further repair and I chucked it in the back with the chairs. I lowered (and secured) the roof before that took off as well and soon we were all huddled inside with the doors shut.

Apart from a very short and very bracing walk across the cliffs the rest of the day was spent in Billy, cowering from the wind. Our sea view was gradually disappearing as the windows slowly became covered in a thick layer of sticky sea salt.

During the night the wind became *really* fierce, the noise was deafening and Billy was rocking alarmingly, sleep was impossible.

'I'm going to have to turn him into the wind, we're side on at the moment that's why we're rocking so much,' I said as I clambered out of bed.

'Be careful,' from somewhere under the duvet.

I evicted a reluctant Nelson from the driver's seat and then gingerly maneuvered Billy round until he was facing directly into the wind. It reduced the rocking considerably but it now meant he wasn't level anymore so we had to turn around in bed or we'd have been sleeping upside down.

Trouble was now though, Billy was facing directly over the cliff and all I could see through the windscreen was the stormy sea far below us which was just a little unsettling. I'm not sure I would have stayed in bed if someone else had been trying to turn around in a howling gale, in the dark and on the edge of a cliff like that. Right on cue a little face appeared through the darkness behind me and peered out through the windscreen.

'Oh my god Tim this is horrible, it feels like we're right on the edge.'

Erm.. well we are pretty much, I thought, but I said.

'Don't panic, it looks worse than it is, we're at least six feet from the edge.'

'Oh well that's reassuring, what's to stop us from rolling straight over the edge.'

'It's ok, his handbrake's on and he's in gear, he's not going to roll anywhere, anyway if we went over at least we'd all die together.'

I went out into the gale and nearly got blown off my feet. I searched around in the moonlight for some rocks and wedged them under Billy's wheels just to make sure. When I got back in I was cold and clammy and my whole body was sticky from being salt blasted.

Now though the wind was blowing straight into the air vents at the back which were right by our heads making a really horrible noise. Cursing, I clambered out of bed again and went back outside into the hurricane to stuff towels into them and we slept fitfully for the remainder of the night. It was still really windy in the morning but maybe not quite as bad, I got out of bed and wandered off a bit for a pee and when I looked back at Billy my heart nearly stopped.

He was literally right on the edge and sloping downhill as well, I don't think either of us would have slept if we'd seen that.

There were a tense few minutes as I moved the rocks from the wheels and then carefully, oh so carefully and with my heart in my mouth turned Billy round again so he was side on to the sea but this time with the side door facing away from the wind.

I put the bed away and carelessly tossed our now practically useless furniture in the back. I also gave a couple of the windows a wash with our valuable drinking water so we could at least see out. We still had to keep the roof down and so breakfast was prepared bent double which was as usual, uncomfortable and inconvenient.

Still, we enjoyed coffee and toast sitting in Billy with a wonderfully unspoilt panoramic Mediterranean sea view.

✦✦✦✦✦

Beautiful though it was we couldn't really stay there with that wind and it didn't seem like it was dying down much so after lunch we reluctantly packed up and headed off.

We arrived in Rosas later that afternoon, it said Roses in the atlas but Pierre had called it Rosas, so Rosas it was.

We drove slowly along the long busy sweeping seafront looking for somewhere to park for the night. There were plenty of campers parked up but no room for us so we continued right to the end.

We came across a derelict petrol station on a small patch of rough ground strewn with all sorts of litter caught in clumps of dry dusty weeds. I drove Billy round behind it parking at the base of a small rocky cliff next to some old abandoned cars, a skip full of rubbish and an old washing machine.

Two skinny, mangy looking street dogs were skulking around the skip, eyeing us warily.

'Bit of a come down but it'll do for the night I suppose, what d'you reckon?'

'Lovely spot Tim, you've really excelled yourself this time' said Suzi looking all around, 'I've always wanted to live on a rubbish tip.'

'Ooh perfect,' I said, ignoring the sarcasm and eyeing the skip. 'Right, I've had just about enough of these bloody things.'

I grabbed both sun loungers from the back and took them over to the skip leaving a trail of foam bits behind me and chucked them in. The two dogs backed away as I approached and then disappeared behind the cars when they heard the crash.

'What did you do that for, there's no point having a table with no chairs is there.' complained Suzi.

'Ah yes the table, thanks for reminding me.'

I dragged the table out for the very last time and tossed that in the skip as well, oh yes that felt good!

'Aww you've frightened those poor dogs doing that,' complained Suzi as she grabbed some bread and went over to look for them, 'they look starving poor things.'

She called to them and they started to come out but then our two went charging over which really spooked them and they disappeared again.

'You probably shouldn't go near stray dogs like that anyway, remember what we were told,' I said to her knowing full well what a waste of energy *that* sentence was.

She then went off in search of them as I put the boys back in Billy. She soon found them, they were cowering behind some bushes and as she approached them they lay down and

126

rolled over, resigned to their fate. She reached out and stroked them both, they were very nervous but after a couple of minutes they relaxed a bit and took some bread. They got worried when I went near them though, they clearly didn't like men.

'It's probably men that have ill treated them that's why.' said Suzi quietly.

I agreed and backed off, they obviously weren't used to human kindness either, probably being more used to receiving a kick or having a stone thrown at them.

A little later on we took a walk along the seafront, leaving the boys busily watching the dogs. We were a bit hungry so we stopped to buy something to eat from a take away food outlet.

Neither of us spoke much Spanish at all yet so we were hoping they might understand at least a little English. I noticed there were some pictures of flags above the counter, amongst them the union jack so it was looking promising.

Apart from the Spanish one, there were three other versions of the menu on the wall, one in French, one in German and one in English which was great, shouldn't have much trouble being understood here then.

There wasn't much on there that we fancied so we just settled for chips, can't go wrong really can you - chips - nice and simple.

I'd learnt to count to ten in Spanish, so holding up two fingers as well so there'd be no confusion I said to the guy behind the counter.

'Dos chips por favor.'

'Que?' said the man behind the counter, screwing his face up in puzzlement.

Hmm, ok then I thought, let's simplify things a little.

'Chips, por favor,'

'Que?' his screwed his face up again adding a look of incredulousness for effect.

'Chips.' repeated I.

'Cheeps?...Cheeps?' repeated he, shrugging his shoulders as well now.

'Si, chips,... chips.' I did a mime of someone eating chips.

Screwed up face, puzzled look, exaggerated shrug of the shoulders, arms out to the side, palms upwards, I was getting nowhere fast.

I knew it would be fatal to do it but I looked at Suzi at this point, she was trying really hard once again not to laugh at my inability to be understood.

I turned quickly away. I knew it wouldn't be long before we both lost control if things carried on like this.

Brainwave, I pointed to the menu where it clearly said 'Chips' with the price next to it.

'Chips,' I said, tapping the menu.

He glanced at the menu and then stared blankly at me shaking his head stupidly, there was more shrugging.

I looked at Suzi again, I knew I shouldn't have and we both burst out laughing straightaway, unable to hold it all in any longer while Mr Chips continued to stare at us - his mood blackening.

I looked over the counter and could see some chips cooking away in the fryer and also some ready for serving... aha!

'Chips' I said pointing to them triumphantly, surely now....

All patience gone, he batted my hand away from the counter, shaking his head vigorously and waving his finger in the air. He was ranting away about god knows what, the fact that we were almost wetting ourselves wasn't helping matters much either.

He brought this thankfully incomprehensible diatribe to a close by slamming a bag of ready salted crisps down on the counter.

'Cheeps!' he spat, gesturing to the cruelly crushed bag in between us. I looked closer, was he foaming at the mouth?

Now it was my turn.

'Cheeps?... cheeps?' I said screwing my face up at him, then I turned to Suzi with shrugged shoulders and upward palms, 'cheeps...cheeps?'

Too much for both of us and we just fell about laughing.

Too much for him as well, red in the face now he became literally hopping mad and he actually started shouting at us. He slammed his fist down hard on the counter and waved us away with both hands, looks like we weren't going to get any cheeps after all then.

I was just about to ask him if he spoke any Australian when thankfully Suzi dragged me away from the counter before things *really* got out of hand. We stood back a bit on the pavement to regroup, still giggling like school kids as Senor cheeps calmly went about his business.

A couple of minutes later two blokes wearing union jack shorts walked up to the counter and one of them said in English.

'Couple of bags of chips please mate.'

Within *seconds* Senor chips had dished out two cardboard cones full of lovely hot, crispy, golden chips for them and they walked away happy.

I know!! ..work that one out if you can!

We had to admit defeat there and instead we treated ourselves to ice cold beers in tall glasses and a pizza (no chips thanks), at one of the many outdoor seafront restaurants. We sat out on the cobbled streets in wicker chairs at a wicker table with a crispy white tablecloth beneath a red and yellow parasol and watched the world go by.

I have to say I was a little wary of ordering but luckily there were no problems this time as the waiter insisted on speaking English to us. On the way back we passed Senor chips' place and gave him a nice big wave and a smile - he didn't wave back.

We got back to Billy shortly afterwards - he was covered in dust and salt from his earlier excursion and looked a little forlorn parked there on that wasteland amongst all the rubbish. Poor Billy, we would have to find somewhere nicer to park him tomorrow.

It was a busy, noisy place with constant traffic which would probably mean little sleep but it would have to do for the night. Not surprisingly we were the only ones parked there but just before we went to bed, a Swiss camper pulled up and parked not far from us.

Some time later we were woken suddenly by a loud banging on the side of Billy and two indignant, startled dogs replied equally noisily.

With my heart pounding I peered out through the curtains and saw two policemen standing there. I clambered out of bed and opened the side door, trying my best to hold two angry dogs back at the same time as trying unsuccessfully to cover my nakedness.

'No camping' said one of them over the din.

He then said something I didn't quite hear or understand and made various gestures which didn't really help, whilst all the time trying not to notice my lack of clothing which was clearly making him a little uncomfortable.

Well what the hell d'you expect Senor Policeman, waking people up at this time of night.

His amigo meanwhile had gone over to the other van and was now banging on *their* door - more barking.

'Right ok then I get the message,' I said 'we'll move now,' could be a little foolish arguing with a man carrying a gun I thought. He seemed happy with that and strolled off back to his car.

Cursing, Suzi threw some clothes on, I didn't bother.

We put some things away in a hurry but left the bed made as the police were still sitting in their car waiting for us to go.

'What time is it?' asked Suzi as we pulled away.

'Two thirty.' I said.

'Bastards!

ɲɲɲɲɲ

We drove back along the surprisingly still busy and brightly lit sea front, there was room to park there now and we did consider parking there for the rest of the night but thought better of it. We didn't fancy getting woken up again, not by the same police anyway so we carried on.

'It's probably illegal to drive naked you know.' said a smiling Suzi.

'Probably, well you've got to kick back somehow haven't you!'

I must say I was feeling quite liberated, driving naked along a busy, brightly lit sea front was going straight into my top ten list of favourite and illegal (probably) things I'd never done before.

We left Rosas and the bright lights behind and a couple of kilometers later we came to some signs at a turning where Suzi said.

'Santa Margarida, isn't that the place Pierre told us about?'

'It is let's try it, I thought he said Santa Margarita, must be the same place though.'

I turned off and followed a poorly surfaced road through the partially lit streets of Santa Margarida. The occasional street lamp revealed a never ending building site with block after block of forlorn looking half built villas; they looked to be shoddily built from large hollow terra cotta bricks. The surrounding area was all overgrown with piles of broken bricks and other building materials long since abandoned.

The place was like a maze with pot holed roads going off in all directions from numerous little roundabouts. These 'roundabouts' consisted of a circle of kerb stones with nothing in the middle apart from some litter caught in the clumps of weeds. We had no idea where we were going or which turning to take but kept on going anyway. Then the road improved suddenly and we passed row after row of smart well lit waterfront villas, all with yachts moored alongside.

Eventually we came to a high wire fence bordering a patch of wasteland with yachts moored on the far side, it looked promising, could we get in there?

We followed the fence until we came to an entrance, the gates were open so I pulled in, half expecting to be challenged by a security guard but we saw no-one. I had to slow right down as it was very bumpy which gave us time to have a good look around. There were just a couple of cars parked near the yachts and a camper over in the far corner.

I made my way slowly across and pulled up close to the boats near a concrete slipway, was this private land? We sat there quietly and surveyed the scene for a while, waiting to see if anyone came out and told us to leave.

A dog appeared from somewhere and started barking at us but apart from that we saw no-one, there were no angry shouts, it looked deserted.

We all got out and the boys ran straight up to the dog and made friends, thankfully. The last thing we needed was a dog fight to announce our arrival at this time of night.

'You might want to put some clothes on now Tim, this isn't a naturist village.'

'Hmm? oh yeah you're probably right,' I said and reluctantly I put some shorts on.

Caine was happy to have a new friend to play with; Nelson just cocked his leg up the dog and sauntered back to Billy.

It looked like a good place to spend the night and seemed pretty quiet compared to Rosas. There was a large apartment building on the other side of the road and we could hear music coming from somewhere in that direction. We were wide awake now so I put the kettle on and we sat in the side doorway enjoying the warmth of the evening, drinking tea and watching the dogs playing happily in the dust.

We were being serenaded by the occasional pinging of rigging on masts, a sound we both enjoyed and we were happy to be parked near the boats. A light shone in one of their windows but apart from that there were no signs of life, there was a nice feel to the place and we liked it straightaway. We climbed back into bed and fell asleep immediately.

We were woken suddenly by a loud bang and a frightened dog landing on the bed. Caine did not like loud bangs and he squashed himself down the side of me and lay there panting heavily.

'Oh my god what the hell was that?'

'Sounded like a firework,' I said, 'either that or someone's shooting at us.'

There was another loud bang.

'Fireworks,' I confirmed.

'At this time of night?'

Nelson was sitting up in the driver's seat with his head the other side of the curtains looking out to see what was going on, he wasn't at all bothered by loud bangs.

He was also looking for the dog he'd met earlier.

'Caine, stop digging your elbows in my ribs will you and can you breathe your dog breath the other way please.' I said trying to turn his head away. There really wasn't enough room for him on our tiny bed and we could have done without the extra body warmth as well.

I woke some time later with a crushing pain across my chest and I was struggling to breathe properly. I panicked a bit until I realized Caine was lying right across my chest with his head on the pillows between us, spark out, snoring away happily.

'Ugh, dog breath to wake up to, how lovely.' I moaned sleepily.

'I thought it was yours,' came the sleepy reply from somewhere on the other side of Caine mountain.

'Charming.'

It was just coming daylight - it was too hot, too cramped and there was little or no chance of getting any more sleep. I dug Caine in the ribs to wake him up and gave him a shove to try and get him off the bed.

He stirred sleepily, yawning luxuriously, then he stood up and stretched, farted loudly and jumped down.

'And a good morning to you too,' giggled Suzi as we both dived under the duvet for safety.

When I opened the side door, last nights dog was still sitting in the middle of the car park, waiting for Caine to come out and play in the dust, which of course he did.

In the daylight we could now see that this place was very run down with clumps of weeds everywhere and cracked concrete all along the water's edge. It was like it had been abandoned mid build, a bit like all those half built houses and villas we'd passed the night before.

We were sitting in Billy having breakfast when to our dismay, we saw a police car driving slowly along the road; they were looking at us as they approached.

'U-oh,' I said.

'Oh no not again.'

We watched as they slowly drove past the gate and then thankfully they carried on.

'Phew, that's ok then,' I said, 'looks like we're allowed to park here, maybe it's private land.'

'As long as the owner doesn't mind.'

'Well we'll find out sooner or later I suppose.'

We decided we were going to try and stay here for as long as we could get away with. Ok it wasn't very pretty but it would do for now, there was water for Caine to swim in and there was a shop just around the corner that we could walk to for the basics. Water may be a problem but we had enough for a day or two so we relaxed into our new surroundings.

It was baking hot, the air was still and we were in full sun - there were no trees for shade and everywhere was dry and dusty. I rigged up a makeshift awning using a bed sheet pegged onto Billy's guttering and his open front door and then tied to a rusty pole. Between that and the parasol we at least had a small area of shade to sit in out of the direct glare of the sun.

The boys spent most of their time underneath Billy where it was coolest and every so often Caine would saunter off to the slipway on his own and lie down in the water for a couple of minutes, then get straight back under Billy and lie in the dust again.

The fridge had packed up altogether now and we were drinking warm water all day long which wasn't very pleasant, but at least it was wet.

'Those Mountains look nice over there' said Suzi the next day, pointing to them in the blue hazy distance.

'They do don't they, let's go up to that village there look.' There was a cluster of white houses nestled on the mountainside, 'we'll need water pretty soon anyway, let's go now shall we?'

It took a while to de-camp and pack things away but then we were off.

We drove inland for a few kilometers and headed for the houses we'd seen which turned out to be a place called Palau Saverdera, a picturesque old town on the lower slopes of the mountains. I wanted to get to the top of town for some reason so I kept on going upwards through the narrow, twisty and attractively cobbled streets.

At the very top we saw a local woman bent over a large stone water trough doing her washing. Nearby a man was collecting water from a pipe in the shade of some lovely big trees.

'That looks like it could be spring water.' I said as I drove up past it and pulled onto a clearing underneath the trees. We collected our jerry cans and went back down just as the man was leaving.

'Ja ja, sein gutes wasser,' he said nodding when I asked him if it was good water.

I reckoned that meant it *was* good water, I also reckoned he was German so I said 'Danke' which immediately used up half of my German vocabulary.

The water was trickling slowly out of a pipe and splashing down onto worn stone cobbles before gathering in a small stone pool. Nelson reached down and had a drink from the crystal clear water, being very careful not to get his feet wet. Caine on the other hand drank his fill while he was lying down in it.

I put a container under the flow and we sat on the stone steps with our feet in the cool water whilst we waited for it to fill up. It took quite a while to fill up both cans but we were in no hurry. It was so tranquil and cool sitting there in the shade with the only sounds being the trickling of the water and the birds chirping away in the trees.

We needed to do some washing so we gathered some clothes together and took them down to the wash area. The trough was constantly fed by water flowing from a pipe which I realised was the overflow from the spring. The woman looked up and greeted us with a smiley 'Buenos dias' as we arrived.

We set about washing our clothes whilst on the other side the woman was smiling and eyeing us intently the whole time.

She obviously couldn't resist it any longer and she came over to our side jabbering away in Spanish and handed Suzi her box of washing powder. She jabbed her finger at it and wagged her finger at ours - apparently hers was a far superior brand and ours should be discarded immediately.

She then proceeded to animatedly demonstrate the 'proper' way to wash clothes.

She chucked all the clothes into the water to soak and left them floating there. Then she took a shirt out and sprinkled some of the washing powder all over it and started kneading away aggressively and slapping it down repeatedly on the wall, talking and laughing away the whole time.

I was becoming a bit concerned for the welfare of our clothes at this point.

Next, and now this is very important so watch closely, she took a big square block of blue soap and rubbed it back and forth along the collar and cuffs - and now we leave it for a while. She then took another piece of shirt in each hand and rubbed the two together vigorously, Jabber jabber jabber, gesturing for Suzi to do the same with the rest.

137

I grabbed my favourite 'Black Island' sleeveless t-shirt quickly before she could start abusing that too and proceeded to wash it myself – carefully, receiving a wry look and a shake of the head for my troubles. Then she waggled a disapproving finger at me and laughed, no no no this was woman's work, no place for a man, I should either be working or drinking beer with my friends.

I was then ignored for the rest of the show, nothing new there then!

Returning her attentions to the collar she reached for a scrubbing brush which she held up proudly, stroking the bristles lovingly, jabber jabber jabber. It was probably a priceless family heirloom passed down over the years from mother to daughter, and then she held up a finger - now just watch this! She attacked the collar venomously, scrubbing away furiously, the dirt never stood a chance.

Our poor clothes were having a bit of a tough time of it but I have to say they were looking very, very clean now.

Every now and then she would take a lunge at the slowly sinking clothes and bash them about a bit. I was wondering how many clothes had drowned in there and were lying lost and forlorn at the bottom of the murky, milky white water.

I was almost tempted to jump in to cool off a bit but then common sense got the better of me.

If I jumped in there and accidentally swallowed some of that water I would be dead in seconds, poisoned by a toxic concentration of hundreds of years of washing powder. My lifeless body would get sucked down into the evil man eating sludge lurking on the bottom, built up from generations of filth, never to be seen again.

If that didn't kill me then I reckon Senora Twankey surely would have.

Demo over and she left her box of powder and the block of soap as a gift for Suzi and then, waggling a finger at our box, she gave her strict instructions not to buy any more of *that* rubbish. She didn't leave the brush though, 'no no no you can't have this brush it's very special' she said clutching it to her chest protectively. I heard the word mama amongst the millions of others.

Suzi graciously accepted the gifts and then Senora Twankey gathered all her clothes into a large wicker basket which she tucked under her arm, wedged on her generous hip and walked bow-legged back down the hill.

We took our now *very* clean washing back to Billy and hung it on a line I'd put up from Billy to a nearby tree, it wasn't going to take very long to dry in this heat. We sat on a low stone wall in the shade of some big trees and had our lunch, all the time wondering if our washing line would be frowned upon by the locals.

We needn't have worried, two Senoras came walking down the dry dusty pathway behind Billy and greeted us happily with 'Buenos Dias'.

When they saw our washing they both stopped to inspect it and had a good old sniff of it, presumably checking to see how clean everything was and more importantly, which washing powder we'd used.

It obviously passed the test as they both smiled and nodded their approval at us before continuing on their way down into the village.

The washing dried in about half an hour and after having a little siesta on the wall we packed up and headed back to base.

ཉཉཉཉཉ

We got back to the boats and parked in 'our place' by the slipway close to the rusty old pole so I could put the 'awning' up again. The dog was sitting there waiting for us, wagging her tail expectantly as we pulled up.

Later that afternoon, we were strolling along one of the pontoons looking at the boats when we saw a yacht approaching under sail, heading directly for the pontoon we were on. It was listing to one side quite a bit and as it drew close to us the captain, (and he clearly was a proper captain as he was wearing a proper captain's hat) shouted across to us.

'I say, ahoy there! would you mind awfully catching the rope.'

We didn't mind at all and quickly leapt into action. There was a woman at the bows holding a coiled up rope which she threw to me as the yacht thumped heavily against the concrete pontoon - I grabbed it and tied it to a rusty ring. Then she went to the stern and threw another rope which Suzi caught, I ran over and together we pulled the yacht in and then tied it up. The captain then plonked himself down heavily in the cockpit.

'Thanks awfully chaps, absolutely buggered I'm afraid, been up all night, sailed from Cannes yesterday, wind got up a bit, sod all sleep, shipping water at a hell of a rate of knots from god knows where, bloody bilge pump not working, having to bail out by hand, tedious, bloody tedious, must get some sleep.'

He looked absolutely exhausted and lay down where he was and fell asleep instantly, the woman had already disappeared into a little cabin at the back.

'Hang on though you're sinking, you can't sleep' I said but he was well out of it, obviously beyond caring anymore, 'and your sails are still up.'

I climbed on board to see what I could do but apart from Pierre's I'd never been on a yacht before and knew nothing about them. I peered down into the main cabin, it was awash with almost a foot of water and now that I was on board I could feel just how much it was listing.

'What do we do now, we can't just let them sink,' said Suzi.

'No we can't can we, we'll just have to bail it out ourselves,' I said as I picked up a bucket which was floating around the cabin.

I scooped up some water and passed it up to Suzi who was now also on board and she chucked it over the side before handing it back down to me.

It was quite a big boat – about three times the size of Pierre's – and it held a lot of water! We scooped and chucked for ages until eventually the water level started to go down. I lifted the floorboards up and carried on scooping water from the bilges, this was going to take hours, meanwhile, Captain snooze snored on.

Just then there was a call from the pontoon.

'Do you need any help?'

'That would be great, thanks,' replied a very hot and sweaty Suzi.

'I'm Mark, I'm from Lady Jane over there,' he said pointing to a cruiser on the next pontoon, 'I can see you're having a spot of bother, is this your boat then?'

'No it's his and its sinking.'

I stuck my head out of the hatch.

'Hi there, another pair of hands would be great and another bucket maybe?'

'Oh I can do better than that, don't go away.'

He walked off briskly and returned trailing an extension lead and carrying a small submersible pump which he handed down to me.

'Here you go drop that right in the bottom, that's it, now pass the pipe to me and.....hey presto!'

He turned it on and it hummed into life with a small but steady flow of water going over the side. I climbed up the steps and sat in the cockpit for a breather, noticing the yacht wasn't listing as much anymore.

'Do you know how to take sails down Mark?' I asked, looking at them billowing gently in the breeze.

'Don't know the first thing about sailing I'm afraid,' he said.

'No nor me, oh well, it can't be that hard can it,' I said as I undid a rope which looked like it might be connected to the sails.

A split second later the boom came crashing down on the roof of the aft cabin, luckily just missing all our heads.

'Ok so it's not that one then,' I said in what I hoped was a casual manner despite the horrified looks from my 'crew'.

I quickly hoisted it back up again and re-tied the rope.

'Think I'll leave the sails up for now what d'you reckon?'

'Good idea skipper,' said Mark chuckling away.

Captain snooze never even stirred.

The boat was a mess with the sails flapping all over the place, ropes everywhere and a weather beaten, exhausted Captain. It reminded me of how Pierre must have felt after *his* voyage, except *his* 'ship' wasn't sinking.

'Oh I know, you're from the orange camper over there aren't you, the ones with the two beautiful dogs.' added Mark.

'That's right,' replied Suzi and we all introduced ourselves.

Mark's boat, Lady Jane was moored here for the summer months after coming down through the French canal system. Apparently these were known as the free moorings as no-one knew who owned them or the land we were parked on, so nobody had to pay anything to moor their boats here.

'This place is for the working class yachtsmen who can't afford fancy marina prices,' he laughed.

'So basically it's a squat,' chirped Suzi.

Mark roared with laughter and I chipped in with,

'It's a yacht squat,'

The following burst of laughter woke the captain briefly, just long enough for him to take in the situation and to say.

'Oh I say damn good show you chaps, damn good show, drinks all round......' then he lay back down and fell asleep again.

'Come on over for a cuppa,' said Mark to us as he turned to go 'it'll take ages to empty all that water out, and bring the dogs over'

We accepted his offer but first I messed around with a few ropes and things and finally managed to bring the sails down without destroying the boat or killing anyone. They didn't look anywhere near as tidy as the other yachts but it would have to do for now.

We went back to Billy for the boys and then went over to Mark's boat. Lady Jane had started life as a lifeboat and Mark had converted it for living by adding a cabin and then later another bigger cabin. It looked a bit strange but it was done out really nicely inside.

'Have you been over to the beach yet?' he asked.

'No not yet,'

'It's quite nice over there so whenever you want to go just give me a shout and I'll take you across in the dinghy,' he offered.

'That'd be nice thanks,' said Suzi, 'what about the dogs though?'

'The dogs can come as well no problem,' said Mark, 'I love having dogs in the boat.'

We took him up on his kind offer and the next day was spent just across the channel on the beach after having been ferried there in his inflatable dinghy. We stayed right by the big boulders which lined the channel as it was quieter there and we could also watch the yachts going in and out.

Suzi really wanted to overcome her fear of deep water so given that we both like to meet our fears head on, it was decided that jumping into the channel from a height would be the best way to do it.

We found a flattish boulder that we could both stand on and then holding hands, prepared to jump in together.

'Don't let go of me,' she pleaded, gripping my hand tightly.

'I won't let go.'

'Promise?'

'Promise.'

'How deep is it?' she asked with a shaky voice, staring down at the deep blue water.

'Deeper than you.' I said - well it *was*!

'I can't do it.'

'Yes you can.'

'I'm really scared Tim.'

'I know you are, there's nothing to be scared of, I'm right here, I won't let you drown.'

'It's too deep.'

'It doesn't really matter how deep it is, you *can* actually swim you know.'

'I know I can but I won't be able to touch the bottom.'

'You won't need to, you can *swim*.'

'I can't do it Tim.'

'Yes you can, look I'm right here, you'll be fine,' I said giving her hand a squeeze, 'I won't let go I promise.'

This went on for quite some time but eventually and after several false starts, she very bravely took the plunge. Holding hands tightly we both jumped off together. It was quite a drop and her head went right under, she came up coughing and spluttering and panicking a bit but I still had hold of her hand.

'Oh my god Tim I can't touch the bottom, I can't touch the bottom, don't let go, oh shit!'

'It's ok, just relax and lie back like I showed you.'

Slowly she relaxed and I was able to let go of her hand as she lay back in the water and floated as she'd done before in shallow water.

After a minute or so she plucked up the courage to swim out into the middle of the channel and back, smiling broadly the whole time before climbing out onto the rocks.

'I did it, I did it, oh my god I did it!' she shouted ecstatically, wet hugs were had and before I knew it she'd jumped back in again on her own.

After that she was in and out of the water every few minutes, she was loving it.

☺ ☺ ☺ ☺ ☺

The couple on the sinking yacht were called Malcolm and Sandy and as a way of saying thank you to us for helping them out, we were invited over for drinkies on their yacht.

Now don't get too excited, it's not quite as grand as it sounds.

We had beers in old plastic beakers sitting on thin, faded and torn plastic cushions in the cockpit of an old wooden yacht desperately in need of some TLC, under an awning made of a tatty old sail strung up over the boom.

Still, there we were, living the high life - having drinks on board a yacht in a marina on the Mediterranean (I use the term 'marina' very loosely there).

Malcolm was an ex navy man with a serious limp and very hairy legs (none on his head) and one useless arm which he could hardly use. Sandy had answered his advert for a sailing companion to crew for him and they were headed to Alicante for the winter. We offered to take them up to Palau the next time we went for water in a day or two which they were really pleased about. They were looking forward to seeing some of Spain other than from their boat.

They had more water containers than we did and Billy's entire floor space was taken up so they had to share the back seat with the boys.

It was a bit of a squeeze but Caine didn't mind at all. Nelson did though, he was disgusted with it all and squeezed himself onto the front seat with Suzi. He was much happier with this arrangement as now he had a great view out of the windscreen; he loved to be able to see where he was going.

They loved Palau and were thrilled to be collecting fresh mountain spring water and to be able to do some washing. I strung two lines up this time as Malcolm had brought a length of rope from the boat. We left it all to dry and wandered down into the town for something to eat as Malcolm insisted they buy us some lunch.

We found a lovely little restaurant tucked away on a back street and we sat outside on a tiny walled terrace with just two tables. We had an enjoyable lunch in the shade of a huge parasol looking out over the red tiled rooftops with the deep blue Mediterranean in the distance.

After we'd eaten, Malcolm ordered another bottle of red wine

'I've been told there's a scrap yard around here somewhere Tim,' he said re-filling all the glasses again, I had said no thanks but that fell on deaf ears, 'I wonder if you'd mind if we looked for it on the way back,'

'Yes sure why not, what are you after?' I replied.

'I need a starter motor, mine's died I'm afraid, can't start the bloody engine to charge the batteries, damned inconvenient.' he said draining his glass again.

'So you've got a boat which is sinking, a bilge pump that doesn't work and an engine that won't start,' said Suzi teasingly with a big cheeky smile.

'Hah! That's about the bloody size of it I'm afraid,' laughed Malcolm, nearly choking on his wine.

'Hmm, he somehow neglected to tell me all that when I answered his ad,' said Sandy rolling her eyes at Suzi.

'Didn't want to scare you off old girl,' said Malcolm with a laugh as he gestured to the waiter for yet another bottle.

'You didn't tell me my cabin roof leaked either did you, or that the toilet wasn't working properly, or the cooker.'

He chuckled away to himself as he downed another glassful.

'So what do you do for a loo then,' asked Suzi.

'Bucket and chuck it,' said Sandy, 'it's not very dignified is it plus you have to watch which way the wind's blowing.'

'I just hang my arse over the side and let rip,' laughed Malcolm.

'So what about when you're in the marina then,'

'It all goes over the side when it's dark, anyway everybody's toilet goes straight out into the water.' he laughed as he filled his and Sandy's glasses up again,

'Oh god, I go swimming in that water,' I groaned.

'Well don't go swimming at night will you, you might bump into something - are you drinking that?' he added, pointing to my still full glass.

'No I'm driving.'

'Dammit, can't let it go to waste,' he said, reaching over.

I was struggling to banish a disturbing image of a turd infested marina as Malcolm stood up, drained my glass and then staggered over to pay the bill.

On the drive back and purely by chance he spotted the scrap yard he'd been told about. He shouted for me to pull in and a blast of foul wine breath found its way into the front, engulfing us both.

It was a chaotic place with hundreds of old cars piled up everywhere and lorry containers scattered about haphazardly, full to bursting with spare parts. I parked Billy next to one which looked like it might be the office.

The only reason I thought it might be the office was because it had a small window in it and I could just make out a door which was partly obscured by a stack of radiators and rusty exhaust pipes. There was a mangy looking Alsatian type dog chained up to a rusty old car chassis and it was whining and straining at the chain in an attempt to get to us.

'I'd give that one a wide berth if I were you,' came the stern warning from Malcolm and Sandy did just that.

Suzi however went straight up to the dog and started fussing it. The dog was in heaven, standing up on its back legs with its paws on her shoulders whimpering in delight and wagging its tail furiously.

A man appeared from the office and walked slowly over to us and shook hands with Malcolm who was already talking to him, in English. He made no attempt to speak any Spanish at all, instead he just spoke louder, all the time breathing his wine breath all over the poor bloke - scrappy took a step back.

Then he threw a couple of French words in for good measure just to help things along a bit. Of course he didn't understand a word he'd said and Malcolm quickly lost patience with him.

'Oh bloody *hell* man,' he bawled, 'what's the matter with you, look it's quite simple, I.. want.. a.. STARTER.. MOTOR!' He slapped the back of his hand into the palm of the other to emphasize each word, 'Oh sod you then I'll find one myself, where are they over here?'

He stomped off in wine fuelled high dudgeon in the general direction of the nearest container.

I turned to scrappy and did a quick mime of starting a car complete with sound effects and the man immediately understood. He laughed and gestured for us to follow him and he took us in the opposite direction to a small container which was literally full of starter motors.

The girls called over to Malcolm who was struggling to open the door of the container he'd chosen and we all had a good titter at his expense as he limped his way back, huffing and puffing away to himself.

The man gestured for Malcolm to search through the motors for himself and then wandered off.

'Stupid little man,' he grumbled, 'why the hell didn't he show us these in the first place.'

We both got stuck in and after looking at dozens of different motors, Malcolm finally found one which was nearly the same at the business end and had the same terminals on but was a slightly different shape.

'Damn it all that's close, bloody close,' he said as he compared it in his mind to the one he already had, 'can't be sure though without seeing mine.'

Well why didn't you bring yours with you then I thought to myself.

'Why didn't you bring the old one with you then you plonker,' said Suzi with a big smile.'

That's my girl!

'It would have made more sense wouldn't it and you wouldn't have had to get your knickers in such a twist would you.' she continued.

He had no answer for that and the girls had another good giggle at his expense as he played with the motor and tried to ignore them

'The holes look to be in the right place but it's a bit wider here though,' he said squinting at it.

'Will it fit d'you think?'

'Could be worth a punt.'

'Better test it before you pay for it though.'

We went off to find scrappy and Malcolm shouted the word test at him a few times accompanied by the word battery and luckily he knew what he meant. He took us to another shed where he tested it and it seemed to be working ok, then he wrote the price on his hand and held it up.

'Good god man you can't be serious, that's daylight bloody robbery!' shouted Malcolm and he turned abruptly and walked away two paces and then just as abruptly turned and came back again.

He snatched the pen off him and wrote a figure on his own hand and showed it to scrappy. This was met by a waggling finger and an apologetic smile, he pointed to the figure on his hand again.

Now it was Malcolm's turn to do some finger waggling.

'Now look here Senor, either you accept my price or the deals off, no way is it worth *that* much and it might not even bloody well fit!.'

Scrappy shrugged his shoulders – not my problem - and pointed to his hand again, still smiling.

Malcolm sighed and said,

'Right senor I'll meet you half way ok? take it or leave it.'

Malcolm then counted out half the required money and slapped it down on the bench, picked up the starter motor and strode out before scrappy could say anything. He counted it, shrugged his shoulders again, gave a little smile and pocketed the money.

As I was leaving I saw scrappy talking and laughing with his friend and waving the money about, he was clearly thrilled with the outcome.

On the way back we passed a rubbish dump and we looked at each other and smiled - we must go 'shopping' there next time we come for water.

ꊂ ꊂ ꊂ ꊂ ꊂ

Later on that same day Sandy came over to Billy and asked if I'd come and help Malcolm fit the starter motor as he was struggling to do it with his one good arm.

We climbed aboard carefully, there wasn't much room now as half the floorboards in the cockpit had been raised to get to the engine below. Malcolm was lying on his front with his head down the hole, there was a clang followed by,

'Oh bugger it you *bloody* thing, oh hi Tim, dropped the sodding spanner.'

I got the feeling it wasn't the first time that had happened - he rolled over onto his back and sighed.

'Not a job for a bloody old cripple like me, need two good arms damn it.'

'Would you like me to have a go?' I offered.

'Are you sure, that would be awfully kind if you would, can't bloody well reach, need another good arm to support myself this one's bloody useless I'm afraid.'

I lay down on the floor and we both peered down at the engine. There was a heady mixture of stale salt water mixed with engine and diesel oil rising up and blending with Malcolm's wine breath.

'I've got one bolt in about halfway so far that's all,' he said, 'slow old job, not enough room to turn the spanner fully, I'll try and hold the starter if you can do the spanner work.'

I reached down, he was right there wasn't much space, just enough for one hand at full stretch. The starter fitted on the lower side so it was out of sight and had to be done by feel - not the best arrangement. It turned out there just wasn't enough room for the two of us as we kept banging heads and getting in each others way and happily Malcolm retreated, taking his wine breath with him. He cursed his useless arm once more and went back to fixing his bilge pump.

The spanner was slippery and I kept dropping it which meant reaching further down and groping for it in the oily water which only made things worse. It was really hot work too, being upside down didn't help much either and I began to feel a bit queasy. Luckily Suzi was at hand and she kept passing me water every so often.

We still didn't know if it would fit properly yet and I could only use one hand to operate the spanner which would only turn a fraction before stopping against the side. I laboured on slowly eventually getting the three bolts tightened fully and happily it fitted into place nicely.

I finally emerged from the engine and once all the excess blood had drained from my head, I dropped straight over the side into the water to cool off leaving Malcolm to connect the wires. Caine was looking down on me from the boat and I knew what was coming next.

Right on cue he threw himself off the boat and landed right next to me. We then had to swim all the way back round the boats until we reached the slipway so he could get out.

I made a point of swimming with my mouth shut after hearing Malcolm's little horror story earlier.

We spent long, hot, lazy, dusty days just trying to keep cool, cowering from the midday sun underneath our various shade makers and drinking warm water all day and all night. Oddly enough, we found drinking a hot cup of tea was more refreshing than the warm water and we lost count of the number of cups we'd have in a day.

The highlight of the day was in the late afternoon when I would run barefoot to the shop and buy two bottles of ice cold San Miguel beer. The pavements were burning hot but our feet had toughened up so much we could now walk on them without getting burnt. The beers were stored loose in a big chest freezer and as I reached in to get them I'd shove my head right in to cool off a bit then I'd race back to Billy as fast as I could as literally within a couple of minutes, they'd be warm.

On one of these mercy dashes I spotted an orange folding plastic sun chair leaning against a wheelie bin. I stopped and examined it, it looked ok apart from one small broken bit, I could mend this easily with some string I thought to myself and took it back to Billy.

One day as we were enjoying our breakfast in the relative coolness of the early morning, Suzi pointed out a huge mound of human excrement right on the end of the wall at the side of the slipway. A length of toilet paper was still attached to the top of it, fluttering around like a little white flag in the gentle morning breeze. It seemed a very odd place for someone to go to the toilet and odder still was the fact that by lunch time it had disappeared completely - where had it gone to? We'd been there all morning and hadn't seen anyone clearing it up, all that was left there now was an ugly dark brown stain in the concrete.

Each night, sleep was intermittent until about 3 a.m. due to the continuous music coming from the bar over the road beneath the apartments with 'Y Viva España' being played seemingly non stop.

Then every so often there would be a really loud bang as someone let off a firework which was then followed by screams and shouts and drunken laughing.

On top of all that there was the whistling - loud piercing whistles which echoed around the buildings followed by more shouts and more drunken laughing.

There was also the frequent sound of cars racing around the narrow streets with tyres screeching, horns blowing and drunken passengers hanging from their windows shouting, singing 'Y Viva España' and laughing (drunkenly).

When it eventually quietened down and just as we'd be drifting off, there would inevitably be the odd party of stragglers staggering along singing bloody 'Y Viva España' at the tops of their voices and kicking an empty beer bottle along the pavement.

We couldn't shut the noise out either as it was still hot during the night and we had to sleep with the side door open just to try and get some air. Nelson was more than happy with this arrangement as it meant he could lie right in the doorway and keep an eye on his surroundings. We felt quite safe sleeping there with the door open with him on guard.

One night we went for a walk around the town and came across a flamenco band playing on a small stage outside a hotel right next to the pavement. There were three men playing guitars and a beautiful senorita dressed in red with jet black hair singing and dancing flamenco. It was a beautiful sound and we stopped on the pavement to watch and listen - we were entranced.

After a time the singer started dragging people from their seats up on to the stage to sing along with her.

'Uh oh,' I said, 'time to go, I don't fancy getting roped into that.'

'Oh for god's sake Tim don't be such a big baby, look, she's only choosing people who are actually staying in the hotel. The night is young, just relax will you and stop embarrassing me.'

Well I didn't relax at all and I was ready to leg it at a moments notice but I was still loving the show, we both were.

A couple of songs later though the singer came out onto the pavement and grabbed some poor unsuspecting passer by and dragged her on to the stage to huge applause and proceeded to thoroughly embarrass her. Immediately Suzi turned to me, faking a huge yawn.

'Oh wow I'm really tired can we go now, we must get back to the boys it's getting late.'

'What, but I thought the night was young, let's stay for another couple of songs,' I said - largely to myself as it turned out as she was off down the street - 'Hey come back you big baby!'

♫♫♫♫♫

The water was running low so we went back up to Palau again to fill up and do some washing.

Senora Twankey was there again and had just finished doing *her* washing, she greeted us warmly but when she saw that Suzi still had the same old washing powder she put her hands on her hips and tut tutted. She then insisted we follow her down into the town, leading us through the narrow streets until we reached a little shop where we all went inside.

She made a sweeping gesture around the dimly lit shop with her hands and patted her chest smiling, ah it was her shop and I picked out the word 'mama' again.

It was like a little aladdins cave (so I wasn't calling her Senora Twankey for nothing then!) with what looked like everything you'd ever need in life filling the old wooden shelves.

She reached up to one of the shelves and brought down a box of 'proper' washing powder and banged it down on the counter triumphantly, talking away non stop. She then produced a block of soap from the depths of a large cardboard box and finally, she reached into the window for a scrubbing brush just like the one she had.

I spied a roll of fine net curtain up on one of the shelves which I thought would make a good mozzie screen for the side door. I asked for two metres of it and as she was cutting it I made a buzzing noise and slapped myself across the face by way of explanation. She understood straight away and roared with laughter and this prompted a further outpouring of tales from a bygone era (I think!).

I paid for the net curtain but she flatly refused to take any money for the other stuff which was really kind of her. We edged slowly towards the door as she prattled on and on – about what we had absolutely no idea. We had no choice but to just stand there and listen to her and anyway, even if we *had* been able to speak Spanish we'd have had little or no chance of getting a word in.

We somehow made it through the door but she followed us out onto the street and carried on talking to us there. Thankfully though after a couple of minutes, she saw a friend walking past and latched onto her and we made good our escape.

We did the washing together and then filled up all the containers with the beautiful crystal clear mountain spring water. Looking up, we could see a tiny, solitary white building perched high above us on the rocky mountainside. It *was* we were told, a chapel named Santuari de Sant Onofre, where long ago there once lived a hermit serving penance.

A footpath led off towards the mountains which we hoped would lead us up to the chapel, and so around midday - which probably wasn't the best time of day to take a hike up a mountain in that heat - we set off.

We took a little food in our money belts to keep us going but water was going to be more important so I took a five litre bottle with me. It was a bit cumbersome to carry but we were going to need it as it would be even hotter out on the open trail. There weren't many trees to be seen, especially higher up which would mean little or no respite from the mid day sun.

We followed the dry dusty pathway through the stubby undergrowth as we climbed slowly and steadily, stopping whenever we could in the welcome shade of a small lonely tree for a drink and to admire the view back down the hillside.

The higher we climbed the steeper it got, the terrain becoming more rocky until eventually there were no more trees to stop and shelter under. The air was so hot and dry I was finding it hard to breathe and I could feel my face burning from the heat being reflected back off the ground.

I was glad I'd decided to carry the five litres of water as it was disappearing fast.

The boys were running ahead of us and as usual kept coming back regularly to check on us. This one time though Nelson came back on his own without Caine, we couldn't see him anywhere and assumed he was ahead of us somewhere so we pressed on.

As we were making our way through an overgrown part we heard the faint sound of water coming from somewhere a little way off the path. We made our way through the short prickly bushes to find Caine wallowing in a tiny pool of water he'd somehow found. He just lay there with a big smile on his face enjoying the feeling of the water on his belly. He looked happy enough so we just left him to it and carried on upwards.

A couple of minutes later there was a bark and a rustling in the bushes and then Caine re-appeared. He charged up the path at full speed and dived on his big brother, he was so happy to be wet again but then got a good telling off from Nelson for making *him* all wet.

The path steepened some more and we made our way carefully between the rocks before eventually reaching the little whitewashed chapel, perched right on the edge of a rocky outcrop at about four hundred metres altitude. The view back down the mountainside was breathtaking and well worth the walk up. We rested for a while on a stone wall and drank some warm water in the welcome shade of a large tree.

The door to the chapel was locked with a massive padlock which meant we couldn't go in which was a little disappointing. A rope was hanging down off the roof by the door which was attached to the bell in the little tower.

'They probably ring the bell to summon the townspeople for services or for funerals and special occasions,' I guessed.

'I wonder what it sounds like,' said Suzi going over to it and grabbing hold of the rope.

'Don't ring it!' I said knowing full well she was going to anyway.

Seconds later the sound of the bell reverberated around the hillside, echoing its merry way right down to the town and beyond.

A chime or two would have sufficed but *oh* no, she must have pulled on that rope for a good minute letting the bell clang away loudly non stop. She had a delighted grin on her face the whole time whilst I looked around nervously, expecting a horde of angry locals to descend upon us, demanding retribution for such an outrage.

About five minutes later as we stood admiring the stunning view down the mountain we heard the now familiar and slightly irritating buzz of a small two stroke motorbike approaching along the dusty track leading around the mountainside.

The bike bounced its way slowly along the bumpy track, ridden by a flat capped man who had both legs sticking out in case of emergency which made it look like he was walking the bike along. Dressed in checked shirt, corduroy trousers and flip flops, he stopped at the chapel, got off the bike which then died immediately by itself and leant it up against the chapel wall.

He said Buenos Dias to us through his cigarette, opened the chapel door using one of the keys he'd selected from the *very* large bunch he was carrying and then got straight back on his motorbike. He rolled it down a slope, bump started it and it roared angrily back to life amid a cloud of blue smoke and then he rode/walked off back along the track - disappearing from whence he came.

We looked at each other slightly puzzled.

'Did he come here specially to do that for us d'you think?' asked Suzi.

'Don't know, bit of a coincidence though isn't it.'

'Maybe ringing the bell means someone wants to go in and pray or something.'

'In you go then.' I said giving her a shove.

There was a welcome coolness inside and we sat in silence for a while before finding a door which led onto a small stone terrace. There were no trees for shade so we just sat on the burningly hot stone wall in the blazingly hot mid day sun and ate hot soggy sandwiches. The water – which was now almost hot enough to make tea with - was nearly all gone but the walk back down was going to be easier so we should be ok.

The lonely sound of a church bell echoed its way up the mountainside to where we were sitting, other than that there wasn't a sound and the view was just spectacular. Far below us we could see the town of Palau Saverdera and beyond that in the far distance, the long sweeping coastline of the Bay of

Roses and the beautifully shimmering deep blue of the Mediterranean.

We lingered there for some time, not really wanting to leave, before reluctantly setting off back down the mountain. Billy was still in shade when we got back and quite cool inside, so after a quick cup of tea we pulled the bed down and had a very welcome siesta.

On the way back we took a detour and found the rubbish dump I'd seen before. It was spread out over a huge area and as there was no one around I drove around until we saw what looked to be the best pile, Pierre was right, there was some good stuff to be found here.

I found some nice pieces of wood which I already had plans for, Suzi found a folding sun chair in really good condition as well as a parasol which was like new. I also found a small roll of plastic mosquito netting, a foot pump for blowing dinghies up with, and the top prize - a double sized airbed without any holes in it.

We loaded our treasure into Billy and headed off.

Just as we were nearing Santa Margarida we passed by a small market on the side of the road, well we couldn't resist a market could we - great places to buy cheap, local produce.

I pulled Billy onto the verge and then we had a quick walk around and bought a few things, not too much though as it would only go off in the heat.

We came across one stall with a huge mound of kiwis, nothing else, just kiwis.

'Ooh look at all these lovely kiwis Tim, we must get some, how much is that in sterling?' she said pointing at the price tag.

When I told her she said excitedly,

'Wow that's good, let's get a bag full.'

The man behind the stall handed us a large paper bag, we filled it up and paid for the kiwis.

We wandered around the rest of the stalls feeling quite pleased with our bagful of bargain price kiwis. We were just passing the kiwi stall on the way back to Billy when I overheard two English women talking.

'Blimey Sal, have you seen the price of these kiwis?'

'Yes I have,' Sal replied, 'they're cheaper in Tesco.'

☺ ☺ ☺ ☺ ☺

The first thing I did when we got back was to blow our 'new' airbed up with our 'new' pump and oh joy - it didn't leak - wow what a find.

I took it straight down to the slip, jumped on and paddled out into the channel, then I rolled off and went under to wash all the dust and grime of the rubbish tip off me.

There were no boats coming in or out so I lay there for a while just floating about and congratulating myself on a great find. I was imagining passing many hours floating around lazily on this just soaking up the sun, occasionally rolling off into the water to cool off a bit, and then climbing back on again to soak up some more sun - oh what bliss.

Just then I heard a splash nearby and here comes Caine powering his way through the water towards me with a 'how dare you go swimming without me' look on his face. He clambered straight up onto the airbed and suddenly there was a loud hiss as his claws ripped through the material and we both went down like a rock, nice one Caine. It went down so quickly I didn't even have chance to grab hold of it and it sank without a trace - I was gutted.

I swam dejectedly back to the slip but then I cheered up a tad when I passed a bikini clad woman in a big red sun hat sitting on the end of the wall writing postcards - she was sitting right on the big brown shit stain.

It made me smile to think that someone would actually want to place their barely covered bottom directly on a horrible looking stain like that. She smiled back at me and I felt a bit mean not telling her about it but by that time the damage was done. Anyway I wasn't quite sure how to go about explaining that one to her so I just let it lie.

When I'd finished sulking over the airbed I went over to Mark on Lady Jane and asked if I could borrow a saw and instead he lent me his whole toolbox. I made a frame from the wood I'd found on the tip and fastened the mozzie netting to it using drawing pins I'd borrowed from Sandy. It fitted perfectly over the slatted windows in Billy which meant we could now have them permanently open.

We had to have the windows open at night for some air but there were a lot of mozzies here because of a large area of wetland across the other side of the channel. It was hard to sleep with them buzzing around our heads and biting us all night long and in the mornings we'd wake up with blood all over our faces from where we'd been swiping away at them.

They could bite through thick denim jeans too and Suzi often came up in big painful lumps and huge red blotches from them, we had to stop them getting in. The large piece of fine net curtain we'd bought from Senora Twankey's shop was now hanging in the side doorway so we now had a nice through draught - if ever there was a breeze that is.

For a change of scenery we left Santa Margarida and drove around to the other side of the channel, parking Billy right next to the large boulders which Suzi had jumped off. It was almost dead opposite the free moorings and the beach stretched all the way down to the large residential marina of Empuriabrava.

We got out and sat on the rocks with our feet dangling in the cool water, Caine of course went straight in to cool off.

A couple of Spanish campers were parked a little further upstream on some scrubland close to the water; it looked like a nice spot to park. There were several adults, lots of kids and dogs and they were enjoying a barbeque on a small beach, they looked like day trippers to us.

Sure enough, as evening approached they all packed up and left, we were pleased about that as we wanted to move over there to spend the night.

'Let's go over there and see what it's like first,' said Suzi - wisely as it turned out.

We walked over and to our dismay saw the whole area strewn with litter and empty bottles. There was a neat pile of carrier bags full of rubbish, dirty nappies scattered all over the place and around the perimeter of their camp there were piles of excrement with dirty toilet paper fluttering about.

'Hmm maybe we won't move here after all,' I said.

'This is disgusting,' said Suzi incredulously, 'how can they leave all this litter behind after them, look at it all. Why not take it away with them, how can you just leave dirty nappies on the ground like that, it's their own country and they treat it like this I can't believe it.'

We were finding that day trippers nearly always left a mess behind them with litter and rubbish strewn all over the place, whereas people who were living in their vans never did.

Needless to say we didn't move there.

As night fell, the beach emptied and soon we were the only ones left there which was perfect. It was nice and dark there as well apart from the lights of Rosas and Santa Margarida just across the water We could hear the familiar sounds drifting across the water from the free moorings but they weren't nearly as loud and we would have had a lovely night's sleep if it hadn't been for the damn mozzies.

Despite the netting we now had up over the doors and windows the little bastards still found their way in somehow. When I say 'little' - they weren't - these were huge buggers with fangs like sabre toothed tigers and a thirst for blood like a swarm of rabid vampires.

Lying in bed we could hear them constantly buzzing around us, then the buzzing would get louder as they got closer and we would take a swipe at them in mid air, what a waste of time that was.

Cover our heads with the duvet? no too hot, can't breathe, we were sitting targets, well lying ones really.

The best way we'd found was to wait until they got really close, hold your nerve until the buzzing stopped which meant they'd landed somewhere, and then slap yourself hard across the face. If you got lucky the buzzing would stop, well for a while at least until another one moved in for the kill.

Either that or it would be the same one you'd missed that was returning for another bucket of blood after having a belch and a good laugh at your expense.

It wasn't funny really, Suzi was really suffering so one night was more than enough in that particular spot.

ꐕꐕꐕꐕꐕ

On our way back to the free moorings the next morning we pulled onto some rough ground near the boatyard, the one Pierre had told us about.

The channel that went past the free moorings ended up here then it went round in a loop and rejoined itself again creating a large island. It was a very quiet spot with just the odd car and camper so we easily found a nice spot by the water and decided to stay for the day.

It looked like a good place to empty the toilet too as the ground was nice and soft and there was plenty of water around. If it wasn't emptied every couple of days now it would really start to stink because of the heat. A week's worth of human waste cooking in a confined space like Billy was indescribable and really had to be smelt to be believed.

Suzi spotted a mast on the far side of the island all on its own.

'I wonder if that's Pierre,' she said.

'No, that's a German flag.' I replied as I peered through our trusty binoculars, 'same colours, but the stripes are going the other way.'

A bit later on we wandered over to the boatyard and had a walk around the boats to see if there was any work going. The first person I spoke to happened to be the yard owner, he told us that most of the boats were in the water now and all the work like painting was done during the winter. He said it would be ok though for us to walk around and ask the owners anyway.

We did find a couple of owners with their boats but none of them needed any help with anything so we went back to Billy. We spent a peaceful night there and returned to the free moorings the next morning.

We went over to chat to Malcolm and Sandy, he'd finally managed to fix the bilge pump and he proudly gave us a demonstration of it working. He still hadn't fixed the leak though so in effect they were living aboard a yacht which was permanently sinking, but at least now they didn't have to keep bailing it out with a bucket all the time.

'Got a bit of a problem up there as well I'm afraid,' said Malcolm pointing to the top of the mast, 'damn light's not working, should fix it really but can't afford bloody boatyard prices, it'll just have to stay broken, I can't go up there with one arm anyway.'

I remembered watching Pierre easily climb *his* mast freestyle to fix *his* lights and then before I knew it I heard myself say.

'I'll have a go, have you got a safety harness?'

'Well yes I have, but no bosun's chair I'm afraid,' he said 'so I've got no way of hoisting you up.'

'That's ok, just give me the harness and I'll climb up.'

'How the hell are you going to climb up there, that's a forty foot mast,' he said as he helped me into the harness and passed me a bum bag with some tools in it, 'There's a new bulb in there too just in case that's the problem, try that first.'

I stood at the bottom of the mast and looked up - oh boy, it *was* a long way up. Never mind, it'll be just like climbing a tree I told myself, something I was pretty good at.

'Hope you've got a good head for heights old boy.'

'So do I' I thought as I reached up, clutched the mast and pulled myself up then wrapped my legs around the mast and held myself there. Well that was easy, just need to keep doing that until I reach the top, how hard can it be?

I worked my way up bit by bit until I'd reached the cross trees which were a little awkward to get past. Once I was above them I put both feet on them up against the mast and stood there for a minute to have a rest and a look around. I felt the mast swaying from side to side as people moved about below which was a little disconcerting.

'Are you ok,' called Suzi from somewhere a long way below me.

I looked down to reply but immediately wished I hadn't, looking around at this height was fine but looking down wasn't so good and my stomach did a somersault - I gripped the mast a little tighter.

'Yeah I'm fine, just enjoying the view,' I said in an effort to reassure myself, 'can you keep still down there please'.

'What?'

'Nothing never mind.' I replied without looking down.

I looked up - hmm over half way, not too far to go now and I grabbed another handful of mast and slithered on up.

I finally reached the top but it felt really disorientating not to have any mast in front of me any more and I could easily have freaked out. Having a panic attack clinging to the top of a forty foot mast was simply not an option and I took some deep breaths to calm myself.

I managed to relax a bit and clipped the harness on to an anchor point, hoping it would all be strong enough to hold me up here if it hit the fan. Next I wrapped my left arm around the mast, hugging it tightly as my legs held me in position with an adrenaline fuelled grip of steel.

'Don't look down now Tim,' I said to myself, 'do not look down - just focus on the light, nothing else, just the light.'

I wished they would all stand still down there as any slight movement down on the yacht made the top of the mast behave like a pendulum. It was swaying back and forth in a sickening stomach churning motion and it would have been so easy to panic.

Also fainting at this point was simply not an option so I closed my eyes, took some more deep breaths and then began.

First I needed to take the cover off the light so I reached down into the bag for the screwdriver. NO! don't look down, oh god no do not look down, just feel for it - that's it, got it. I gripped the screwdriver tightly with a trembling, sweaty hand - don't drop it Tim. I undid the screws and put them between my lips, screwdriver carefully replaced in the bag.

I took the plastic lens cover off carefully, gripping it with my left hand which just about reached it, don't drop it whatever you do. I reached down and put it in the bag and then I took the bulb out and put that in the bag as well.

I held onto the mast with both hands and took a few deep breaths before continuing.

I found the new bulb in the bag, fitted it and thankfully the light came on - oh happy days. I couldn't stay up here much longer as my legs were sweating and weakening. I was losing grip now and kept sliding slowly downwards and I had to keep pulling myself back up again.

'Yes it's working, I say Tim it's working now!' shouted an excited Malcolm from some forty feet below me. No kidding Sherlock, I *can* see it y'know, it's about an inch from my face!

I was just reaching into the bag for the lens when suddenly my whole world lurched sickeningly to one side and I clung on to that mast for dear life. What the hell were they doing down there, no don't look down you idiot.

I closed my eyes and gripped the top of the mast so tightly my muscles were trembling.

'Hey huh huck's hake keek skill!, I hissed through the screws as I swung back the other way again – oh my god stoppit!

'I say what was that?'

I took the screws out and compromised with,

'Keep bloody still!'

I wasn't enjoying the view quite so much any more and my legs were about to give up on me, whose daft idea was this anyway. It was a full minute before I could relax my grip and carry on.

I got the lens out of the bag with trembling fingers and refitted it, thankfully without dropping anything. I was having visions of the damage a screwdriver could do if dropped from up here and made a mental note to tie any tools to some string next time.

Next time? - there won't be a next time!

Anyway, job done and I unclipped the safety harness before sliding slowly down the mast until my feet reached the safety of the cross trees once more. I very quickly discovered that my legs simply wouldn't hold me up so I just sat there for a few minutes to regain my composure. I did contemplate jumping off at this point but thought better of it - it wouldn't have ended well.

I reached the deck and received a slap on the back from a delighted Malcolm.

'Bloody good show young man, bloody good show, can't thank you enough.'

'Wow it's hot up there,' I said as I struggled out of the harness.

We all sat in the cockpit underneath the canopy and Sandy supplied us with cool beers in their old faded and stained plastic beakers. My legs were still weak and wobbly from clinging on for so long and there was a definite tremble in my hand as I downed the very welcome beer.

'This beer's nice and cool,' said Suzi between gulps, 'have you got a fridge then?'

'Not a fridge as such, come down and have a look,' she said beckoning as she got up and went down the steps into the cabin.

We both went down and watched as she took the cushion off one of the bench seats and then lifted the wooden lid off. Inside was full of lovely cool things you'd normally find in a fridge only everything was sitting on top of a huge block of ice. We put our hands in to feel the delicious coolness - I nearly jumped in.

'How long does the ice last?' asked Suzi.

'A couple of weeks at least,' replied Sandy, 'even in this heat.'

'Wow that's brilliant,' crooned Suzi, she looked at me, 'can we have one in Billy?'

'No room,' I said sadly and had one last feel of the ice before climbing the steps back up into the cockpit.

൛ ൛ ൛ ൛ ൛

We went back to the rough ground near the boatyard late one afternoon with the intention of getting a nice quiet night's sleep for a change. Also I needed to empty the toilet again as it was really stinking, and it was very unpleasant trying to sleep with that smell filling our nostrils.

I pulled Billy up close to the water, squeezing our way in between two huge clumps of reeds. There was just about enough room to get out and sit in front of Billy at the water's edge. It wasn't the prettiest location but it was so peaceful and private and no-one could park near us. I set about mending the chair I'd found whilst Suzi wrote letters and did her diary.

A little while later, two large camper vans pulled off the road and drove around for a bit obviously looking for somewhere to park up for the night.

Next thing we knew one of them pulled up right next to us, driving all over the reeds, flattening them in the process. It drove back and forth flattening a huge area of them and finished up side on to the water and so close to Billy there was hardly enough room to walk between us. Then the other one pulled in next to it so that they were L shaped.

We were outraged - there really was no need to pull that close to us, there was plenty of room elsewhere.

Four adults and five kids poured out of one camper and two adults and three kids from the other. What a racket, they took over the whole area and even brought their chairs right in front of Billy and sat there right next to us by the water.

The peace and tranquility was utterly shattered.

They laid two big ground sheets down on the cruelly flattened reeds, then on top of that they unrolled a large piece of plush looking carpet upon which they then set up tables and chairs and parasols. Within minutes the whole place was filled with eight screaming kids charging around on bikes, riding round and round Billy, squeezing between the gaps, banging into him (and us) and annoying the boys in the process. The toilet was outside in the long grass as we couldn't cope with the stink in Billy and this was now being used as part of their obstacle course.

There was only so much of this Nelson was going to take before he made his feelings clear.

The six adults had no control over the kids whatsoever and were quite happy to let them run riot over everything, including us. Caine would usually have been thrilled to have so much company this close but even he was put out.

Next they set up a stereo with big speakers and blasted loud music out which of course meant they now had to shout to one another. Conversation between ourselves was now practically impossible and all letter writing ground to a halt.

All fourteen of them sat down at the tables for supper and then afterwards, a couple of the women brought two of the younger kids around to our side of Billy where we were now sitting. They went into the long grass about ten feet from us and flattened a patch of it so the kids could go to the toilet there.

We looked on incredulously as they both had a good old shit and were then taken back, leaving their deposits behind in full view and well within smelling range.

We were totally ignored by everyone, as if we weren't there at all and a couple of minutes later the women came back with two more kids and did the same thing all over again without even bothering to clean up after themselves.

As you can imagine, we were well upset by this time and reluctantly decided to move somewhere else for the rest of the night as it looked like they were here to stay. We packed everything away and I had to move a couple of their bikes before I could reverse Billy out, these were angrily tossed into the long grass right where their toilet was – oops!

We ended up over by the noisy main road and annoyingly still well within earshot of our neighbours. Eventually all the kids were in bed and just the adults and the loud music remained. At long last they all went to bed and peace returned once more, but as if to serve as a reminder that they were still there they left bright lights on outside, spoiling the darkness.

The thought of waking up in the morning and seeing that rabble was just too much for us and so we decided to go back to the free moorings to sleep.

We packed things away yet again and then I realized I hadn't emptied the toilet - it was still sitting over in the long grass all by itself, it had to be done now that's for sure - then I had an idea.

I started Billy up and reversed out.

'Wait you've forgotten the toilet,' said Suzi seeing it sitting all forlorn by itself in the long grass.

'Oh no I haven't,' I said as I left Billy running and got out, closing the door quietly behind me.

I picked up the loo and carried it over to our Belgian neighbours and walked onto their carpeted area. I quietly removed the lid, holding my breath trying not to retch from the stink and then poured the entire contents out all over the carpet.

It glugged out slowly, thick, gooey and evil smelling and I watched contentedly as it crept menacingly across the shagpile.

I went over to the water and filled it up a bit to swill it out, emptying that out on top of the thick stuff which thinned it all down nicely, making it go even further. It slowly made its way off the edge of the carpet and then spread across the plastic groundsheet and surrounded the table and chairs.

I sauntered off back to Billy with my heart full of joy and drove off, blowing the horn as I went past them in the hope that they would wake up and find my little leaving present while it was still fresh - so to speak!

☺ ☺ ☺ ☺ ☺

We stayed at the free moorings for the next few days until we felt like a change of scenery. We were also yearning to find ourselves a quiet spot far from the *maddening* crowd.

I'd seen a lake called Panta de Boadella on the map which wasn't too far away in the foothills of the Pyrenees. We reckoned it would be quieter and maybe a bit cooler for the boys, so we set off early one morning stopping at Palau to fill up with water to save hunting around for it later. We also bought a few large loaves of bread, loads of olives and fruit and headed off.

Somewhere along the way we passed acres and acres of vines so we picked and stashed a fair few bunches as well as some baby sweetcorn, so we wouldn't starve over the next few days.

We found the lake without too much trouble and I pulled Billy off the road parking near some trees not far from the water. There was a sloping bank leading all the way down to the shore where people were swimming and splashing about. Several camping cars were dotted about the place, as well as a few tents and several cars - it was going to be hard to find somewhere quiet to park up.

'Oh god this is no good, it's like a bloody camp site,' groaned a disappointed Suzi, 'let's find somewhere else.'

'Look over there that looks like a nice spot,' I said pointing across the water to what looked like a long beach on the far side of the lake. We looked at the map and saw what could be a track leading all the way round the lake.

'Right, let's see if we can find it,' I said and we all jumped back into Billy and drove off in search of the track. A short way along the road Suzi spotted an overgrown track leading off in the direction of the lake.

'Could that be it?'

'Soon find out,' I said as I reversed back and turned off, immediately having to slow to a crawl because of all the bumps and pot holes and low branches which were at windscreen level.

We crawled along at walking speed as I had to try and avoid the huge craters and low branches at the same time. There were some horrible scratching noises as Billy's side was swept by the scenery and every so often he would ground on a lump in the middle of the track as the wheels went down into a crater.

'This could end badly couldn't it, what happens if we meet someone, there's no room to pass.'

'Let's hope we don't then,' I said.

'Poor Billy, you're hurting his tummy, fancy bringing him down here,' said Suzi throwing me a concerned look.

'What? it was your idea.'

'No it wasn't.'

'Yes it was, you made me come down here.'

'Don't be ridiculous, I just pointed it out that's all, maybe we should go back.' she said, both feet up on the dashboard to brace herself against the rocking and rolling of Billy.

'Not going back, for one thing we'd have to reverse all the way back and the exhaust would probably get ripped off in the process. Another thing, there could be somewhere really beautiful waiting for us at the end of all this and anyway we just don't go back do we so there, end of.'

Luckily so far we hadn't met anyone, not surprising really, I wasn't expecting much traffic.

'Mind this one,' said Suzi pointing to a particularly large branch. It didn't look like it would bend very much so I had to go around it.

Suddenly Billy dropped down into a really deep hole, there was a sickening thump from directly underneath us and he came to a dead stop. We looked at each other as I put him in reverse, no way was he going forwards and luckily, although it took a bit of an effort he managed to scramble backwards out of the crater.

'Is he ok d'you think?'

'Well he's still going and he sounds the same as he did before so let's hope so,'

'You could have damaged the sump doing that and oil could be leaking out and we wouldn't know,'

'Ah yes but Billy keeps his engine in the back remember and he grounded somewhere near the middle, so the engine should be fine. Anyway what d'you mean *I* could have damaged the sump it wasn't my fault, you told me to swerve to avoid that branch so it's more your fault than mine!'

'Oh don't be so stupid you're the driver, you made him go into that hole you plonker.'

'Well you could have warned me about it couldn't you it was on your side, why don't you watch where we're going.'

Just then a branch whipped in through the window and whacked me in the face.

'Hah! that'll teach you to be cheeky!' giggled Suzi delightedly.

'That's not funny,' I said wiping the blood from my stinging face as I deliberately steered Billy over to the left so that the branches came in *her* window. It almost worked but she was one step ahead of me (as usual) and she shut her window quickly.

'Hah hah - tosser!' she said laughing triumphantly.

We bounced and lurched our way slowly along the ridiculously overgrown track, it seemed like a never ending journey and not one I cared to do again in a hurry. I was hoping it would get a bit better the further we went but it only seemed to get worse. It took almost an hour to get to the end of the track but when we finally emerged from the undergrowth it was like we'd arrived in paradise.

We ended up right at the water's edge on a never ending lakeside beach with a shady grassy strip running along the top beneath a line of overhanging trees. Across the vast expanse of deep blue water the rugged mountains rose majestically to give a magnificent backdrop to the paradisiacal scene.

To top it all off we were the only ones there apart from just a couple of tents pitched up in the shade. There were no camping cars at all which came as no surprise really as no-one in their right minds would contemplate bringing a camper along that track - especially not one which was their only home and was carrying all their worldly possessions!

We drove along the shoreline for a bit and pulled up under the trees on the grass with the side door facing the water, then we all got out to survey our new surroundings. Billy was on a slope and was a long way from being level so I dug a hole in front of both tyres on one side and then drove him forward a bit until he was nice and settled in the holes and very nearly level.

After that we all went down to the water where of course Caine ran straight in and lay down to cool off whilst Nelson did his usual delicate paddling - I walked in a bit.

'Oh my god that is freezing!' I exclaimed and I walked quickly out again.

'Is it really that cold?' asked Suzi disbelievingly.

'Wow that actually hurts,' I said rubbing my legs, 'no swimming for me that's for sure, why is it so cold?'

'Caine's not complaining though is he, he's loving that.'

He was just lying in the water with a big happy grin on his face, enjoying being really cool for the first time in ages.

We had lunch next to Billy on the grass under the trees wallowing in the tranquility of our new surroundings - there wasn't a sound to be heard.

'Oh my, I could stay here forever,' purred Suzi, awestruck by the scene.

'Me too,' I replied stretching out on the warm grass.

As I was lying there I noticed a wet patch under Billy so I took a closer look and my heart sank when I saw water dripping from his water tank.

'What are you looking at?' asked Suzi.

'Looks like there's a leak in the water tank, must have happened when we went down into that big hole you made us go into.'

'Oh very funny, can you fix it?'

'Not sure, I'll have a go but it looks like it's around the tap which makes it a bit awkward and I'm going to need something which sticks to this stuff,' I said trying to figure out what it was made of, 'it's a sort of rubbery plasticky material, hmm could be tricky.'

'Is it leaking much?'

'Yeah it is really, at this rate it'll be empty in a few hours.'

'Oh no that's a shame, what a waste of water, can't we catch it in something?

'We haven't got anything; the other cans are all full.'

'Put the boy's water bowl under it then, at least they can drink it,'

'What's the point, they've got a whole lake to drink.'

We could have caught it in our big washing bowl but again there was a whole lake full of water to do our washing in so we just had to let it leak out. Still the grass would benefit from it and I imagined that soon there would be a lovely lush deep green patch in the middle of all the other paler green moisture starved grass.

We were parked quite close to an old stone ruin which had the remains of what looked like an old bell tower. The boys were exploring their new surroundings and had wandered over to it. After a short while Nelson came back to Billy on his own leaving Caine barking at something. He went on and on barking non stop so we went over to see what all the fuss was about.

We found him standing just by the ruin looking into what must have been a room at one time. There was no roof left and one outside wall had fallen down completely leaving just the other three.

He stopped barking when he saw us there next to him but his hackles were raised and he was still chuntering away and growling, staring intently into the enclosed space. There was nothing there that I could see apart from a few stones on the floor, just three walls and nothing, yet he was seeing something which was disturbing him or frightening him.

Nelson wasn't bothered by it at all and he wandered around the room sniffing and cocking his leg merrily. I walked around the back of the ruin to see if I could see anything or anyone but

I saw nothing, and when I got back he was still standing there staring into the room and growling at nothing - or so it seemed.

We stayed with him for a while, eventually calling him away and he reluctantly came with us but then he kept stopping and turning around, growling at whatever it was he was seeing or sensing. By the time we got back to Billy his hackles were back down and he seemed a bit more relaxed but he was still chuntering away quietly and keeping an eye on the ruins.

We decided it was best to move further away from the ruins for his sake, so we put everything back in Billy and drove further along the shore for a few hundred metres. We found a lovely spot right next to a small stream which fed the lake and I dug more holes for Billy's wheels to drop into to help level him.

It was even more peaceful here and there wasn't a soul to be seen anywhere - unless Caine could see one, but he seemed more relaxed now that the ruins were out of sight.

The down side to being where we were now was that the sun disappeared quite early and we were left in the shade from early afternoon onwards. This would never do so we put everything away again and moved back almost to where we'd been in the first place. Almost but not quite and we made sure we couldn't see the ruins before we set up camp again.

For the third time that day I dug holes for Billy's wheels to drop into to make him more level.

The sun stayed with us a bit longer here but it still went down behind the hills far too early. As we looked out across the water we saw the far shores of the lake bathed in glorious evening sunshine until quite late.

'Reckon we're on the wrong side of the lake,' I said glumly.

'What did you bring us all the way round here for then you idiot!' came the stern reply, 'first you hurt Billy's tummy and then we end up in a place with no sunshine, plus Caine's all upset as well, what *were* you thinking of, we can't stay here.'

'I thought you wanted to stay here forever,'

'Changed my mind.' she said laughing.

'Me too, I don't like it here either the water's too cold, we'll go back round to the sunny side tomorrow - mind you it'll be sunny here first thing in the morning.'

We gathered some wood from around the trees and lit a small fire to roast some vegetables on - and to keep warm as it turned out.

It seemed to go quite cold as the night drew in and we huddled closely around the fire, our fronts were nice and warm but our backs were quite cold. Once the initial cold of the evening had passed though, it felt a bit warmer and we slept with all the doors open.

There were no mosquitoes for some reason so we didn't need the netting which allowed a little more air to circulate which was nice for a change. We would have had a lovely night's sleep had it not been for Caine who kept waking us up by going outside all the time and growling in the direction of the ruins.

Nelson stayed outside all night and every time one of us looked out he was just lying there quietly in the moonlight, not sleeping, just watching.

In the middle of the night (cue Mr. Joel) we got out of bed and strolled naked along the shoreline in the moonlight with the boys - we went the opposite way to the ruins for Caine's sake.

By the morning the water tank was completely empty and we were left with just over ten litres of water. The sun was just peeping up over the mountains on the far side of the lake, the temperature was rising quickly and we sat outside on the grass enjoying a nice cup of coffee and some very crunchy toast. The bread we'd bought in Palau wasn't exactly fresh any more but nevertheless it was delicious and we still had one huge loaf left.

I filled our solar shower water can up with ice cold water from the lake and put it up against Billy's wheel in the sun. In a couple of hours we had nice warm showers and then afterwards we lay on the warm ground soaking up the rays and let the sun dry us.

Before we left I wandered off into the trees, dug a hole and emptied and cleaned the toilet, then we packed everything away again and set off back along the long bumpy track.

Eventually and without further mishap, we got back to the first place we'd stopped at when we reached the lake and drove around for a bit looking for a place to park.

There were still quite a few camping cars scattered about, two were French, two were Belgians and one German, as well as a few tents and day trippers. Far too many people for our liking but we found a nice spot set back a bit by some bushes under the trees, well away from anyone else - it would do for the night.

It looked like someone had just vacated the spot judging by the tyre tracks and the large wet patch on the ground where their sink had emptied out - at least that's what we hoped it was.

We stayed by Billy most of the time, relaxing in the sunshine, writing letters and diaries, snoozing in the shade and people watching.

Caine got fed up of waiting for us to take him down to the water, so every now and again he would wander down on his own and lie in the cold water to cool off, much to the delight of all the children who were splashing about in the shallows.

When he'd cooled off enough he'd come back without shaking himself and lie in the shade still dripping wet. Nelson kept his distance from him and just sat quietly in the shade, people and dog watching.

Sometime during the night we were woken by some grunting noises and a rustling in the bushes right next to Billy, there was a dull thump and Billy rocked a bit, more grunting and rustling.

'Can you hear that noise,' I asked groggily.

'Yes I can, sounds like someone having sex,' came the whispered response through he gloom.

'Do they have to do it up against Billy?'

Then the smell hit us, wafted in through the open slatted windows on the warm night air.

'You have got to be kidding me,' I hissed, 'someone's having a shit right next to Billy.'

I got out of bed and holding my breath, peered out through the slatted windows. I could just make out the shadow of someone squatting down right by Billy. I closed the windows and me and Caine went outside to investigate. Nelson wanted to come too but he opted, as he always did, to stay with Suzi and protect her.

We got there just in time to see a fat naked man emerge from the bushes carrying a loo roll and walking slowly away from Billy towards one of the camping cars. He hadn't noticed me at all and he didn't even appear to hear Caine who was growling at him constantly. We followed him to see which van he went into and then returned to Billy.

'Who was it?' asked Suzi.

'The guy from that Belgian van over there,' I said nodding in their direction, 'the blue one.'

There was a pattern beginning to emerge here I thought.

'Belgians again, is that what they do then, use other people's space as their toilets?'

'It's beginning to look like it isn't it,' I said, 'well they can bloody well have it back,' I said as I reached for the toilet spade.

'Ugh no don't touch it!'

'Oh don't worry, I won't.'

I went back out into the night and following my nose, fought my way into the bushes and eureka, I found it. I scooped it all up together with a good amount of soil so it didn't touch the spade and carefully carried it over to the blue van.

There was a small caravan step with a rubber mat on top by their door so I carefully slid the precious cargo off the spade, leaving it sitting on the step, still complete with toilet paper. To round things off nicely Caine cocked his leg on it before we left and then we went down to the water to wash the shovel - the water was cold but not as cold as over the other side for some reason.

We were awake at first light, long before any one else and strolled down to the water for our morning washes. Well that cold water certainly woke me up I can tell you but I still managed to have an all over wash - meanwhile Suzi and Nelson bravely got their ankles wet.

'I'll have mine later when our water's warmed up,' she said wisely.

The sun was just creeping up the beach towards us as we were having our breakfast by Billy. The bread was really stale now and the crust didn't give in without a fight but it was fine toasted. We would probably have to leave today sometime as we needed food and had less than five litres of water left.

I also had to find something to mend the water tank with.

'Hey here we go, this should be interesting,' I said as I saw the door of the blue van opening.

'Oh my god I'd forgotten about that,' said Suzi giggling through a mouthful of toast.

A woman was just about to step out until she saw what was on her step - she stared at it for a few seconds and then disappeared back inside. There was a raised voice and then the man stuck his head out and looked down at it clearly puzzled, then he looked over at us.

All four of us were watching him intently and we both gave him a big wave and a smile.

He was being scolded from within by his wife who slapped him around the head a couple of times before propelling him out of the door.

He took avoiding action, missed the step and fell forward, landing heavily on the ground. He got no sympathy from her indoors at all, just a torrent of Belgian abuse and venomously spat instructions to clean his mess up - well that's what we reckoned she was saying anyway.

We were both in hysterics watching this pantomime unfolding.

'Hah, that'll teach him,' I managed, trying not to choke on my toast.

'She thinks he did it there last night, he must have been really pissed,' laughed Suzi.

'It proves the old adage doesn't it,' I mused, 'never shit on your own doorstep!'

We roared with laughter and they both looked over to see what we were laughing at, poor bloke – he looked really confused.

I must say it was very satisfying to watch him clean up as his wife hurled more abuse at him from the doorway, tossing several empty bottles outside at the same time.

'And you can take your empty bottles over to the bin while you're at it as well, then go and have a wash you disgusting creature, you stink!' she shouted in Belgian as she threw a bar of soap and a towel at him.

You didn't have to speak Belgian to understand that!!

All the time he was cleaning his mess up he kept looking over at Billy with a confused look on his face trying to figure out what the hell was going on. His wife just stood in the doorway the whole time with her arms folded glaring at him.

A little later on I penned this piece of poetical brilliance....

A big fat man from a big blue van had far too much to drink,
He came in to our garden and created quite a stink.
He staggered off and left us with a heap of steaming waste,
I gathered up the evidence and took it back post haste.
Oh what joy when in the morning he did open up the door,
His wife kicked him up the arse and he landed on the floor.

We packed up shortly after and headed back to Santa Margarida and the free moorings. Along the way we picked and stashed a couple of huge sunflower heads from a field and put them on Billy's dashboard to dry out in the sun.

We also stopped at Palau again to stock up with water and food and I bought another ten litre jerry can from Senora Twankey's shop whilst we were there so we could last a bit longer between water trips.

When we got 'home' to the free moorings we parked in the same spot by the slipway and that all important rusty pole and set up camp once more.

It felt good to be back.

A lovely Spanish family with two teenage girls arrived every day with a couple of jet skis and hired them out to holidaymakers. The girls had hours of fun flying around on them when they weren't being hired out. When they were they took to a very tatty, multi patched but still leaking inflatable dingy and countless times each day, dad would have to drag it up the slip and pump it up again. Several of the patches were peeling off so it was no wonder it didn't hold any air.

Most days poor old dad would toil away trying to mend the punctures, cursing the whole time whilst his daughters hung around, impatient to get back on the water.

Another patch finished and he would stomp off huffing and puffing while the girls shoved it out, jumped in and paddled off.

Then one day they paddled the once again half sunken dinghy round to the slip and dad reluctantly came over and emptied it, cursing away as usual whilst the girls giggled away at him. He dragged it halfway up the slip and stood staring down at it muttering obscenities which only made the girls giggle even more. Then he shouted at it, gave it a really good kick and stormed off.

The girls cheered and ran after him, then they all got into their car and drove off, returning about half an hour later.

A brand new dinghy was brought out and duly pumped up, the girls were hopping about in excitement, come on dad hurry up will you!

The dinghy was launched and the girls hopped aboard shrieking with delight, then they disappeared out of sight around the boats somewhere - we could still hear them though.

Dad then dragged the old sorry looking, half inflated dinghy up the slip by its rope and as he was dragging it past Billy he stopped and held out the rope to us. He pointed to the dinghy and then gestured for me to take the rope; he had clearly had quite enough of it and was offering it to me.

I was of course delighted and he was more than happy to off load it and hurled some final insults at it before leaving.

I dragged it under our awning so I could work on it without getting fried, and I was just looking over it to see what needed doing when Mark stopped by. He lent me some glue and some rubber off another old dinghy he'd once had and he also gave me some other stuff to try mending Billy's water tank with, which I planned to have a go at after the dinghy.

'Tim, shouldn't you be mending the water tank first instead of playing around with that old thing,' said Suzi, 'I mean come on, which is more important?'

'You're absolutely right as usual my sweet, I must get my priorities right mustn't I.' I said and I immediately set about mending the dinghy.

Using Pierre's inside and outside patching technique I did the most obvious hole first, then I pumped it up a bit using the foot pump I'd found on the tip and took it down the slip and submerged it – aha - bubbles!

I marked the spot where the bubbles were coming from with the chalk which Mark had also lent me and dragged the dinghy back to Billy.

Once that one was mended I half pumped it up again and took it back down to the water. No bubbles from that one anymore but then I found another leak near the front.

I repeated this procedure five times altogether and eventually sometime later that afternoon there were no more bubbles to be seen anywhere. One was a bit trickier to do than the rest as it was by the fitting that the painter was fastened to.

'What's a painter?' enquired a puzzled Suzi.

'This is the painter,' I said holding up the rope on the front of the dinghy.

'That piece of rope is called a painter,' she said frowning, 'why?'

'No idea.'

'How ridiculous, what a stupid name for a piece of rope, you can't paint anything with it can you.'

'Well I'm sorry but that's what it's called.'

'Pffft! well I'm not calling it a painter, it's just a piece of manky old rope.'

She was right of course, it *was* just a piece of manky old rope and I was tittering away to myself as I finally pumped it up properly and then launched it. Caine leapt in straightaway and I held my breath waiting for a hissing noise as he pierced the rubber but thankfully there was none.

Then, using my hands as paddles I made my way slowly around the boats with Caine standing up in the front keeping a watchful eye on Suzi. She and Nelson were making their way over to Lady Jane as Mark had invited us over for a cuppa. He was also teaching me the basics of navigation, something which I hoped would come in handy some time later.

I tied the dinghy up to Lady Jane using the painter, oh sorry, I mean piece of manky old rope, and then climbed on board.

Caine looked up bewildered.

'Hey how the hell am I supposed to get up there guys?'

'Just be a good boy and stay there for a while, can you do that d'you think?' I said as we all settled down in the cockpit, knowing full well what the answer would be.

Well the answer came in a series of howls and excited barks quickly followed by a huge splash as he attempted and failed to leap up onto the boat. As he pushed off, the dinghy shot back and he just dropped into the water coming up coughing and spluttering. He attempted to climb up the side of the boat, failed again and then swam off looking for somewhere to climb out.

A couple of minutes later he came charging down the pontoon and leapt straight onto the boat with water pouring off him, he hadn't even stopped to shake. He greeted everyone happily and then he did shake, drenching us all in the process. When the temperature is around 35c. it's really not that bad when a dog does that, it's actually quite refreshing and dries in no time.

The next morning we all piled into our 'new' dinghy and we hand paddled our way across the channel to the beach on the other side. I tied the dinghy to a rock and we spent the morning there sunbathing, swimming and people watching.

Two German guys came along and laid their towels and things out on the sand near us. We could tell they were German by their towels -they were both in the colours of the German flag!

One of them stripped off completely, it wasn't a naturist beach but he wasn't bothered and neither was anyone else. He then applied sun cream - using the tips of his fingers only - to his entire body, it took ages and we were intrigued.

His friend, who wasn't naked, put cream on his back for him as he carefully and very particularly wiped his hands clean on a towel and then stood and slowly turned himself around. He did this for at least an hour, rotating slowly the whole time. Eventually he got down onto his hands and knees with his legs wide apart and did the same rotating trick in that position - he got some funny looks.

He was obviously after the ultimate all over tan, and he was certainly succeeding.

There wasn't a white patch to be seen anywhere and as Suzi so delicately pointed out, he even had a nice even tan on the underside of his scrotum.

☺ ☺ ☺ ☺ ☺

We went across the channel to the beach in the dinghy every day after that - it was cooler being by the sea.

So far my patch work was holding up well and I hadn't had to pump it up once. I'd also mended Billy's water tank with that fiberglass stuff Mark had lent me and so far that was holding well too. Not sure about the long term though, only time would tell.

Nice though it was, we became a bit bored with the daily routine of being there so we thought we'd head south for a bit to see somewhere different, and also to find out if it was actually any hotter. Everything was carefully packed away, all except for the dinghy which I paddled round to Lady Jane and tied it alongside. After a visit to Palau for water, bread and other foodstuffs we set off down the coastal route.

We stopped at several places along the way like L'Escala, Estartit, Palamos and Lloret de Mar but they were all hideously overcrowded and built up. Needless to say we didn't stop anywhere for very long, we couldn't anyway, there was no room. It was just impossible to find anywhere quiet to park and for Caine to have somewhere to swim and cool off, it was hotter here already and we hadn't travelled that far yet really.

We were disheartened, we couldn't go any further South, it was too just hot for the boys. Instead we turned away from the coast and the crowds and found ourselves heading into the tree lined hills - maybe we'd find a nice lake or river to camp next to.

We were really tired, it had been a very long day driving through all those crowded places and we desperately needed somewhere quiet to park for the night. The sun was going down as we came across a pull-in on some rough ground with a track which led us through the trees - it looked promising. The track ended at a small clearing in the woods, there was no one around and I parked Billy near some bushes, perfect.

We sat out on the grass by Billy and relaxed, enjoying a very welcome cup of tea and the peace and quiet. There wasn't a sound to be heard, not even any bird song which suddenly struck us as a little odd considering we were deep in the woods.

'Something's not right about this place,' said Suzi looking all around, 'it doesn't feel right.'

I was getting the same feeling.

The boys were having their dinners when suddenly they both stopped eating and froze, listening intently to something we hadn't heard.

Nelson the protector as he was known, being the bravest, left his food and walked off, staring into the woods and growling continuously with his hackles raised. Caine had other priorities - he finished his food first and then joined him.

I decided to check it out, they wouldn't behave like this for no reason, there must be someone nearby. The light was fading fast now and I took my yobbo clobberer with me just in case.

It was a piece of driftwood I'd found on the beach in France, it resembled a baseball bat but with a slight curve and a v shape at the top. I always kept it handy as a weapon just in case, but luckily so far I hadn't needed it.

'Be careful Tim, I've got a bad feeling about this place.'

'I'm not going far,' I replied.

I kept Suzi in sight and stood by the boys peering into the trees, looking all around but I couldn't see anyone or anything so I went back.

'Did you see anything?'

'No, nothing,' I said.

'Well the boys aren't happy here, something's not right, we should really go.'

I knew she was right, she always was but we were knackered and really needed to rest here for the night.

'It's probably just an animal don't worry,' I said unconvinced, 'I'll go and have another look,'

'I'm coming with you, I'm not staying here on my own,'

This time we went further into the trees, Nelson went on ahead as Caine squoze in between us, more for protection rather than to protect.

We came across a large flat rock about three feet tall in a small clearing. There were what looked to me like blood stains all over the top of it and all around the base completely encircling it were the remnants of a fire - it looked like an altar of some sort.

I suddenly shivered and went all cold, we looked at each other and we both felt the same.

There was a strong sense of foreboding about the place and it felt like we were being watched but we could still see no one. I had a flashback to a Peter Fonda film we'd seen called 'Race with the devil' which really didn't help the churning feeling in my stomach.

I decided not to mention it.

Nelson still had his hackles up - I expected him to cock his leg up against the rock but he wouldn't go near it. Caine was still firmly squashed in between us, hmm maybe it is time to go.

As we were turning to leave there was a rustling in the bushes and a mangy black dog appeared. It slowly skulked its way across the clearing snarling, teeth bared, eyeing us all warily and then it lay down by the altar.

Another dog appeared and did the same, then another until all three were lying by the altar guarding it. Normally the boys would run straight up to any new dogs to say hello but not this time, they just froze.

Ok, definitely time to go now and we all hurried back to Billy, only now with Caine bravely leading the way with Nelson!

I thought I caught the shadow of someone through the gloom but couldn't be sure.

It was almost dark when we got back, we'd left all the doors open and things outside but as far as we could tell everything seemed to be ok. There was a car parked in the trees not far from Billy which we didn't like the look of but it was too dark to see if there was anyone in it. We hadn't heard it arrive and it definitely wasn't there when we got here - how was that possible?

We hurriedly chucked everything back into Billy hoping we weren't leaving anything behind as we had no torch - why the hell didn't we have a torch? – and then we all piled in and scarpered.

It would have been so easy to lose our way trying to drive out of there in the dark and in a hurry but luckily we found the road straight away, no traffic coming, good let's go.

Almost immediately there were headlights behind us, where did they come from, was it that car that was in the trees? they were very close behind us now.

We were tired, it was dark, we were lost in the hills and now we were being followed by devil worshippers.

The atmosphere was very tense in Billy as we drove through the night, going god knows where and with those lights right behind us. I wasn't going fast and there was no traffic, they could easily have overtaken us if they'd wanted but they chose to stay behind us.

We'd been driving for a good half hour when suddenly the lights vanished as suddenly as they'd appeared - very strange considering there were no turnings or lay by's around. I kept on going though, I mean I wasn't being paranoid or anything but they could still have been following us, just driving without their lights on!

Eventually we came to a very small village, there was only one streetlight and as we passed under it I could see that there was no-one behind us.

We both relaxed a bit but I got strict instructions to keep going - I was more than happy to oblige.

After a time we passed through another small village and I was relieved to still see no-one behind us. As we were leaving the village we came across a lay-by with a lorry and a camper parked up for the night, this would have to do.

I pulled in, we were knackered before and in need of sleep but now we were wide awake so there was no point going to bed just yet. We needed to gather our wits and relax a bit first. It was almost 3am and we had absolutely no idea where we were so I put the kettle on and made tea (as you do) then we all went outside for a stroll along the grassy verge.

It was all very quiet, but a normal quiet this time, very dark and no traffic which we were pleased about. I had a tin mug of tea in one hand and my yobbo clobberer in the other.

We went to bed then but neither of us slept and after about half an hour it started to get light so we got up again. We wanted to be away from here - somewhere far away from here.

Over brekky we groggily discussed our options.

Which way now?

Well we're not staying in this area that's for sure.

Agreed.

Going further south is out of the question, it's too hot for the boys.

Agreed.

We could always go back to Santa Margarida, ok maybe it's a bit boring and not that pretty but at least it's safe. We also know people there, and there's water for Caine to cool off in.

'Safe' sounded good to us and the motion was carried unanimously.

We had no idea where we were so we just continued along the same road until we came to a town which was actually in our atlas. Turns out we were somewhere in the hills inland from Tossa de Mar.

We headed north, stopping on the way to pick and stash some kiwis, grapes and baby sweetcorn.

It felt good to be back in Santa Margarida again and to drive through it's now familiar abandoned streets, we knew our way around here now.

When we arrived back at the free moorings it was still early and most people were in bed. Everything was as we'd left it and happily there was no-one in 'our spot' by the rusty old pole - it was nice to be back.

Up with the roof - down with the bed - sleep.

ꝶ ꝶ ꝶ ꝶ ꝶ

We were woken shortly after by a rustling noise at the slatted windows, this was followed by a slight thud as something landed on the sink. We both looked up and there was a polythene bag sitting there with something inside it. We looked at each other puzzled, then I looked out of the window to see Mark walking across the dusty car park on his way back to Lady Jane carrying a bag of shopping.

Caine was watching him lazily from the driver's seat, Nelson was probably doing the same only he was outside somewhere, neither of them barked at him - they knew him well enough now. I looked in the bag.

'Two croissants,' I said, 'he's just stuffed two croissants through the window for us, ooh and they're still warm as well.'

'Wow that's kind of him isn't it, looks like it's time for breakfast then,' said Suzi yawning.

'Or we could go just back to sleep and have them later,' I said hopefully, flopping back down on the unmade bed.

'No let's have them now while they're still warm and fresh, it'll be a nice treat for us,' she said digging me in the ribs, 'come on Polly, put the kettle on you know I can't go back to sleep once I'm awake,'

The thought of fresh croissants was enough to get even me out of bed, despite the fact I hadn't had nearly enough sleep.

Another sweltering day was idly spent sheltering from the heat of the sun beneath our awning, drinking endless cups of tea and swigging warm water. We'd found another sun chair on our second visit to the tip, and also a small folding table so together with the chair I'd found in the skip and had since mended, we now had a full compliment of patio furniture.

We were sitting there quietly dozing in the mid-day heat, minding our own business when there was the sound of a large vehicle really close to Billy, Suzi turned to me and said.

'Sounds like someone's parking up next to us, surely not, they've got the whole car park to choose from.'

'Oh no it's not more Belgians is it?' I groaned.

We looked at each other in dismay and then we both laughed but neither of us got up to look. We heard voices followed by a heavy thump and then the vehicle drove off – phew!

'Well?' asked Suzi.

'Well what,' I replied.

'Aren't you going to have a look and see what it was?'

'No you go and look, I'm busy.'

'Yeah busy doing nothing, go on you look, you're nearest,' she said smiling.

'No I'm not, you are,' I said as I gulped some more warm water from the bottle.

'Go on you're supposed to be the man around here, anyway I'm too hot to move,' she lied.

Curiosity got the better of me in the end and I got up to see what had occurred but I somehow very clumsily managed to spill half a bottle of water over her head as I got up.

'Whoops sorry my darling, how very clumsy of me,' I laughed as I made my escape.

'Ugh you tossing tosswanker!' she shouted after me.

'Language Susan!' I shouted back.

I went round the other side of Billy and stared in disbelief at my discovery.

'Oh you have got to come and see this,' I said.

Still dripping with water Suzi appeared and we both stared.

There was a huge block of ice about four foot tall just sitting there right next to Billy. I fell to my knees in the dust, wrapped my arms around it and hugged it.

'What's that doing there?'

'Who cares, I love it, it's mine,' I said as I rubbed my face all over it.

'Are you enjoying that Tim?' laughed Mark who was passing by on his way to the shop.

'I think I'm losing him Mark,' laughed Suzi, 'do you know anything about this?'

'No, maybe it's for one of the yachts.'

'Well let's make the most of it while it's here then,' I said getting to my feet.

I went into Billy and got a carton of fruit juice and the water bottle and placed them on top of the ice block. Then I covered it all with a towel, it was in the shade at the moment but soon the sun would move round and it would start to melt.

After half an hour or so we both went to have a drink of water from our new fridge, it was really cold and so refreshing - what a treat in the middle of a baking hot day.

To our surprise we also discovered two bottles of San Miguel beer under the towel.

'Where did these come from?' I said a little puzzled, 'I didn't put them here.'

'Oh I know, I bet Mark put them here on his way back from the shop, isn't he kind.'

We retreated beneath our awning once again and drank the ice cold beers with big happy smiles on our faces. That was three treats we'd had now, big day for us!

The ice block was in full sun now but it was hardly melting at all, even so I got some more towels and covered it completely. A bit later on there was a knock on the side of Billy and Malcolm popped his head round.

'I say sorry to disturb, just got back, thanks awfully for looking after our ice for us.'

Oh well, it was nice while it lasted I suppose.

With heavy hearts we emptied our 'fridge' and both of us had a good drink of ice cold water while we could. It would be a very long time before we had another.

Mark had made his way over and we both offered to carry the ice over to Malcolm's boat. We laid the ice block down carefully on the bed sheet that Malcolm had brought over and then, grabbing two corners of the sheet each we lifted.

Unfortunately it was an old sheet and suddenly there was a ripping sound followed by a dull thud as the ice block landed in the dust - and on my foot.

'Oh bugger,' said Malcolm.

'Oh crap,' said Mark.

'Ouch!' said I.

Suzi and Sandy were trying (not very hard) to suppress their giggles whilst I nursed my foot after I'd pulled it out from underneath the ice block.

Malcolm then limped off to his boat without another word and came back with one of his sails. 'This'll be bloody well strong enough that's for sure,' he declared triumphantly.

We laid the sail down in the dust and rolled the ice block onto it. They're not easy things to handle you know - they're all wet and slippery.

This time we made it all the way along the quay and down the pontoon to Malcolm's boat, without further incident or injury.

Just before we went aboard, Malcolm dipped a bucket in the water and sluiced it down to get rid of the dust. Think I'd rather have taken my chances with the dust rather than with what might be floating around in *that* water!

It was quite heavy and a bit cumbersome to get on board and down the steps into the cabin but we managed it without any major mishaps.

Sandy had emptied out their fridge locker in readiness and we carefully lowered the new block into the bottom of it, I was so hot and sweaty by this time I almost jumped in after it!

I said farewell and gave it one last stroke before leaving.

The next morning as we were walking over to Lady Jane for a cuppa we noticed Malcolm's boat wasn't there. Mark said they'd left sometime during the night, presumably on the next leg of their voyage down to Alicante.

We never saw them again.

It was yet another relentlessly hot, dry, dusty day and we were sitting under our array of very dusty and now very faded shade makers, writing letters to friends and family. Well Suzi was anyway, I was trying to but without much success, communication being one of my many failings - apparently.

I sat there for ages, struggling to start even one letter home but there were simply too many distractions.

By distractions of course I mean all the beautifully tanned and practically naked women who were strutting about and posing shamelessly as they sailed past on board their swanky yachts.

Family would just have to wait I'm afraid and instead I wrote this -

The weather here is very hot,
Further south go, we can not.
We'll have to wait here for the summer,
Very boring, what a bummer.

The place just here is full of whistles,
Caine is lying in the thistles.
Noisy people, wankers, jerks,
Setting off loud fireworks.

The sun is very very hot,
Another poser on a yacht.
That woman in the big red hat,
She's sitting where somebody shat.

The countryside is full of litter,
Making us feel very bitter.
Plastic bags, bottles, shit,
There'll soon be nowhere left to sit.

In Rosas with itchy feet,
Writing this in mended seat.
Parasol above my head,
Siesta time, let's go to bed!

The next morning we got some food together and made our way round to Lady Jane in the dinghy as Mark had invited us all on a day out and a trip up the coast - we were very excited.

When we got there he had the cover off the engine compartment under the cockpit floor and was making sure everything was ok after not being run for several weeks. We tied our dinghy to the pontoon in the dual hope that it would still be there when we got back, and also we hoped it might deter someone else from taking over Lady Jane's berth while we were gone.

Pretty soon the big Perkins diesel engine roared smokily into life, shattering the early morning silence.

I stood at the pointy end waiting for Mark's instruction to untie the mooring rope - Suzi was at the blunt end doing the same thing.

We cast off and Lady Jane moved gracefully away from the pontoon with Mark's inflatable dinghy following along behind, ours looked tiny left there all by itself.

I stood in the bows as we made our way slowly down the channel, (hah, my turn to pose now - ok Lady Jane was hardly a floating gin palace but who cares, it felt good) and out into the open sea, past Rosas, heading north.

The sea was a deep strong blue beneath a cloudless sky as Lady Jane cut her way effortlessly through the water. I sat up on the cabin roof lost in my own little world, enjoying the cool salty breeze on my face. Apart from the steady hum of the engine the only sound to be heard was the water breaking against the bows.

We passed several yachts sailing silently along with their sails full of the warm early morning breeze and I was envious - I wanted to do that - we *would* do that. We planned one day to buy a yacht and sail around the world which is why I was enjoying learning navigation.

We motored steadily for a couple of hours, Mark was following a chart of the coastline (a proper chart not a road atlas like Pierre used!) and he showed me where we were going, he even let me steer Lady Jane for a while.

He took over the controls again as we pulled into a delightful rocky cove with a small sandy beach and I went up front in readiness to lower the anchor. There were a few yachts and cruisers anchored around the bay but still plenty of room for us without getting too close to anyone.

I lowered the anchor gently when Mark gave me the nod, he'd given me instructions on how to do it properly and I hoped I wouldn't cock it up. The water was about twenty feet deep and I could clearly see the small puff of sand as the anchor hit the bottom and started to dig itself in.

Mark shut the engine off and Lady Jane dropped back and took up the slack in the rope - we were anchored.

It was an idyllic setting and we were in heaven, complete solitude and silence and what a wonderful way to travel and to see beautiful places like this.

We went ashore in the dinghy, the beach was deserted and we sunbathed, swam and snorkeled the morning away before having lunch, then we all piled into the dinghy again and went back to Lady Jane. I climbed up onto the cabin roof and then dived off, trying to reach the bottom where it was nice and cool. I made it, even managing to sit on the bottom for a while before kicking off again in search of oxygen.

I grabbed hold of the anchor rope then and pulled myself down hand over hand until I reached the anchor itself, it had dug itself so deeply into the sand I could hardly see any of it - Lady Jane wasn't going anywhere.

Whilst Mark was having a siesta down below we went up front to the small piece of deck in front of the cabin to do some sunbathing.

Because of Lady Jane's eccentric home built design it was a bit tricky to get there as there was only a very narrow walkway along the side of the boat and no side rail at all. It was only just wide enough for one foot at a time and the cabin roof didn't have anything helpful like a grab rail on it to hold on to so it was quite a balancing act.

Nelson was never very happy if Suzi went out of sight even for a short time and he felt compelled to follow her even if it *was* against his better judgement, as this time it most certainly was. He hated getting wet and did not like the look of all that water directly below him one little bit.

Back home in Wales if it was raining, and believe me it rains a lot in Wales, he would simply refuse to go outside, even to go to the toilet. He would hold it all in for literally days on end, we'd open the door for him and he'd get as far as the threshold, take one disgusted look at the weather and then turn around again.

So very reluctantly, being driven by loyalty, devotion and the compelling need to protect his Suzi at all costs, he very carefully began to make his way along the narrow walkway.

He was doing ok and it looked like he was going to make it until suddenly and unfortunately for him - Caine saw what he was doing.

He leapt up and charged after him not being in the least bit careful and he of course had to get to us first. Well there simply wasn't enough room for both of them on there and he just barged his way past Nelson who just disappeared over the side with a resounding *sperloosh!*

A few seconds later he surfaced again, coughing and spluttering, he was absolutely mortified and with us laughing at him as well, oh the indignity of it all.

Still in a bit of a panic he tried without success to scrabble his way up the side of the boat. He quickly gave up on that idea and as he slowly regained some composure he swam round to the dinghy and tried - unsuccessfully again - to clamber on board there.

He managed to get his front feet over the wooden transom at the back and then just looked up, pleading with someone to get him out. I dived in and swam over to him, gave him a shove up the arse and he plopped into the dinghy with a soggy splat.

He gave himself a good old shake and immediately started cleaning himself. Trouble was now there was water sloshing around in the bottom of the dinghy which he couldn't avoid so he climbed up onto the rounded side of the dinghy and sat there precariously, looking all spikey and feeling very sorry for himself.

Mark, woken from his slumber by all the noise pulled the dinghy tight up against Lady Jane and I lifted a soggy Nelson safely back on board.

Sadly and all too soon it was time to go, Mark fired up the engine once more and then motored forward slowly whilst I pulled the anchor up and stowed it on deck.

We both sat in the bows on the way back down the coast, reveling in the magical light of the late afternoon sun - Nelson stayed in the cockpit!

It had been a memorable day out and one that we would remember fondly for many years to come.

We motored back up the channel to the free moorings, anxious now to see if our dinghy had been pinched or not. As we approached the pontoon we breathed a collective sigh of relief to see it still tied there and no other boat in Lady Jane's berth.

It was the perfect end to a perfect day.

One day somewhere around the end of August the weather suddenly changed, it went distinctively cooler with a sunless grey sky.

Also we suddenly became aware of a lack of noise and looking around, we noticed a lot of the yachts had left, leaving empty spaces everywhere. There were no cars in the car park either, the Spanish family with the jet skis didn't turn up and there was an eerie silence about the place, it was weird.

The place had turned into a ghost town overnight.

'This is weird,' said Suzi looking around all puzzled, 'where is everybody?'

'Don't know, strange isn't it.'

We went over to Lady Jane to find Mark busy fettling the engine so I went down below, put the kettle on and made us all a cup of tea.

'Well that's it,' he said, 'the seasons over now, finished. I'll be leaving tomorrow, heading back up through the French canals and back to good old Blighty. You'll be off down to Alicante for the winter now then will you?'

'That's the plan,' I said, 'Benidorm or Alicante, we just weren't expecting to be going so soon that's all.'

'Best to go now though, this place is like a ghost town out of season and once it rains this car park just turns to sludgy sticky mud, it's horrible and you won't be able to park here.'

'Time to up sticks then,' said Suzi later on as we walked back to Billy.

'Looks like it,'

There was a cool wind blowing as I took down the now redundant, faded and torn shade makers for the last time and threw them in the bin along with the parasol.

I let the dinghy down and folded it up, but try as I might there simply wasn't enough room in Billy for it and sadly I had to admit defeat. It was with a heavy heart that I tied it to the rusty pole in the hope that someone nice would come along after we'd gone and give it a loving home.

We spent one last night there planning to set off the next morning. It was the first time for a long time that we hadn't gone to sleep with 'Y Viva Espana' ringing in our ears - we were almost missing it!

We said our goodbyes to Mark the next morning, arranging to meet up the following year on the French canals. From there we drove up to Palau to fill up with spring water and to stock up with enough food to last the next few days.

Knowing from our previous little excursion that we weren't going to like a lot of the places along the way, we drove all the way down the Mediterranean coast that day, stopping only for short breaks here and there.

We were disgusted with Benidorm, it was so built up and hideously overcrowded with holidaying brits sporting union jack hats.

There were English newspapers on sale everywhere, all day English breakfasts, bloody union jack flags flapping all over the place, blotchy red and white people in their union jack shorts, British pubs selling British beer, English voices everywhere, British vehicles all over the place - it was our worst nightmare.

We drove in fascinated horror through all this crassness and down towards the beach, thinking maybe we could park somewhere along the seafront away from it all. Huh, no chance, the long sweeping beach was crowded, the pavements were crowded and even the road itself was crowded. There were people crossing continuously, presumably going back and forth from the beach to stuff in yet another all day English breakfast. They'd probably swill that filth down with a pint of bloody Watney's red Barrel or something equally disgusting, then waddle back down to the beach carrying trays full of beer with the Daily Star tucked under their arms to get some more sun on their already blistered and peeling lardy white flesh.

We didn't even stop, not that we could have parked anywhere even if we'd wanted to - we drove right to the end of the seafront and just kept on going.

We couldn't get away fast enough.

Alicante was no better and we hated it straightaway, we couldn't contemplate staying there for even a week let alone an entire winter.

We didn't want to stop there but we'd had enough for one day and it was getting dark. We'd travelled over 600 kilometers since leaving Santa Margarida that morning, we were tired and at a bit of a loss.

We drove around in despair eventually finding a small space tucked away between a shed and some trampolines right at the end of the seafront. It was away from all the lights and the crowds and fairly quiet, we reckoned we'd be all right for the night and then get the hell out tomorrow - to where we had no idea but staying here wasn't an option. It was very disheartening to be feeling like this about the place especially after waiting so long to get here, so many people we'd met along the way were headed here for the winter, it was the place to be - apparently.

Well it wasn't the place we wanted to be that's for sure!

Over breakfast the next morning we were discussing our options and studying the atlas, looking for somewhere close but quiet where we might park up for the winter. We had the atlas open on the table and as Suzi poured some coffee she spilt a drop on the opposite page which she quickly mopped away with her hand.

We both looked down at the atlas and our eyes were drawn to the coffee stain, we looked closer and then together we both said.

'Portugal,'

We looked at each other, this was something we hadn't thought of.

'Hmmm, Portugal,' I said thoughtfully.

'Portugal, ooh yes I like the sound of that,' said Suzi excitedly, perking up again, 'well you can't argue with a coffee stain can you, it's a sign.'

We both laughed, already feeling much better and it was decided - we would go to Portugal.

'Hmm, right then,' I said, 'If we took this road here it would take us to Granada and then on to Seville, after that it's Portugal. It's quite a long way but It looks like a nice route, it would take us across the Sierra Nevada.'

'Ooh goody, I've always wanted to see the Sierra Nevada.' said Suzi brightly, perking up even more.

'Ok then, decision made - look out Portugal here we come.' I said putting the atlas away and sharing out the last dregs of coffee. We ventured into the town only as far as the first shop and bought enough supplies to last us for the next few days.

I saw a tap by a wall on the seafront on the way back so before we left I topped up Billy's tank which happily still wasn't leaking.

Good job Tim!

רו רו רו רו רו

We'd been warned by quite a few travellers about taking that particular route across the Sierra Nevada. There were horror stories of people in campers getting stopped by bandits and being robbed at knifepoint.

Don't stop anywhere along the way they all said, and whatever you do don't park up for the night. When you're sleeping they pump gas in through the air vents or they climb onto the roof and put it through the skylight. The gas renders you motionless, unable to move a muscle but it doesn't knock you out so you're fully conscious and aware of what's going on but you just can't move. They then break in and at their leisure, rob you of everything valuable and then usually rape the woman.

Were these stories true and would they stop us taking the Sierra Nevada route?

Well this was something we'd been looking forward to doing for a long time now so of course it didn't stop us. We just stared fate straight in the eye as usual and set off. I had my yobbo clobberer on the dashboard in front of me though just in case. I wasn't going to go down without a fight and neither would the boys come to that - we felt quite safe.

We passed through Murcia and then Lorca before heading inland towards Granada. The road climbed steadily with the countryside becoming more and more rugged and less populated the further inland we went. At the side of the road and in the middle of nowhere in particular we passed a home made and hand painted sign saying 'Beware of Bandits'.

We just looked at each other and laughed, was that for real or was somebody having a laugh.

Anyway we kept on going, the scenery was breathtaking and we were not going to miss this for anything. It looked just like cowboy country and apparently a lot of westerns had been filmed in this area. I half expected to see a posse charging towards us on horseback, racing down the hillside and across the plain through the trees with guns blazing, leaving a trail of dust hanging in the air.

We were so in awe at the beauty of our surroundings that of course, we did what we were advised several times *not* to do under *any* circumstances and stopped for a while to have a cuppa. I pulled off the road and parked under a tree for some shade.

Now that we'd stopped there was no breeze, the sun was fierce, the air heavy and still and it was hard to breathe. I took some pictures as we wandered aimlessly around the hillside marveling at the beautiful landscape. Afterwards, I made the tea and we sat and relaxed for a time beneath a shady tree.

Nobody came and attacked us so we set off again.

We were happily trundling along slowly in the sweltering heat - don't drive slowly we were warned, that would only make it easier for the bandits to stop you, no, you must go as fast as you can its much safer that way.

But how could we drive fast through scenery as beautiful as this, it had to be taken slowly and we were looking all around us with open mouths uttering 'wow' or 'oh my god look at that' every few seconds.

Anyway I couldn't go too fast, I was taking pictures out of the window as I was driving along.

We had all the windows open as well which was something else we'd been told never to do. Suzi and Nelson were sharing the passenger seat with both their heads hanging out enjoying the warm breeze and the incredible views.

Up ahead in the distance (I saw a shimmering light?) – no, through the shimmering heat haze I saw someone standing in the middle of the road and alarm bells started ringing.

'Hey look, there's someone in the road,' I said.

There was no traffic and as we got nearer the first thing I could make out was a man with a shock of unkempt blonde hair. He was dressed scruffily in a faded and baggy red t-shirt and holey cut off jeans, he had nothing on his feet and there was a tatty red holdall on the side of the road next to him.

He was waving his arms in the air, trying to get us to stop for him.

'Looks like he needs a lift,' said Suzi, 'what's he doing out here he must be roasting, we'd better pick him up.'

'What? he could be one of those bandido types,'

'Well he doesn't look much like a bandido to me, anyway what does one look like?'

'Oh I dunno, they probably dress in scruffy clothes and stand in the middle of the road flagging people down. They'll probably have a gun hidden away in their holdall as well. Not only that, their mates will be hiding behind the trees waiting to pounce if someone daft enough like us stops.

'Oh stop it will you there's no-one for miles around.' she said, not even looking around to check, 'anyway he looks ok to me.'

'How do you know, you can't see him properly yet,' I joked - he looked ok to me too actually.

I still looked all around though trying to see if there actually was anyone hiding behind the trees but I saw no-one.

He stayed in the middle of the road smiling, I slowed down but wasn't going to stop for him, I just didn't want to run him over - Nelson had his eyes on him now too. He didn't move and I had to swerve to go around him, and then just as we were passing him he got down on his knees in the road with his hands together begging us to stop.

Oh good one mate, I knew that was going to work and sure enough,

'Aww Tim look at him he's on his knees bless, we can't not stop now,' said Suzi looking at me.

'Huh! typical bandido tactic that is.' I said jokingly.

'Oh stop it, we can't just leave him here in this heat poor thing he looks done in, come on stop let's pick him up,'

I knew all along we were going to stop for him and I said 'Ok tell you what let's let Nelson decide shall we.'

By the time we'd stopped we were a good distance ahead of him and he picked up his bag and ran after us, I couldn't help looking all around again. Nelson was on full alert now and I grabbed hold of him as el bandido approached Billy, I had one hand on Nelson and the other on my yobbo clobberer.

He ran up to Suzi's window putting a hand on Billy's door in his excitement. Whoa that's pushing it a bit señor I thought, expecting a reaction from Nelson but there was none. I have to say he had a very disarming smile and he thanked us over and over again for stopping, putting his hand on Suzi's shoulder - well that should clinch it.

Normally such an outrageous action from a stranger simply wouldn't be tolerated and I fully expected Nelson to fly at him and sink his teeth into his face but there was still no reaction. No warning growls or even raised hackles - obviously he had no problems with him.

We both relaxed and not for the first time we trusted his impeccable judge of character, we both knew straight away that this guy was no bandit. I relaxed my grip as el bandido babbled on and on in Spanish - he kept mentioning Granada so we assumed that's where he wanted to go.

He was obviously very thirsty and he showed us his empty water bottle, Suzi immediately handed him one of ours which he drained in one go so she gave him another. He was so grateful and I just knew he wanted to lean in the window and hug and kiss her but he had the good sense not to push his luck with Nelson right there in his face.

He opened the side door, climbed in and of course Caine greeted him like an old friend. Nelson just turned and gave him a filthy look but stayed on the front seat with Suzi, 'Ok Caine calm down, no need to go overboard.'

From then on he babbled on and on continuously in his happy smiley way and every so often we would hear the words

Granada and Alhambra, we guessed he was urging us to visit there. After a while he went very quiet - we both looked round and our 'bandido' was fast asleep on the back seat with Caine sprawled across his lap.

He got out in the middle of nowhere just before we reached Granada and Suzi gave him another bottle of water to take with him. He mentioned Alhambra one final time and thanked us yet again, then he said his goodbyes to Caine and disappeared into the undergrowth.

We didn't stop in Granada to visit the Alhambra, nor did we stop in Seville, beautiful though it looked. Something was pushing us on towards Portugal so we just kept on going, eager to reach the west coast before the end of the day.

We hit the coast again somewhere between Huelva and Jerez, it had been a long days travelling and we were tired and in need of somewhere to park for the night. We'd done just over 700 kilometres since leaving Alicante that morning and 1400 since leaving Santa Margarida two days previously,

I turned off on to a small track which if we were lucky would lead us to a beach, if not then we'd probably end up at someone's house.

We got lucky and ended up on a lovely big beach with massive sand dunes and a huge sandy car park, this would do nicely. There were a few campers of differing nationalities parked here and a few day trippers in cars. We managed to find ourselves a quiet spot well away from the other vans right up against a low stone wall and overlooking the sea.

The waves were huge and there were quite a few surfers in the water - it looked like a surfers hot spot as nearly all the vans had surf boards either on the roof or leaning up against them.

We all got out to stretch our legs and to drink tea after the long journey and as the evening closed in all the cars slowly disappeared one by one until just the campers were left. Later on we sat on the sand watching the sun going down over the horizon before falling into bed - we were asleep in seconds.

We would have liked to stay there for a few days to relax and recharge our batteries a bit, but during the day it got really busy with day trippers. We spent a very long day hemmed in by cars and people with no space of our own, it wasn't at all relaxing. Once everyone had gone though it became very peaceful again and we had our corner of the beach all to ourselves once more.

We collected armfuls of driftwood from the beach to make a small fire, then we roasted some potatoes and drank warm beers as the sun went down.

Nice though it was, we really didn't fancy another day like that so we decided to press on early the next morning and get to Portugal.

It was late morning by the time we reached Ayamonte - the last stop before Portugal. A typically bustling Spanish town with narrow cobbled streets and whitewashed buildings. It stands on the banks of the River Guadiana which forms a natural frontier between the two countries.

We followed signs for the ferry which would take us across the river to Portugal. The traffic was crazy, there were cars and bikes going everywhere, nobody seemed to be following any rules so I ended up doing the same. At one point I needed to turn right across two lanes of traffic so I did just that and the traffic had to stop for me, it was great fun! There was some inevitable horn blowing but I don't think they were that bothered really.

Eventually we made it safely to the river where miraculously I found a parking space right by the harbour, trouble was there were no trees for shade. It was a hot day and we needed to get some shopping which meant leaving the boys in Billy for a while.

We closed all the curtains to keep the sun out and opened all the windows wide for them, we knew they would never jump out. We also knew no-one would be putting their hands in either!

We walked a short distance to the local indoor market where we bought some lovely olives and olive oil. It was a lively, noisy little town, the pavements were crowded and we found ourselves stepping into the road quite often which was a little hazardous to say the least.

The traffic was just chaotic and going much too fast for the narrow streets - there was much horn blowing going on. Small motorbikes and scooters with young girls on were buzzing around everywhere, beeping their horns and shouting across to each other as they rode along, weaving in and out of the cars seemingly in a big hurry to probably go nowhere in particular.

We got our shopping done quickly and then retreated to the relative safety and tranquility of the harbour where we were parked. We needn't have worried about the boys, it wasn't too hot in Billy at all as there was a nice cool breeze coming off the water. They weren't even panting and hadn't touched their water bowl.

We had lunch on a wooden bench next to Billy where we had a lovely view of Villa Real de Santo Antonio in Portugal on the far side of the river - the boys were underneath Billy in the shade

If we looked behind us it was utter chaos so we concentrated our attentions on the scene across the water, it looked so peaceful from here but then I suppose if we were over there Ayamonte would have looked peaceful too.

'Hey look,' said Suzi pointing to a dog going down the slip on the far side of the harbour, 'that dog over there looks just like Caine.'

I looked round at the boys, only Nelson was there.

'That's because it is Caine,' I said.

He'd toddled off on his own to go for a swim.

There were children playing on the slip and they were laughing away as Caine plonked himself down in the water.

Once he'd cooled off a bit he stood watching them, asking them to throw their ball for him which to his delight they did. He spent a good half hour over there swimming and fetching their ball and generally entertaining them before waddling back to us soaking wet, leaving a wet trail all the way down the pavement.

The ferry was going back and forth across the river about every half an hour, so after lunch we packed everything away and drove around the harbour to the terminal. We bought our ticket and Billy rattled his way onto the ferry, a few minutes later we set sail for Portugal leaving the noise of Ayamonte behind us.

It didn't take long to get to the other side and pretty soon we were rattling our way off again and on to Portuguese soil.

There was an immediate and overwhelming feeling of calm and tranquility about the place, we could feel it even as we drove off the ferry and up onto the street. We parked at the first opportunity which luckily was in the shade of a lovely big tree, perfect.

We now needed some Portuguese Escudos so we left the boys in Billy and went to look for a bank. The streets were quite busy but everyone was walking along slowly and calmly, no-one was rushing, no-one was shouting.

The traffic was also going past slowly and calmly, there was no horn blowing, wow what a difference, it was as if a blanket of tranquility had come down and wrapped itself lovingly around us.

We stood transfixed and just gaped in awe at our new surroundings.

It was weirdly and wonderfully peaceful and considering how busy it actually was, there was hardly a sound to be heard. It was a surreal experience for both of us and we instantly fell in love with the place.

I had the feeling we were going to like it here.

Up Sticks

Portugal

We went into the first bank we came across, cashed a eurocheque and with a pocketful of escudos, returned to Billy where we found a policeman waiting for us.

Unfortunately the dogs had taken quite an exception to this stranger loitering suspiciously around Billy and were kicking up a real fuss, despite the fact that we'd asked them several times not to shout at policemen. Luckily though he didn't seem bothered in the least and thankfully, when they saw us approaching they quietened down enough so we could hear what he was saying. It didn't make any difference if we could hear him or not really as we didn't have a word of Portuguese and he spoke no English so we were getting nowhere fast.

He was very calm and patient though and almost apologetic about it and eventually after a lot of hand gesturing and finger waving it clicked, we shouldn't be parked here. We were parked on the left which is the wrong side of the road as we would then be facing the oncoming traffic when we pulled out - not allowed, very sorry but you must park over there on the other side.

He was happy that we now understood him and he smiled, shook our hands and wished us a safe journey. We got back into Billy and spent the next few minutes trying to decide which way to go next. I was just putting our Spanish pesetas into the drawer along with our leftover French francs when I looked out of the window and saw our nice policeman still standing patiently next to Billy.

It looked like he was waiting for us to go so we thought we'd better get a move on.

I started Billy and was just getting ready to pull out when he stepped out into the middle of the road and stopped the traffic in both directions before guiding us out safely, clearly pleased to be of service to us.

Not wanting to upset him by trying to turn and go the other way and seeing as though we'd turned left when we drove off the ferry we decided to carry on going that way. We parted with a smile and a wave and a cheery 'Adios' from Suzi - okay it wasn't Portuguese but it would have to do for now.

We followed the river Guadiana downstream with a lovely warm breeze coming in through the open windows as Billy trundled along happily, his tyres making a very pleasing sound on the shiny cobbled road. Off to our left was the widening river estuary and on the opposite side, a row of dirty run down houses.

The road then turned away from the river and we left Vila Real de Santo Antonio behind us, the cobbles now being replaced with a poorly surfaced and uneven road.

This long straight road led us through the trees for a kilometer or so until we emerged in the seaside resort town of Monte Gordo, a nice looking town with a colourful array of shops, bars and restaurants. A wide, attractively cobbled boulevard lined with palm trees ran all along the beach front and apart from a few large hotels and apartment blocks, most of the buildings were fairly low rise.

Normally in a town the traffic would be manic with everybody rushing around everywhere, all trying to bully me into going faster and not allowing me to change lanes when I needed to. This usually ended up with us being ushered in the wrong direction, taking a wrong turning or just whizzing through somewhere without really seeing it properly.

Today things were different - I was able to drive really slowly so we could have a good look around as nobody seemed to mind. There was no impatient driver right up Billy's backside honking his horn trying to get past like we'd become accustomed to. No angry little motorbike weaving around behind us, in fact the traffic seemed quite content to just pootle along at our speed for a change.

The car behind us was black with a green roof with something on top, at first I thought it was a police car but it turned out to be a taxi and even he was happy to follow behind patiently.

We drove all along the front and ended up parking right at the far end of all the buildings on some litter strewn rough ground by the sand dunes.

Tea was duly made and we drank it sitting in Billy's side door surveying our new surroundings and feeling nice and relaxed for the first time in ages.

'So Tim, what is it with you and rubbish tips?'

'Hmm….?'

'Out of all the lovely places we've passed you had to choose here,' she said, 'why?'

'Erm…well it's nice and quiet.' I replied searching for an answer I just didn't have.

'Of course it's nice and quiet, no-one in their right mind would stop here for a picnic.'

'Well *I* stopped here.'

'Exactly!' she spluttered, spraying out a mouthful of tea.

'Mind you don't choke on your tea my darling,' I laughed.

'And it stinks as well,' she added, wrinkling her nose up in disgust, 'either that or you need a wash.'

'Well you're full of compliments today aren't you, anyway I had a wash last week.'

'Think I'd better do the driving from now on, you're obviously not to be trusted.' she said smiling.

'Not a chance matey, I'm not letting you loose with poor old Billy, you'd crash him straightaway.'

'Cheeky git,' she said throwing the remains of her tea into my lap, soaking my shorts.

'Ow that's hot!' I yelped, jumping up, pulling the shorts away from my skin.

'Serves you right for being so rude then,' she giggled, 'ha ha, it looks like you've wet yourself.'

'Oh yeah very funny, right, that's the last time I make you a cup of tea, what a waste.'

'Aww don't sulk,' she pouted, tickling me under the chin, 'you're not sulking are you my darling? argh no don't!' she squealed when she saw what I was planning to do with *my* tea, 'I've got delicate skin it's ok for you, you can take it you've got rhinoceros skin.'

We both laughed.

'Yeah well maybe I have, but not on my willy.' I winged, nursing myself gingerly, 'anyway I wouldn't waste good tea on you.'

Instead I held the cup down low so Nelson could drink the dregs - he loved his tea.

'Well, we'd better move on then seeing as you don't like it here,' I said as we did the washing up.

'Why don't we just stay here for a while and re-charge our batteries instead, we're both still tired from all that travelling,'

'What stay here, are you sure?' I said peering out of the door at the virtual rubbish tip we were parked on, 'is it growing on you then?'

'No not here you *plonker*, let's stop in Monte Gordo for a while, there's a nice big car park over there look.'

She was right as usual, and so after I'd changed my shorts, (the tea was drying into a rather suspicious looking stain) I turned Billy round and we headed back into town heading for the big car park we'd seen on the way through.

There were quite a few cars parked there but we managed to find a place right on the far edge by the beach. Despite the fact that the car park was quite full and there were a lot of people still on the beach it was strangely quiet. We sat on the edge of the car park where it stepped down onto the beach and soaked up the tranquil atmosphere of our first Portuguese beach scene.

There were paths leading away from the car park across the soft white sand to beach bars with their bamboo awnings and wicker tables and chairs under brightly coloured parasols. The soon to be familiar smell of sardines being barbecued filled our senses, wafted along by the gentle onshore breeze.

Later on, when all the cars had gone I turned Billy round so that his side door was facing the sea and we had supper as the sun gradually turned bright red and started sinking slowly into the sea.

The night air was still and on the far side of the car park the traffic moved slowly along the main street. Taxis were pulling up regularly at the large white building we'd parked next to which we later discovered was a casino. There was a constant flow of people in and out of the place and also quite a few people on the streets but oddly, hardly a sound to be heard.

It was as if we were watching a film and someone had turned the sound right down.

We both felt an overwhelming sense of calm wash over us as we stood there gazing at the scene for what seemed like ages. We could feel the tension from all the miles we'd just done simply melting away. What a contrast to the bustling, noisy Spanish resorts we'd so far experienced.

We had the best nights sleep in a long time that night and woke early and refreshed the next morning, ready for our first mission which was to find a good bakery.

As luck would have it as we wandered through the cobbled streets we saw a young boy leaving a house with a loaf of bread in his hand.

The door was open and the heady aroma of freshly baked bread wafted out of the house as we approached. I knocked on the door and a tiny woman dressed all in black invited us into a darkened hallway where she proudly showed us a table laden with huge loaves of crusty bread. She picked one up and patted its bottom lovingly, offering it to us questioningly.

Suzi nodded and smiled, took the loaf and gave it a good old sniff which seemed to please the woman no end. She then lifted a white cloth from a large whicker basket full of crusty bread rolls with creases down the middle. They looked really delicious and we were unable to resist them, more nodding and smiling and then she handed us two.

'Ooh, no no, we want more than two please,' I said holding my hands out for more but she waggled her finger at us before replacing the cover over the rolls.

'Very sorry but I can't let you have any more because that's all I've made and most of them are pre-ordered. If I gave you any more than two then there wouldn't be enough for everyone else.'

That's what we reckoned she was saying anyway.

This message was conveyed by her patting the rolls and counting on her fingers, then pointing to a piece of paper pinned to the wall with a list of names on it and numbers next to them - her customer list.

She then put the two rolls in a small plastic bag and wrote the amount down on a scrap of paper. She didn't have a bag big enough for the loaf and said next time we must bring our own bag like other people do (we worked out that's what she'd said as we sat on the sand later eating our breakfast).

I gave her an as yet, unfamiliar bank note and she handed me some as yet, unfamiliar coins as change which I pocketed quickly (it's ok I'll count them and work it all out later).

Will you be wanting any rolls tomorrow?

Yes we will and we'd like six if possible please.

I'll make more tomorrow and then you can have six,

That's very kind of you thank you very much.

No problem, see you tomorrow and don't forget to bring a bag.

It's amazing how you can have a conversation with someone when neither of you can understand a word the other one's saying.

We went straight back to Billy for a breakfast of coffee and some truly delicious buttered toast made from the big heavy and holey sourdough type loaf.

According to the hastily scrawled note that Senora Pao had handed us the big loaf was called 'pao grande' and the rolls were 'papo secos'.

These were the very first words we learned in Portuguese!

ꙥ ꙥ ꙥ ꙥ ꙥ

Our second and distinctly less appetizing Portuguese lesson came later that afternoon after all the cars had gone and we had the car park to ourselves once more, well apart from a couple of other campers that is.

We were sitting on the edge of the sand just by Billy with our legs dangling over the low wall, enjoying watching the sun go down when we heard someone calling. We looked up to see a tiny little man and his tiny little dog walking across the car park in the direction of the beach bars, he was hunched over and had a strange staggering gait.

'Boa tarde!' he called again holding his hand high up in the air in a greeting to us.

We waved back but that wasn't good enough, he wasn't satisfied with just a wave.

'Boa tarde!' he shouted yet again and he laughed to himself as he re-adjusted his cap. He'd stopped by this time, determined to get something out of us.

'Buenas Tardes!' I called back, well one of us had to say something and that's all I could come up with at the time. He seemed pleased enough to hear a response though even if it was in the wrong language, and he cackled away to himself as he continued on towards the bar

We were used to saying hello in Spanish now after having been in Spain for the last couple of months so it sounded a bit strange to us.

'What did he say?'

'Not sure,' I replied as I reached for the Portuguese phrase book we'd bought earlier, 'let's have a look shall we.'

'Ah right then, looks like you say 'bom dia' in the morning, 'boa tarde' in the afternoon and then 'boa noite' in the evening according to this.'

'So when does the afternoon become the evening then, does it say?'

'It says there are no hard and fast rules but it's usually around sunset time, same as in Spain really.'

We spent some time learning these and a few other words, and then a little later on as we were eating, the same tiny little man and his tiny little dog came staggering away from the bar. He stopped in the middle of the car park again, this time with hands on hips and an expectant look on his face.

'Boa tarde!'

We were ready.

'Boa tarde!' we both shouted back.

He was thrilled and threw his head back laughing, he said something else then but of course we had absolutely no idea what he was on about. Still he seemed happy enough with his teachings for one day and he gave us a big gappy smile, clapped his hands in delight and staggered off, laughing and chuntering away to himself as he went.

He'd only gone a few paces when we heard him making a really horrible noise.

Unfortunately for us we both looked over just in time as he noisily dragged the contents of his throat up and gobbed it all out in the direction of his little dog who promptly caught it in mid-flight and ate it.

'Oh no no no,' gasped Suzi incredulously, 'I didn't just see that did I?'

'Well *I* did but I wish I hadn't,' I said, fork poised halfway to my mouth with gooey cheese sauce dripping from it, I looked at it and put it down.

'Oh my god I feel sick,' groaned Suzi putting a hand over her mouth - she stood up quickly and turned away.

We looked at each other in disbelief - supper was abandoned and the boys ate a hearty meal that night!

Early the next morning, as we were eating breakfast on the sand he came staggering along again, singing and chuckling away to himself. He was always staggering, either he was permanently drunk or he had bad hips or something, anyway he raised his hand and shouted across to us.

'Bom dia!'

'Bom dia!' I called back, hoping he wouldn't come over to us and luckily he didn't, it looked like he was on a mission.

'Who's that?' asked Suzi turning to look.

'No don't look Ethel!' I said, shielding her eyes from the inevitable.

'Why, who is it?'

'Gobadog,' I replied.

'Who?' then she spotted him, 'oh no not him, not while we're eating again please,' she groaned, picturing the events of the day before.

He stopped then and shouted something else to us - of course we had no chance of understanding what he'd said and I suspected very few people would have. When he got no response he turned and staggered on and thankfully we were spared a repeat performance from the night before.

There was a skip near one of the beach bars and he headed straight for it. He was so tiny he had to reach up to grab the side of it and then he pulled himself up and leant over into it, balancing precariously on the edge whilst his little dog waited patiently below. He ferreted around in the rubbish, sliding further and further down into the skip until just his feet and legs were sticking out over the side. Something flew out and landed near his dog who immediately ate whatever it was, then something else followed it and that disappeared inside the dog as well.

Suddenly there was a loud curse as his feet vanished and he fell in. More cursing followed by a laugh and then his head shot up again, he was laughing hysterically to himself and rambling on about something as he clambered back over the side and dropped to the ground.

In his hand he had a carrier bag with the remains of what looked like a loaf of bread in it. He saw us watching him and he held it up triumphantly for us to see. He gave his little dog a piece and then had some himself before carrying on towards the bar - so that was their breakfast sorted then.

He started to drag his throat up again and both of us instinctively turned away just before the grand finale - we didn't want to spoil breakfast as well.

It was so peaceful and relaxing parked there at Monte Gordo, our days were spent exploring the town and walking with the boys along the seemingly never ending beach under cloudless blue skies. We walked barefoot for hours along the warm white sand as the deep blue waters of the Atlantic crashed down relentlessly against the shore.

Going left, we would walk all the way to the wide estuary of the river Guadiana at Vila Real de Santo Antonio, where we'd sit on the giant boulders of the sea wall to have our picnic before heading back.

Going right, after a kilometer or so we would pass a couple of beach bars at a little place called Cabeço, then it was Altura and then Manta Rota.

We kept walking until we reached a natural break in the sand where the sea came in and we could go no further. The beach continued on the other side but according to our atlas, it was actually an island called Ilha de Cabanas which was separated from the mainland by the Rio Formosa, we would have to go exploring there soon.

On our way back we left the shoreline and went up through a break in the sand dunes at Cabeço. There were two beach bars there, one on either side of a large sandy car park and they both looked to be closed up for the winter. We saw no-one about and there were no campers or cars anywhere, it looked like it would be a nice quiet place to park up - we would have to explore here soon too.

We were nearly back at Monte Gordo when Suzi spotted something rolling around in the shallows so we went over to see what it was. It was a terracotta pot bellied vase with a hole in the bottom; it looked to be unbroken so I picked it up to have a closer look at it.

As the water drained out of the bottom a long probing tentacle of a squid appeared over the top, followed by another, then another.

I put it down on the sand gently and we watched transfixed as yet more tentacles crept slowly over the top, feeling their way down the side followed by the head until it was out completely. It flopped down onto the sand where it slithered and dragged itself slowly inch by inch back down towards the water and freedom once more.

The pot, we later discovered was a purpose-built squid pot laid down by the fishermen which must have come loose and got washed up on the beach. The squid finds its way into the pot where it thinks it's nice and safe - which it is until the fisherman drains all the water out and then out it comes.

We were happy we'd found this one and it was so heartwarming to see it make its great escape - we kept the pot.

We'd just finished lunch when someone poked their head around the front of Billy.

He was short and wiry with bandy white legs, a deeply wrinkled face with piercing, weak blue eyes, and as it turned out, quite a piercing voice as well.

'All right how's it going? I'm Len from the white Mercedes over there,' he began in his cockney accent, pointing at an old Mercedes van at the far end of the car park.

We all introduced ourselves and he continued.

'Just got back from Holland as it goes, yeah we arrived this morning, we always come down here for the winter, everyone in this town knows who I am. Yeah I know all the bar and restaurant owners around here you'll see, just say you're friends with Len and they'll give you a good deal you mark my words. You should come out with us sometime and I'll introduce you to some people, show you how to have a good time, you look like you could do with it.'

He laughed at his joke and continued,

'Did the van up myself, yeah had it a couple of years now, I'll give you a guided tour sometime, show you the right way to kit one of those things out. Most people who do their own vans haven't a clue how to do it you know but I've done it right, designed and built it myself, it's a real clever design.

I know all the best places to camp as well, I'll show you on the map sometime or even better you can follow us around, yeah that's a better idea, we'll be off to Tavira in a couple of days you'd be better off coming with us.

Yeah we've been working in Holland for the last four months, been doing that for years now, then the rest of the year we're down here living the life of Riley. Four months work and eight months holiday, now that's clever, not many people can say that can they. Mind you we have to do twelve hour days six days a week to earn it and its hard work too but well worth it.

Tell you what we'll stop by after tea and take you out, I'll show you round a few places, help you with the language and all that it'll be a laugh, see you later.'

He turned abruptly and walked off, neither of us had said a word, we just looked at each other and burst out laughing. Suzi breathed a sigh of relief.

'Wow, he can talk can't he.'

'About himself yes.'

'Oh god I think my ears are bleeding,' she said rubbing them.

'Don't fancy a night out with him then?' I asked, knowing the answer.

'Pfft! what do you think.'

We had an early supper that night and then went for a nice long walk along the beach to make sure we weren't there later when Len called round to 'take us out and show us a good time'.

We went west towards the setting sun, a brilliant red ball sinking slowly into a steel blue sea.

We walked until it had disappeared completely then turned round and ambled our way back slowly, endlessly throwing sticks for Caine to swim out for which Nelson promptly pinched off him as soon as he reached the shore again.

It turned out to be a really long walk and it was quite late when we got back, we were tired and looking forward to relaxing with a nice hot drink before bed.

I was just about to close the side door when....

'You ready then?' came an all too familiar voice - my stomach tightened as Len's face appeared in the doorway.

'What?'

'We're just off out, you coming? you said you were.' (no we didn't!)

'Did we? I don't remember that do you?' I turned to Suzi who shook her head vigorously.

'No, we're just about to go to bed, another time maybe.'

'What, you can't go to bed yet it's still early, you've got to come.' (no we haven't).

Just then a woman's face appeared next to his.

'Oh please come, I could do with some female company, it's nearly all men in these places, oh please say you'll come.'

'This is Shirl by the way,' he said.

I'm not sure how it happened, or even why, but we somehow found ourselves going out with them.

The next few hours were spent tediously going from one bar to another while I sat there listening to Len all night, I couldn't get a word in, not that I really wanted to. The girls were getting on all right and were having a normal two way conversation which I was trying to listen in on but couldn't. I can't remember saying very much the whole time, I do remember yawning a lot though.

He made a big show of talking loudly to the locals and even *we* could tell that his Portuguese was very poor. He'd found some friends of his at the bar and had now invited them to join us at our table.

They were quite a striking looking couple due mainly to the fact that they were both very hairy. He had long dark hair slicked back, a moustache and a beard - he looked like a werewolf. She also had some sort of frizzy mop on her head but no beard, well not on her chin anyway. Instead she had what looked to me like a full beard under each arm - she had more armpit hair than I did and they were both an alarming shade of red from overdoing it on the first day.

Happily for me they were now on the receiving end of Len's attentions and I was left in peace. I was able to look around and people watch whilst listening in on different conversations trying to pick out some new Portuguese words.

I was wrenched abruptly from my reverie when I heard Len loudly mention our names as he annoyingly proceeded to tell them all about us (something he knew absolutely nothing about). It was at that point that I became aware of the fact that I'd been staring at her very hairy armpits for some time, oh god how long had I been doing that?

'These two know all about Spain,' he began, (what? no we don't), 'travelled all over the country they have (no we haven't), tell them Tim, go on tell them about how you drove here.'

I opened my mouth to speak but Mr Wolf raised his hand.

'Huh! there's not a lot you can tell us about Spain that we don't already know sonny (sonny?), been going there for donkey's years we have,' he took a swig of beer and wiped his mouth with the back of his hand before continuing, 'go on then, tell me which way you came.'

I had a feeling I wasn't going to get to the end of my next sentence but I gave it a go anyway.

'Well we drove from the South of France down the Mediterranean coast as far as Alicante, then headed inland for the Sierra Nevada....'

'Oh god no what did you go that way for, (I was right!) there's a much quicker way than that. You want to avoid going inland altogether mate there's nothing going on there, it's not like the real Spain around those parts is it, I mean it's not like Torremolinos or Benidorm is it!'

We looked at each other incredulously and laughed which didn't seem to please him very much, or Len for that matter and thankfully they went back to talking between themselves. Mrs. Wolf had her arm resting on Mr. Wolf's shoulder as they talked, those hairs really were quite long you know and I was trying hard not to stare at them.

A few minutes later I heard Mrs. Wolf ask Len,

'So what are property prices like around here then?'

'Oh you'd be better off talking to these two about that, they actually live here,' he said gesturing to the pair of us.

We looked at each other in bemusement, (no we don't).

'Oh really, you live here do you? (no) how wonderful,' smiled Mrs. Wolf as she thankfully lowered her arm, 'how long have you been here then?'

'Erm… well about three days,' I replied dryly as Suzi tittered into her beer.

Mrs Wolf looked at Len, a little puzzled.

'Oh right, whereabouts do you live then?'

'Well we live in Billy and today we're on the car park by the Casino but tomorrow we could well be living somewhere else, who knows.'

Too much for Suzi and she plonked her beer down quickly and roared with laughter at the bemused faces staring back at us.

Why were we the only ones finding all this amusing?

It kind of went a bit quiet then and for some reason they didn't really talk to us much after that.

☺ ☺ ☺ ☺ ☺

Every third Sunday of each month there was a real treat for market lovers. It was the famous street market at Vila Nova de Cacela which according to Len, was one not to be missed.

Well for once he was right; it was a *huge* market taking up most of the streets in the town. We had to abandon Billy at the end of the long line of cars parked on the verge and walk into town from there. Cars would be parked on both sides of the road causing chaos for any through traffic and the later we got there the longer the line and the longer the walk would be.

It was well worth the walk though and we'd soon be slowly jostling and bumping our way through crowds of old people standing around talking, avoiding donkeys and dogs and trying not to trip over huge sacks of produce laid out haphazardly on the floor.

We never actually managed to 'avoid' any donkeys though as Suzi would always stop and say hello to them and give them a fuss and a cuddle. She'd end up in conversation with the owner as well and despite the fact that neither of them could understand each other it would be a good ten minutes before we were able to move on again.

Still, she was happy to have shared the closeness of such a beautiful animal for a few minutes, plus we'd also increased our Portuguese vocabulary by two or three new words.

Of course the olive stall was one of our favourites with its rows of huge wooden barrels full of olives of all different shapes, sizes and colours. The stall holder always insisted we try them before buying any - we didn't need much persuading on that score. We'd sample some from every barrel and always come away from there with a few plastic tubs of various kinds.

The smell of fresh bread would then lead us to one of the many bread stalls laden with huge loaves where we'd buy the usual 'Pao Grande' and some 'Papo Secos'. The flies would be swiped off before grubby hands grabbed the bread and stuffed it into a second hand carrier bag.

The fly swiping it seemed was an act of kindness reserved specially for foreigners as I noticed when a local bought a loaf, the flies were simply ignored and disappeared into the bag along with the bread.

Progress was slow around the crowded streets as no-one was in any kind of hurry to go anywhere in particular. A lot of people just seemed to be there to meet friends, stand around and have a good old chat and clog up the streets.

Huge sacks full of red and yellow lentils, split peas and an endless variety of beans surrounded one little man in a flat cap. He was busily scooping, weighing, smoking and talking all at the same time and the cigarette never left his mouth once. We came away from there with two more second hand carrier bags full of an assortment of practically everything he had there.

My carrier bag burden was growing steadily.

At times the noise would be deafening as on top of the general hubbub of the crowd and the stall holders calling out, every so often we would walk right past huge loudspeakers which were right at ear level. They would either be blasting out music or some frenetic, ear piercing voice would presumably be bigging up someone's stall somewhere. These speakers were free standing on the pavement and I never did discover where the voice was coming from.

My ears would be left ringing as yet another carrier bag was added to my growing collection making it even more hazardous to thread my way through the crowds and progress was slowed even more. At least this one was light if a little bulky as it was filled with various items of clothing selected from huge piles all laid out on the ground on sheets - the whole lot costing less than £2.

The pumpkin man was next on the list, always a favourite with Suzi for some reason. He only had a small table but his little van next to him was crammed full of pumpkins, or 'Frade' as he called them. There was a huge one on the table in front of us and the man asked how much she wanted, not in weight just in size, it didn't really matter she just wanted to see him cut it.

He took a huge knife and hacked a hefty slice off, then he deftly cut all the seeds out into a bowl, popped the pumpkin into a bag and magically came up with a price for it. Suzi was delighted as usual and her little eyes lit up as he handed it to her, her day was made and my burden grew heavier.

Whilst we were there she got chatting to an English couple, the woman for some reason also enjoyed the pumpkin buying process.

They were called Alice and Brian and they wintered regularly on the Algarve in their old camper, opting to stay on camp sites rather than rough camp like we did. We discovered they too lived in Wales, just a mere ten miles from where we lived.

I could tell this wasn't going to be a quick conversation and I was getting uncomfortable standing there talking (or rather listening!) Apart from my already aching feet and legs the heavy carrier bags were biting into my hands and I needed to put them down. I looked down at the cobbles to make sure they were clean first and good job too; there was a dollop of something disgusting looking right between my feet so I shifted over until I found a clean patch before thankfully setting them down.

Brian had a carrier bag too, but more sensibly he had a rucksack on his back for all their shopping. I was thinking what a good idea that would be as it would save me carrying all these heavy bags around everywhere. However that thought was quickly banished as I had a nightmare vision of me knocking little old ladies over or destroying people's stalls with it.

We eventually parted company and my beast of burden duties were once more resumed as Brian sauntered off with his rucksack and his single very light looking carrier bag.

'Cheap cheese, cheap cheese!' called a man in a white coat when he saw we were foreigners.

He had an apé - one of those little three wheeler motorbikes crossed with a tiny tiny van - the rear doors were open and it was full of neatly wrapped rounds of cheese.

'Cheap cheese, cheap cheese!' he repeated when he saw he had our attention.

We shuffled on over and he quickly offered us a taster whilst he told us all about the cheese. Sadly it turned out that 'cheap cheese' was the only English he knew so we didn't learn very much about it really except that we think he made it himself - and that it was *very very* good!

We both tried some and had to agree with him, it *was* very very good, smooth and creamy and given the colour and texture we decided it must be goat's cheese - great, we'll have two rounds please señor. He wrote the price on one of the rounds and showed it to me, it didn't seem that cheap to me but I wasn't in the mood to argue at that point.

I only had a 5000 escudo note left on me so I handed it to him as he gave me the cheese to carry, thanks very much señor.

I stuffed the rounds into one of the bags and grabbed the change giving it a quick check, it looked about right.

Suzi then cheekily helped herself to some more samples and popped one in my mouth along with an olive from one of the bags - delicious.

I was then jostled out of position by a couple of well built and not to be messed with Portuguese ladies who had descended upon the cheese van. Carrying several heavy carrier bags in each hand as well as a handful of change is no easy feat especially in a crowd. Suzi had already disappeared in search of god knows what leaving poor old me to thread my way through the thriving throng (try saying that with a mouthful of cheese and olives!)

Eventually I found her with her arms around yet another donkey which gave me chance to put the bags down (check the ground first!) and put the change back in my money belt.

Eventually and thankfully, after walking round the whole market at least twice we made our way back to Billy; did I say I liked markets? We were pleased to see the boys weren't too hot as all the curtains were drawn and the windows were open, they were fine and hadn't even touched their water bowl. We chucked all our bags in the back out of the way, except for the all important-food ones of course.

Tea was made, a blanket laid out and we sat on the grassy verge in the warm sunshine to enjoy a late lunch. All the tubs of olives were spread out between us along with a bowl of cloudy cold pressed olive oil for dipping the bread into, fresh tomatoes and some of the cheese.

As a palate cleanser we had grapes with slices of freshly picked oranges in a hand painted Algarvian bowl. We knew the oranges were freshly picked as we'd just picked and stashed them from some trees by the side of the road on the way to the market!

The ritual of the olive stone spitting began again much to ours and also the boys' delight as they enjoyed crunching on them after they'd ricocheted off us.

All the time we were eating I was mulling over the price of the cheese we'd bought. When I counted how much change he'd given me I said.

'Well nice though the cheese is, it wasn't particularly cheap.'

'Why, did he rip us off then?' enquired a bulgy cheeked Suzi.

'No I don't think so, I'm just saying it wasn't that cheap that's all.'

I was studying the label as we were talking and then I noticed there was a picture of some sheep on it.

'Hey it looks like its sheep's cheese not goat's cheese going by the picture, look.'

I showed it to her and then the penny dropped for both of us and we fell about laughing.

'Hah hah that's really funny, he was saying 'sheep cheese' not 'cheap cheese' all along.'

'Yep so not his fault after all then, he never said it was cheap did he!'

'No he didn't did he, so this is not so cheap sheep's cheese!'

We tittered over that for the rest of our delicious feast which was then followed by a relaxing siesta in the warm sunshine before packing things away properly and heading back to Monte Gordo.

☺ ☺ ☺ ☺ ☺

Each day we'd see Len walking across the car park on his way to the shops and then each night we'd see them both going out on the town. He never came over to chat to us anymore and they never came to call for us to go drinking either - we were puzzled, was it something we'd said?

Anyway the time came for a change of scenery and some solitude so we decided to go and explore Cabeço. We left Monte Gordo on the EN125 and turned off left after a kilometer or so. The road took us through the trees and past a row of newly built villas on our left - then up ahead the road forked.

'Which way now then, left or right?' I enquired of my navigator.

'Oh I dunno, you're driving you decide,'

'Come on, you're the navigator which way, quick we're nearly on the junction.'

'I don't know....left!'

I turned right at the last second.

'Too late,' I sniggered.

'Tosser!'

We soon ended up on the huge sandy car park we'd seen on our beach walks – the one with a café/bar at each end and a bank of dunes in the middle. I pulled Billy up to the bank and we got out to survey our new surroundings.

Apart from a couple of cars and a lorry at one bar we were the only ones there, the other bar was closed for the winter and we had the whole place to ourselves.

Over the next few days we enjoyed a lovely peaceful time there, the odd camper came and went during the day but we were the only ones who stayed there overnight. There was a handy water tap outside the lorry bar which the owner was happy for us to use and we walked into Monte Gordo along the beach most days for fresh papo secos from our bread lady.

It was also easy to empty the toilet there as the surrounding countryside was all sandy so it was easy to dig a nice deep hole amongst all the trees.

Often we would sit and have our meals in the sunshine on the whitewashed steps leading down from the closed bar onto the beach and just watch the world go by.

The evenings were calm and quiet with the only sound coming from the small waves breaking gently on the shore. Then later on as darkness fell a row of lights from the night time fishing boats would appear all along the horizon. We collected driftwood off the beach and each night we would have a small fire in the dunes to keep us warm as the cool night air came in. We'd roast some potatoes or chestnuts, drink cheap wine and sing silly songs as the sun went down – good times.

We made ourselves at home there and stayed for several weeks, it was nice not to have to keep moving all the time. Most days a Police jeep would drive around on patrol and give us the once over, they seemed happy enough that we were behaving ourselves and left us alone.

We were by Billy one day when Alice and Brian, the couple we'd met at Cacela market turned up. They'd been for a long walk along the beach and had spotted Billy so decided to call in for a cuppa. It was quite a cool, cloudy day with a brisk wind off the water taking the edge of the temperature and they looked quite cold and windswept, well Brian did anyway.

Tea was made and we sat outside on the sand dune and chatted, of course as soon as they sat down the boys went up and introduced themselves, Brian wasn't impressed.

'Ok, you've said hello, now go and sit down now please there's good dogs,' he said politely, secretly wishing they would just bugger off and leave him alone.

Nelson did, he'd checked Brian out and was satisfied he wasn't a threat to anyone but as usual Caine didn't give up. He loved everybody immediately and expected the same in return;

the more Brian tried discreetly to shove him away the more he insisted they became friends.

In the end they compromised, Caine accepted Brian's indifference towards him and Brian endured the indignity of Caine sitting right next to him, leaning against his leg with a wet sandy paw resting on his knee.

'Would you like to sit inside Alice?' asked Brian shivering, his knuckles white from gripping his mug of tea so tightly.

'No I'm fine out here thanks, it's quite sheltered really.'

Brian looked longingly towards Billy wishing he was inside, out of the cold wind and away from this pesky dog - through chattering teeth he said.

'Are you sure you wouldn't prefer to be inside in the warm Alice?'

'No I'm ok, really, stop fussing Brian!'

'Are you sure, you look quite cold Alice.'

He could take it no more and after a few more minutes Brian stood up, dislodging Caine's paw and as he brushed the sand off his trousers he said.

'Bugger it then I'm going to sit inside I'm bloody freezing!'

He'd obviously hatched a cunning plan in his head whereby he could at last get warm and get rid of his new unwanted friend at the same time. With tin mug of tea in hand he made a dash for Billy and was just about to close the side door when quick as a flash, Caine leapt in and jumped up onto the seat next to him.

We all laughed and with his plan foiled, Brian admitted defeat and sat down heavily. Caine saw the chink in his armour and plonked his paw on his arm spilling some tea onto his already dog-soiled trousers. He then lay down right next to him on the seat with his head across his lap, content with this breakthrough whilst Brian sat there enjoying the warmth but having to endure the bloody dog.

He was a good sport though and along with the rest of us he eventually saw the funny side of things and from then on whenever they called round the same thing would happen. Caine never gave up on him and slowly Brian came to accept him, he couldn't have disliked him that much really or they wouldn't have bothered coming to see us.

They left us with an invite over to their van for tea and home made cake as they had an oven in their van and Alice enjoyed baking - cake sounded good to us.

The next afternoon we walked along the beach into Monte Gordo and went onto the campsite to visit them as they preferred to go on to a site rather than rough camp like us. We left the boys in Billy as we didn't think it would be fair for Brian to have to put up with Caine's attentions in his own home.

We soon found their van - a Ford 'A' series with its big upright windscreen and sliding front doors - parked amongst the pine trees with table and chairs outside and washing on the line. They'd obviously made themselves quite at home and didn't intend moving until it was time to return to the UK in a few months time.

Brian had done the van out himself and made a pretty good job of it too.

To start with the front passenger seat swiveled right round to face the 'room' which was a really neat space saving design. There was a small woodburner which Brian had made from an old gas bottle, two bench seats which converted into the bed, several book shelves, various handy lights here and there and a small cooker with an oven. There was lots of cupboard space and even a separate toilet cubicle, what a luxury that would be!

To be able to cram so much into a van this size and still have plenty of room impressed me, I was already busy making mental notes for when we upgraded Billy to something bigger for us all to live in comfortably.

Although it was quite a lot bigger than Billy we wanted something even bigger so that we could have a permanent bed and put an end to all the tedious making and un-making and the putting away of the duvet etc.

We tended to go to their van rather than have them come to ours as there was more room in theirs and it also meant we could take advantage of the showers on the campsite which was an added bonus!

We visited each other often over the coming weeks and months and became good friends.

Whenever the weather was calm and the waves weren't too big, it would be a common sight to see at regular intervals along the beach, men standing around in the water holding onto a pole.

They were clam fishermen and they would shuffle along in the shallows for hours on end with the cold water up to their waists. They would have hold of the long pole and wiggle it gently back and forth, at the bottom of the pole is a wire cage which moves slowly through the sand picking up the clams which gather in the long net attached.

Every now and again and accompanied by the raucous seabirds, they would come out onto the beach to empty their nets and sort through their catch. They would also take this opportunity to answer the call of nature which was another reason why we chose to sit on the steps - these 'shufflers' as we called them used the sand dunes as their toilets.

Quite often we'd go up into the dunes and sit down in the lovely warm white sand to soak up some sunshine. We'd breathe in the gorgeous and ever present curry smell only to find we were right next to a pile of shit lurking half buried by the drifting sand.

Interestingly enough, there was never any sign of toilet paper so we assumed they cleaned themselves up when they went back into the water.

One time however we were just about to move when we were treated to an intriguing spectacle.

A huge black dung beetle had rolled up some of the drying shit into a ball twice the size of itself and was rolling it up the sand dune towards the reeds. It was making steady progress until another beetle came along and tried to pinch the ball off him. The first beetle who we named George turned and chased the intruder away - we called this one Paul.

George then ran back to his ball which had rolled back down the slope and started the climb all over again.

Paul moved in again, there was a scuffle and George chased Paul off again, the ball rolled back down and George was back to square one.

This time he'd almost got the ball to the top when Pesky Paul attacked again, George turned and chased him off and the ball rolled all the way back down again.

Paul, seemingly defeated scuttled off out of sight whilst George breathed a sigh of relief and started all over again.

He was nearly at the top once more when Paul returned, this time with reinforcements - he'd brought Ringo and John along with him and between them they'd hatched a cunning plan.

Ringo and John went one side of George, Paul the other, in a pincer movement if you like - well they *were* beetles after all!

Once again Paul made a lunge for the ball. George had had quite enough of this and with steam coming out of his ears he turned on Paul and chased him off good and proper.

Seizing the moment Ringo and John shot forward and between them they quickly pushed the ball up the slope and out of sight.

Paul had gone for good this time and George returned triumphantly only to find his ball had disappeared. He was beside himself, running this way and that, looking everywhere for it but it was nowhere to be seen. He was clearly distraught at the loss of such a prize and he sat quite still for a time and had a little cry before slowly moving off in the opposite direction.

Poor old George, our hearts did go out to him but still it was good to see Paul getting by with a little help from his friends!

A regular feature was a male jogger who went past quite a few times every day, he was tall, well tanned and wore only trunks. Nothing unusual in that, quite a few people jogged along the shoreline - this guy was a bit different though.

If he was jogging away from the sun he would have his trunks pulled down at the back so that his bum could get tanned, and if he was heading into the sun he would have the front pulled down so he could get his willy done.

He was very thoughtful though and obviously didn't want to offend anyone by exposing himself to them. Whenever he approached someone walking or jogging he would pull his trunks up to cover himself and then once he'd passed them he would pull them back down again.

Pretty smart really, he'd devised the perfect way to get exercise and an all over tan at the same time. He didn't seem that bothered about us seeing him though as he still kept his trunks down whenever he went past. He obviously thought we were far enough away not to be able to see anything but we could, quite clearly.

Maybe he had tunnel vision or something and just didn't see us sitting there, Nelson was a bit hard to miss though. He was fascinated by him for some reason and whenever he saw him approaching he would go and sit halfway down the beach and stare at him intently as he jogged past, but the man never even looked at him.

An end comes to all good things though and slowly one by one other camping cars of various nationalities turned up. Word must have got around that this was a good place to park and not get moved on by the police.

Trouble was they all wanted to park nearest to the sea and it became a little too cosy there for our liking so we moved across to the far side of the car park by the trees where it was quieter.

There was actually a better view of the sea from there and I was also able to string a clothes line up from Billy's mirror to a nearby tree when we did our washing.

It was now November and the weather was still nice and sunny, the days were warm but the nights were becoming a bit chilly.

The Algarve is such a sunny place,
Where life moves at a slow, slow pace.
We're soaking up some winter sun,
Watching beetles having fun.

George had won himself a prize,
A lovely dung ball twice his size.
But the other three were really sly,
They left him all alone to cry.

That jogger man looks rather silly,
Trunks half down with floppy willy.
He's coming back, oh look that's rum,
He's getting a sun tan on his bum.

We like to stretch out on the sand,
Ugh, be careful where you put your hand.
So now it's on the steps we sit,
Avoiding all the shuffler's shit!

☺ ☺ ☺ ☺ ☺

Christmas was approaching and we were eagerly waiting for parcels from friends and family back home. Each morning we'd take a leisurely stroll along the beach into Monte Gordo to check for post.

Now they say that an Englishman will form an orderly queue of one, well we very quickly discovered that in Portugal nobody queues at all.

At the post office all the locals just stand or sit wherever they want to and as if by some sort of sixth sense, they all seem to know whose turn it is next. It was hard to know where to stand and wait and with all the people coming and going we very quickly lost track of where we were in the 'queue'. Everyone else somehow seemed to know though and when it became our turn, they would look at us expectantly, waiting for us to go next.

When we got to the counter I asked for posta restante and handed our passports over.

The rather large and unsmiling woman behind the counter scowled at them for a couple of seconds, did a slow blink and sighed. She snatched the passports from my hand and begrudgingly slid off her stool which gave an audible sigh of relief and went off into the next room to check. She then waddled back over and plonked herself back down with a heavy sigh as the stool cushion harmonized by hissing all its air out again. She slapped the passports down on the counter and snapped 'Não!'

She was very grumpy and before we had chance to say anything else she'd invited the next customer to the counter and we were dismissed.

Every day it was the same scenario - same grumpy belligerent woman, same old scowl, sighs and hissing stool, same result - a short sharp 'Não!'

We could see her in the next room going through a huge pile of parcels and each day we held our breath expectantly. Surely she would find at least one in the middle of all that lot for us, but each day we would leave disappointed.

The days became weeks and we were getting a bit concerned, there should have been lots of letters by now and at least four parcels that we knew of. Where were they, they couldn't all have got lost could they?

Back home they were concerned too; they'd all gone to a lot of time and trouble, not to mention expense to get these parcels together for us, it was all very upsetting.

The pile of parcels we could see in the next room were now looking very familiar, they were the same ones that had been there all along. Well that's just typical isn't it we thought, here we are, desperate for our parcels and whoever that lot belonged to weren't even coming to pick them up.

Then one day, somewhere around the middle of December the situation had become quite desperate, and desperate times call for desperate measures.

We were waiting patiently for our turn to be served, well I was anyway but unfortunately Suzi was not - she doesn't do waiting very well. All of a sudden and without any warning she just walked forward, slipped under the counter and went into the other room where the parcels were.

This didn't go down very well for some reason and there were angry shouts from the staff - the loudest one from grumpy - and then one from Suzi 'Oh my god this one's ours, and this one look!'

By now grumpy was off her stool and had waddled over, huffing and puffing away angrily - Suzi was right, they *were* for us.

I interrupted grumpy's ranting to give her our passports to prove to her that they were for us. She studied them briefly and triumphantly declared that we were wrong and that the names didn't match. She jabbed a stumpy finger at them as she showed them to us, 'look they don't match, they are not your parcels and you must leave immediately.'

'Oh come on that's not my name it's my place of birth!' I said, turning to the page with my name and picture on it 'this is my name here - look.'

She wasn't convinced straightaway but then it slowly dawned on her and she finally backed down when she realized her mistake. There was no apology however and we still had to retreat back to our own side of the counter. She could have let us have them straightaway to make up for her stupidity couldn't she but no, we had to go back and wait our turn like everyone else.

Still, we were now very excited at the prospect of at least some of those parcels being ours and we both waited impatiently for what seemed like an eternity. Even Suzi's constant glaring didn't seem to speed the waiting process up very much, but then our turn came. We went up to the counter expecting her to go and get our parcels but she just stared at us blankly and I actually had to ask her again for Posta Restante.

'Passaporte?'

I turned to Suzi and we looked at each other in disbelief.

'Seriously?' I said to her.

As Suzi stifled a laugh I turned back and with a calm I wasn't feeling, handed the passports over. She grabbed them off me and with a sigh went off to check whilst the poor old stool took a deep breath.

She came back with two parcels, put them on the counter and went back to the pile. Two more were brought out, then two more, followed by one very big one and also a huge pile of letters until most of the counter was taken up. The whole pile of parcels in that room that we'd been looking at every single day for the past few weeks had been for us all along - we were overjoyed and angry at the same time.

Now though we had a problem as we couldn't carry that little lot back across the beach, we'd have to drive in and pick them up. How do we explain that one to old grumpy chops especially as she was now serving someone else.

Luckily for us someone else appeared from the back room and we somehow managed to explain to them that we would return later to pick them up and so all the parcels were duly returned to their original places.

We were so excited we practically ran all the way back to Billy. We had a line of washing out so we had to hastily bring that down and put it away before heading back into Monte Gordo.

We waited our turn, walked up to the counter and I asked ol' grumpy chops for our posta restante, gesturing to the room where our parcels were, I was met with the usual cold stare.

'Passaportes,' she said curtly, holding her hand out.

Well we didn't have them with us, we'd left them in Billy hadn't we, you know, more or less assuming that they wouldn't be needed now that she knew who we were – how wrong we were!

She flatly refused to go and get our parcels until we'd shown her our passports - again.

I noticed that the door in the counter was closed this time so no chance of nipping through, and no amount of persuasion would convince this sour faced jobsworth to hand them over without proof of identity. We had to admit defeat and went back to Billy to get our passports and of course when we got back we had to wait our turn to be served again.

Eventually and after a considerable amount of impatient waiting on behalf of you know who, we reached the counter and after checking our passports yet again, grumpy reluctantly marched off to fetch our parcels. She plonked them all down on the counter with a straight face, no smile, no apology or anything and then with a sigh and a hiss, she plonked herself down on her stool again and we were dismissed.

There were so many parcels it took several trips to ferry them back to Billy in relays. We drove back to Cabeco where we discovered someone parked in 'our place' so we went over to the very far corner well away from everybody and dived on the parcels.

It was an exciting time for us and within seconds Billy was full of wrapping paper and cardboard boxes. As well as several handy items of clothing each, Suzi's mum had sent us several big jars of marmite (just in time!) and what looked like a year's supply of tea bags. There were also several packets of digestive and rich tea biscuits, endless tins of baked beans and a new diary for Suzi.

The boy's food store was also replenished with treats and biscuits of every kind, squeaky toys for Nelson and a frisbee for Caine.

From my mother there were yet more tea bags, clothes and several editions of the local newspaper plus another huge bundle of junk mail - thanks again mum!

It then took us the rest of the day to find enough space to store everything!

We drove a short distance along the coast as far as the small seaside town of Manta Rota, a place we'd walked past several times on our beach walks but never actually driven to.

We passed through the narrow streets which led us out onto a huge grassy area right by the beach; there were a few other camper vans there already so it looked like it would be ok to stay. We drove around for a bit looking for a good place to park and seeing as it was getting quite windy we ended up settling for a spot close to the dunes for a bit of shelter. From there it was just a short walk through the dunes and onto the seemingly never ending beach of beautiful white sand and crashing breakers.

Later, we took our water containers and wandered back over to the entrance where on our way in we'd seen a local woman getting water from a huge water wheel. It was set up on a large square of concrete with steps leading up to it, was about six feet tall and painted green.

I placed a container under the pipe and turned the wheel, nothing happened for a few seconds and then sperloosh! - a big dollop of water gushed out. It was one sperloosh per rotation of the wheel or thereabouts so it took quite a lot of sperlooshes to fill our containers up. It was good fun spinning the wheel though and we both took it in turns - the water was pure and delicious.

Suzi had brought our washing bowl over so we did some washing as well whilst we were there at the wheel and then carried it all back to Billy. I found a long stick not far away and stuck it into the sandy ground - it went in easily. I then tied the washing line to Billy's mirror, across to the stick and then down to the ground where it was fastened to an anchor peg. It wasn't the strongest washing line in the world and it was sagging so much in the middle that the clothes were almost touching the ground.

Later that day as we were walking the boys along the beach, the wind picked up, it clouded over and started raining heavily. By the time we got back to Billy we were all completely drenched and of course so was the washing. It was now wetter than it was before and the line had sagged so much that most of the clothes were now dragging on the ground.

While Suzi rescued the washing, I quickly took the wooden prop out from the roof and lowered it before it took off in the wind. This of course meant we couldn't stand up anymore and we had to sit down as we struggled out of our wet clothes.

Two soggy people, two soggy dogs and a pile of soggy and soiled washing in a VW camper is a lot of sogginess in such a confined space. The boys were curled up in the front seats which were now just as wet as they were and we were going to get wet bums next time we went anywhere.

I dug the small gas fire which we'd brought with us and so far never used out of the locker and connected it to the gaz bottle. Thankfully it worked and it actually gave off a good heat and warmed us up in no time.

The rain didn't look like stopping anytime soon and we sat there for hours holding various items of clothing in front of the fire to dry them. We were nice and warm now but the fire was giving off fumes so we had to open the front windows a bit which of course let the howling wind and rain in. The boys were getting drenched all over again, as was Billy's dashboard and everything else in the front but we had no choice.

The fire was also causing other problems, if there was anything not already wet or getting soaked by the rain it was now coated in a healthy layer of condensation.

After a time the wind eased enough for us to have the roof up again. Unfortunately though, this made it really cold in Billy as the heat would very quickly escape through the thin flappy plastic. As well as that because the plastic was so cold there were rivulets of condensation running down it and dripping all over the place.

A compromise was reached in that most of the time the roof was kept down to keep warm, the downside of this was that it also meant sitting down all the time. The roof would only go up if we needed to do anything that required standing up like cooking so towels and clothes would have to be stuffed all around the bottom of it to catch all the condensation. Every now and again these would need wringing out, so as well as losing all the heat it also meant that there was another pile of wet things which needed drying.

Whenever the rain eased from monsoon to just torrential we would all dash out for a quick walk to stretch our legs and ward off insanity. Unfortunately this of course meant all of us getting wet all over again so the drying process was never ending. It was pretty miserable and long hours were spent just sitting there hardly moving, playing cards or backgammon and not even being able to see out properly because of all the condensation on the windows.

Apart from us there was only one other van left now, a blue one and it looked like a Brit. We had exchanged distant waves once or twice but apart from that we saw very little of them.

To stretch our legs we would take it in turns to go to the kitchen and make tea.

'Going to the kitchen' meant standing up, (bent double though because we couldn't be bothered to put the roof up just for a few minutes) then walking one pace to the sink to fill the kettle up, a small sidestep to the cooker, brew the tea and then make the return journey back to 'the lounge'.

Eventually it stopped raining, two days and nights later and we woke to a clear blue sky and bright warm sunshine. The first thing we did was hang the washing out again, well the clothes which didn't need re washing after being on the ground anyway. Anything wet which wouldn't fit on the line was hung all over Billy to dry in the warm sunshine. All the cushions which made up the bed were wet underneath so they came out as well, the front seats were like sponges, we were definitely going to get wet bums next time we drove anywhere.

We left everything like that and went for a nice long walk on the beach to stretch all our legs properly and to blow away the cobwebs; the boys deserved a good walk after being stuck in the front seats for two days.

After all the rain the field was now only half the size it was as it was now part lake, but luckily we'd parked on slightly higher ground as had the blue van so we were all ok. Getting out would be a problem though as it meant we would have to drive through the water and with the ground as soft as it was I didn't want to risk Billy getting stuck. We had enough food to last for a while so we decided to stay there until it dried out.

The people from the blue van were busy drying themselves out as well, their van was also covered in clothes and they had their cushions out in the sun the same as us. We reckoned the others had high tailed it because they knew the field would get flooded, oh well never mind there were worse places to be stranded. The weather was glorious, the beach was deserted plus we knew no-one was likely to come and park right next to us; it was such a tranquil time.

One thing we'd learnt over the last couple of days though was that we were definitely going to need something bigger than Billy to live in. It was ok when the weather was nice as most of our living was done outdoors but when it was wet and cold like it was now, it was pretty miserable and uncomfortable and not at all fair on the boys.

This was the first time since we'd left home that we'd experienced a prolonged spell of wet, cold and windy weather and it was no fun, something had to be done before next winter. We kept looking over at the blue van imagining how much easier things would be at times like these if we lived in something of that size. It wasn't huge, about the same size as Alice and Brians, but at least there would be enough headroom to be able to stand up and walk about a bit.

We waded over to the water wheel to fetch water and also found a local shop for some basics; we'd be ok for a few more days now while we waited for the ground to dry out. On our way back past the water wheel we met the couple from the other van and got chatting, they were called Jill and Tony and they invited us over for tea and a look around their van. It was originally an ambulance which they'd kitted out very simply themselves. Gemma, their little girl called it an amberlunce so it was now called 'Amber' and they were on a six week tour of Spain and Portugal.

We got on really well with them and over the next few days we had a lot of fun together, going for long walks on the beach, having meals together, always in Amber though as there was more room for all of us. Suzi would usually cook something and then we'd take the food over and we'd all eat together.

We collected driftwood from the beach, (there was no shortage of that after all the bad weather) and have camp fires every night. The ground was dry now and Tony had brought Amber over and parked her right behind Billy in the hope that the two vans would shield the fire from attracting attention over in the village.

Unfortunately the downside to parking up and not going anywhere at this time of the year is that the battery quickly goes flat because lights are needed at night and over a few days the battery drains if the engine hasn't been running. Our back up battery went flat a long time ago so we were relying on the engine battery for lighting power. There was only one small light in Billy so we didn't use much battery power and anyway most of the time we preferred to use candles. We'd heard that citronella candles were good for keeping the mozzies away well that's a laugh, we found that they just seemed to attract the little buggers.

Amber didn't have a back up battery and they had more lights than Billy did, they even had a small TV as well so all this combined with not driving anywhere for the last few days had taken its toll.

Anyway, one morning Tony tried to start Amber, he turned the key and…nothing, not a sausage, the battery was completely dead. No problem, we had some jump leads tucked away somewhere which Suzi's dad had given us so I dug them out. Billy started straightaway and got a nice round of applause and some cheers - good old Billy. I maneuvered him close to Amber so that we could connect the cables and hooked them up.

Turns out they weren't the best quality cables because as soon as they were connected they started smoking, then they melted and caught fire!

Me and Tony leapt into action and bravely extinguished the flames and once the girls had stopped laughing plan B was put into action. Tony took the battery off and we all piled into Billy and headed into Monte Gordo to a garage which he knew of.

Nelson was suitably disgusted with all those people in Billy and he took up his position on the front seat with Suzi and kept his back turned. Caine of course was delighted to have so many friends around him.

We dropped the battery off to be charged up and then parked in our usual place by the Casino. Later that afternoon we drove back to the garage to pick the battery up, the man said it wasn't fully charged yet but it would have to do for now and so we headed back to Manta Rota.

There was enough power in it to run their lights but Tony didn't risk trying to start the engine as they weren't planning on going anywhere.

Running the interior lights had drained all the power from the battery again so the next day another trip into Monte Gordo was called for and we all squoze into Billy again and drove back to the garage. We got there a bit earlier this time so the battery would have a little longer than last time to charge up,

It was decided that we'd all move to Monte Gordo so that the battery could be charged properly so as soon as we got back to Amber everything was packed away. Amber started but only just, then we moved to Monte Gordo but we parked on the other side of the Casino as they'd parked there before.

We realized then that we'd all been parked there for quite a while, one either side of the Casino and we'd never met. Their side was like a proper car park with palm trees, flower beds and no sand. It was all nice clean tarmac with a cobbled boulevard running along the front by the beach. This would be a much better place to be when the next storm hits we decided, as poor old Billy wouldn't get sand blasted like he did before.

Me and Tony carried the heavy battery over to the garage together and left it there for the next two days to give it enough time to charge fully. They were leaving for the long journey home soon so a good battery would be essential.

We all moved back to Manta Rota for one final night of wine fuelled sing songs around the camp fire. They left early the following morning and we watched as Amber trundled slowly away from us across the field and out of sight.

Later that same morning I wrote this:-

Sitting down to write this pome,
Now that Amber's lot's gone 'ome.

We've lots of empty hours to fill,
The weather here is sunny still.

Alone again it's kinda sad,
Thinking of the fun we had.
Parked up in a flooded field,
Waiting for the rain to yield.

We all endured that stormy weather,
Then finally we got together.
Some memorable nights at Manta Rota,
Where all of us out drunk our quota.

Chestnuts roasting on the fire,
The full moon rising higher and higher.
That week we had was mucho fun,
Then sadly our new friends had to run.

Maybe next year, maybe never,
We will all get back together.
We really hope they hit the trail,
And join us o'er hill and dale.

We never did see them again.

A few days later we moved back to Cabeço and parked in our original spot by the dunes, some of the vans had gone so there was plenty of space again. One day a big green traveller's truck pulled slowly onto the car park and parked by us.

It was a Brit and it had no windows but there was a chimney sticking out of the roof so it was being used for living in. We declared right then that we would get something just like that for us all to live in. It looked really big parked next to Billy and in fact it was so big we could almost have put him inside it.

It wasn't long before Suzi got chatting to the people in it. The truck belonged to Paul, a new age traveller and he was giving a lift to Steve who he'd picked up somewhere in Spain as his motorbike had broken down and was now in the back of the truck. They were both on their way to an inland lake called Santa Clara which apparently was a popular park up for travellers.

The truck was an old Leyland FG350 which had started life as a bread van and Paul was more than happy to give us a guided tour of the inside.

As it turned out there wasn't much to see inside apart from a dirty mattress and sleeping bag on the floor, a small wood burning stove and a very old sofa roped to the side of the truck. His toilet was the great outdoors and he did all his cooking on a small single burner camping stove. There were a few cardboard boxes and black bin bags kicking about and Steve's motorbike was roped to the side just like the sofa. He had no washing facilities but then he *was* a new age traveler so that wasn't really very high on his list of priorities.

Hardly a palace but it was the space which impressed us most, that and the wood burner of course what a luxury that would be, not forgetting the permanent bed, we really wanted a permanent bed. In short, we wanted a lorry at least as big as Paul's, one that we could design ourselves and do up really nicely.

He told us of a truck he'd heard about which might still be for sale, it was a Leyland FG like his but a bigger version which sounded good to us. His truck was massive compared to what we were used to, we could easily live comfortably in it so the thought of something even bigger got us quite excited.

The bloke who was selling it lived somewhere in the French Pyrenees, he wasn't sure exactly where but he gave us his phone number so we could contact him when we were next in the area. We'd already planned on going back to France in the spring to find some work so we could check it out then.

I roughly measured the inside of his truck and when we got back to Billy we immediately put pen to paper and drew some initial designs.

That night to our dismay Paul and Steve lit a huge bonfire right in the middle of the car park. It was far too big for our liking but they wouldn't listen to us and just kept piling more wood on. The fire attracted people from the other vans and soon there was quite a gathering around the fire all chatting and drinking. Paul and Steve disappeared for a while and then we saw them putting huge loudspeakers on the roof of his truck. Next thing we knew, Bob Marley was blasting out at full volume entertaining anyone living within a couple of miles.

Now we like Bob Marley and we like camp fires but this was just asking for trouble. We weren't happy about it at all and just knew it would attract attention from the police and we really didn't want to spoil things and get moved on from here. They didn't really care as they were only here for one night and we did think about moving but for some reason decided to take a chance on it. We spent a very nervous evening, enjoying the fire and the music but always looking over our shoulders.

We really should have listened to ourselves as around midnight, the police turned up in their jeep and they were not impressed. They kept saying 'No camping!' over and over again and told us to put the fire out immediately as it was a fire risk and as far as I could make out the music could be heard in Monte Gordo.

We were kicking ourselves - if we'd left earlier we wouldn't have been known to the police who were now busy taking all our numbers and telling us to be gone by the morning. Annoyingly Paul and Steve insisted on arguing with them in English which not only annoyed them further but was a complete waste of time anyway as they didn't speak a word of English except for the 'No camping!' bit. They waited around for half an hour and watched whilst we put the fire out and then left.

One good thing I noticed though was how much Portuguese we could now understand, we understood more than we could speak but we were taking to the language quite easily. Late though it was we decided not to wait until the morning; instead we packed up and left immediately for Monte Gordo. We reckoned the Police would be keeping an eye out here for a few days at least so we planned to avoid going back for a while.

We got a really nice greeting from gobadog in the morning who seemed really happy to see us again. He laughed and clapped his hands in glee when we returned his 'Bom Dia' and in celebration, he dragged his throat up enthusiastically and gobbed it all out on the floor. He didn't have his little dog with him that morning so sadly that one went to waste.

We'd very quickly learnt to watch where we were walking as spitting seemed to be a very popular pastime with the local people. If we didn't actually see it in flight then the sound could always be heard wherever we went. If ever there was something ominous looking on the pavement (and there very often was) it was safe to assume that it wasn't bird shit and sadly, walking barefoot had now become a thing of the past. One dollop of that sticky mess stuck between the toes was more than enough to curtail *that* particular pastime.

One morning we were sitting outside a busy café enjoying a cup of coffee in the sunshine, just passing the time of day and watching the world going slowly by. Parked just across the road from us was a donkey and cart which it seemed, was still a main form of transport for some people in the area. Suzi had just returned from having her obligatory cuddle with the donkey when a gleaming black Porsche pulled up and parked behind it which naturally turned heads and raised a few eyebrows amongst the locals.

All eyes were on the young female driver as she touched up her already immaculate make up in the mirror before stepping out carefully and properly so as not to reveal too much leg. She was very classily dressed in expensive designer clothes and clutching a briefcase - clearly a high flyer.

Her high heels wobbled on the cobbles and everyone fell silent as she bent to close the door. She straightened up, tossed her hair and smoothed her skirt down then she dragged her throat up noisily and gobbed it all out, right into the middle of the road before clip clopping off into the distance.

☺ ☺ ☺ ☺ ☺

Our first Christmas abroad was spent parked on the front at Monte Gordo.

We took a backpack with food and drink and set off for a long walk along the beach. Even though it was yet another beautifully sunny day under a cloudless blue sky, we were well wrapped up as there was a cool sea breeze blowing. Because we'd been here a while now we'd become acclimatized to the temperatures and were feeling it quite cool. If we went back into the dunes where it was more sheltered it was pleasantly warm but not warm enough to strip off. However, the people who had come to the Algarve for the winter or just for

Christmas were obviously finding it quite warm and were wearing lighter clothes and sunbathing.

We carried on past Manta Rota until we came to the break in the beach where the sea came in. We had a lovely picnic in the soft white sand up by the dunes followed by a short siesta before setting off back. As we neared Monte Gordo again the boys made friends with a Portuguese man walking the shoreline and we got talking.

His name was José and he lived and worked in Paris. He was staying for just a few days before heading to his parent's house after having a holiday in Morocco. All this we learned from a combination of Portuguese and French as he spoke no English at all.

Far from being a barrier we saw it as an opportunity to learn Portuguese and so we saw quite a lot of him over the next couple of days as he would often call round to Billy for a coffee and a chat. He would soon be leaving for his home town of Sesimbra - a very beautiful place just South of Lisbon which he insisted we must visit.

I'm still not really sure how it happened but we somehow found ourselves agreeing to give him a lift. I blame Suzi - she likes giving people lifts! We weren't planning a road trip so soon but it could be fun and it seemed like a good opportunity to visit somewhere new and also continue our Portuguese lessons.

And so the very next day after nightfall, José turned up with a rucksack on his back and carrying two big heavy holdalls. We had wanted to go earlier in the day so we could see the scenery but no, it had to be after dark for some reason. He wanted to stow his bags away somewhere but there was no room in any of the cupboards for them (they were all full of tea bags!) so they were just stacked up on the floor.

266

All aboard and we set off eastwards along the EN125. I had the route all planned and was intending to take the main road up towards Lisbon, turning right somewhere near Albufeira. José as it turned out had other plans, he reckoned he knew a better way so no need for a map. Fair enough I thought, he probably knows his way around here better than I do so I was quite happy to follow his instructions.

We were pootling along quite nicely and had just passed Faro when suddenly…

'Vire à direita!' came a shout from the back which I didn't understand.

'Que?' I shouted back just as his head appeared between the seats.

'Vire à direita,' he repeated, pointing to a turning on the right which we were just about to pass, 'Aqui aqui.'

'Ahh turn right – well why didn't you say that then!' I hit the brakes and with tyres screeching, swerved sharply and took the turning. His head disappeared, there was a crash followed by a shout and a couple of seconds later he re-appeared between the seats laughing.

'Ha ha ha, maluco!!'

That night we were to learn turn right, turn left, go straight on, go faster and slow down but more importantly, we learnt how to swear at other drivers – it was a lot of fun and he was a good teacher!

We arrived safely in Loule and he guided us to the town centre where there was a lovely nativity scene set up in the town square. He insisted we all get out and have a walk around which we did but it was really cold and five minutes later we were mobile again.

It looked like we would be taking the scenic route to Lisbon then, as instead of heading back down to the main road José guided us out of town heading north. If this was going to turn into a sight seeing trip then we had the prospect of a long night ahead of us.

Steve Earle's 'Guitar Town', one of our favourite travelling albums was playing on the stereo and we were singing along loudly with him much to José's delight. His head popped up again and he asked who it was.

'Steve Earle,' replied Suzi .

'Quem?'

'Steve Earle!' we both shouted between lines.

'Ahh Stivurl, gosto gosto,' he laughed and from then on all three of us were singing along with 'Stiv' at the tops of our voices.

The road deteriorated rapidly and our pace slowed, surely this can't be the best road to Lisbon, where the hell was he taking us? It wouldn't be so bad if it was daylight and we could actually see the countryside but it was pitch black, tedious and uncomfortable.

The plus side to having a passenger in the back was that whenever a cupboard flew open and vomited its contents all over the floor he was on hand to shove everything back in again, it saved us a job anyway.

I felt a slap on the shoulder and his face appeared between the seats again.

'Pare aqui,' he said matter-of-factly, pointing to a lay by just up ahead with a couple of cars in it - he wanted me to stop.

'Aqui?'

'Sim sim, aqui aqui', he repeated and so I pulled into the unlit lay by.

'Agora café,' he announced.

'Café aqui, onde?' I couldn't see one anywhere.

'Sim, bom café aqui,' he assured us, laughing at our confusion as we looked at each other doubtfully.

We all got out of Billy and he led us through a gap in the hedge where we followed a narrow, well worn path up through the trees, emerging at a small house set on a rocky terrace. José opened the door without knocking and we went in.

We were in what appeared to be someone's front room which had been converted to a café/bar; José obviously knew the owner and was greeted warmly, as were we. Apart from the man with a towel over his shoulder behind the counter there were only two other men in there, they were sitting at a table by a small open fire, quietly drinking their beers.

A television perched high up in one corner was silently playing a football match which no-one was watching. A big black dog walked nonchalantly into the room and sniffed us all in turn before turning and quietly walking out again. We sat on stools at the bar and Jose ordered coffees.

Three espressos appeared on the counter accompanied by three small glasses of water and a bowl of what looked like some sort of beans.

José drank his coffee in one swallow quickly followed by the water, gesturing for us to do the same, which we did. He was right, it was really good coffee here, thick strong and sweet (well mine was sweet anyway!)

Now the water, drink the water quickly, that's it, good. The owner was pleased with our performance and we learned that the coffees were called 'bicas' not espressos.

We moved onto the beans which were round and flattish and pale yellow in colour, they were delicious and José demonstrated the right way to eat them. He popped one in his mouth and chewed for a bit, then a few seconds later took the skin out and placed it in a small bowl - the rest of the bean was then eaten. He had a couple more before leaving the rest to us and the bowl emptied fast, much to the obvious delight of the owner, and José.

'Gosto?'

'Sim gosto,' we both replied.

'Feijão?' asked Suzi as we reckoned they were beans.

'Nao feijão,' replied Jose and the owner shook his head in agreement. They both struggled for an English word for them but failed, the two men by the fire didn't know and the owner's wife who was called into the room didn't know either. Books were consulted and even phone calls were made to friends but all to no avail, defeat was admitted and we left without knowing the answer.

We continued our torturous, bone jarring journey through the night, feeling a little more awake now after the coffee. Some time later we entered a small, sleepy, nameless town and following José's instructions I parked Billy near a small cobbled square. All around the perimeter there were orange trees adorned with twinkling white fairy lights and dominating the centre of the square was a brightly lit nativity scene.

'Boa laranjas aqui, prove,' said José, urging us to try the oranges which we did but immediately wished we hadn't. They were really bitter and we spat them out quickly much to José's amusement.

'Nao para comer!' (not for eating) he said laughing, pointing at Suzi's screwed up face, well I knew *that* was a mistake.

He was so busy laughing he didn't see it coming and a segment of orange hit him in the face with a soggy splat. He turned and fled when he realized there was more on the way and Suzi gave chase. He took cover behind the nativity scene dodging bits of orange until her ammunition ran out and then he crept back out slowly with his hands in the air.

A truce was called and he took us down a dimly lit street leading off the square. He stopped at what looked to us like a tatty old garage door which had been painted red many years before. There was a smaller door within the big one and after looking up and down the street he opened it and went in.

Inside, was a small whitewashed room full of late night revelers, all of them men, all talking quietly amongst themselves and enjoying a beer. At one table a game of dominos was in full swing and a thick cloud of cigarette smoke hung in the air. Luckily for us most of it was up in the darkness of the high, open raftered ceiling. There was no music playing and no TV stuck up in the corner, the only sound being the low hum of voices.

There was a bar of sorts over in the far corner which had been crudely made from rough timber. Two wooden barrels served as tables with the seats being upended wooden beer crates. There were a few wooden chairs here and there which were occupied by the luckier ones but apart from that everyone else was standing.

Heads turned in our direction as we made our way slowly towards the bar - ah foreigners.

'Boa noite,'

'Boa noite,'

Everyone greeted us in turn and we were made to feel very welcome in what was most likely their secret drinking place. José ordered, and three 'bicas' were placed on the shiny bar top, it wasn't shiny from varnish or polish but worn that way from years of use.

He then began telling them the story about the orange eating episode which brought smug smiles and knowing looks from amongst his audience and even a comforting pat on the shoulder for Suzi. I got the impression we weren't the first poor travellers to be fooled into that one.

More coffees appeared on the bar and no, he didn't want paying for them they were on the house, not sure if it was some form of recompense but it did have something to do with the oranges.

We stayed for about ten minutes and then left, getting a quiet 'Boa noite' from everyone on the way out.

Looking back at those tatty old garage doors amongst all the others we would never have known there was a bar in there and we would certainly never have found it on our own.

'Musica!' came the shouted instruction from the back.

'Que musica?'

'Stivvurl!' came the reply.

'Ok then, Stivvurl it is, I said as I shoved the tape in.

Suzi turned the volume up really loud and we all bellowed out the songs as we rattled and banged our way along.

We had no idea where we were but then we were quite used to that by now. We knew we were heading for Lisbon because we kept seeing signs for Lisboa, in fact wherever we went in Portugal there would always be a sign for Lisboa. Even on the remotest of insignificant junctions in the middle of nowhere there would always be one, none to anywhere else just the solitary one to Lisboa.

There was little or no traffic, partly because of the hour but mainly I suspected due to the appalling condition of the road, surely there must be a better route to Lisbon than this. José appeared between us again.

'Café, pare aqui,' he said pointing up ahead, seems like more coffee was needed. I wasn't so sure but I pulled into the car park of a small roadside bar and was just about to park when Jose cursed.

'Oh merde policia!, vai vai!' he hissed urging me to keep going. There was a police car parked outside the door of the bar and we could see the officers inside at the counter.

'What, I thought you wanted coffee?'

'No no no, no café aqui, vai Tim vai,' he insisted, laughing nervously and waving me on with both hands.

'OK then no coffee,' I said shrugging as we left the welcome smoothness of the car park and hit the road again.

From there on the road narrowed as we climbed into the hills, the pot holes became bigger and more frequent, our speed slowed even more, and then it started snowing! Well that wasn't in the script when we planned our nice warm sunny winter!

We were all freezing at this point as well because Billy's heater was rubbish. It was on full blast but there was no hot air coming from it at all. This was due mainly to the fact that Billy kept his engine in the back and by the time the heat had made its way to the front it had gone cold. Visibility was practically zero as well now and we crawled along straining to see the road ahead through the now, heavily falling snow.

Some hours later and just before dawn, our arduous journey was thankfully over and we arrived safely in Sesimbra, parking outside José's parent's house in four inches of snow. I helped him with his bags; they were really heavy, what the hell was in them?

There was no-one home and no-one had been there since the summer holidays. A fact confirmed by the damp musty smell about the place - it felt colder inside than it did outside.

He then very proudly gave us a guided tour of the entire house. Every room was completely covered in busily patterned ceramic tiles, all four walls from floor to ceiling as well as the floor. He kindly offered us a bed for the night but when I put my hand in the bed it felt really cold and damp. We just couldn't contemplate stripping off in this walk-in fridge of a house and then slipping in between two sheets of ice so we decided to spend what was left of the night sleeping in Billy.

It was really cold but at least we had Caine as a hot water bottle and we also kept the roof down which helped to keep the warmth in.

ꙮ ꙮ ꙮ ꙮ ꙮ

I got up a couple of hours later when it came light, put the gas fire on and got back into bed while Billy warmed up.

Getting back into that narrow bed was no easy feat I can tell you, and looking at it with Suzi and Caine still snoring away happily it's hard to believe there was ever any room in there for me in the first place.

I squoze myself feet first into the narrow gap which Suzi had very thoughtfully left me, sliding in from the top end and doing my best not to knee her in the head. I then encountered the immovable Caine mountain and I tried to nudge him out of the way a bit but he wasn't budging so I had to really force my way down, eventually dislodging him enough for me to get in properly.

Well I may have managed to get into bed ok but now of course I hardly had any duvet and it was literally freezing. No matter how hard I pulled there was no more coming my way and trying to pull a duvet from underneath 40 kilos of sleeping dog is no easy feat, especially in my usual early morning weakened state. As well as Caines dead weight there was Suzi and her legendary vice like grip on the duvet. I don't know what it is but some sort of strange metamorphosis seems to take place. She turns green and becomes freakishly strong so between the two of them I didn't have a hope of getting warm again.

Eventually I gave it up as a bad job and did what I should have done in the first place - I got up and made the breakfast.

Sounds easy but it wasn't. The roof was still down and it had to stay down if we were to warm up at all so I was either bent double or I was on my knees. The bed was still down so that it was covering the cupboards and drawers where things like the crockery and cutlery were kept so I had to lift the end of it to get things out. It was the pillow end and sleeping beauty was still snoring away so the fun part was letting it down again with a crash. It was surprising how many times I had to go into those cupboards you know!

We had breakfast on the bed and then we all went for a walk around the town in the rapidly melting snow. Later on José took us to the petrol station and filled Billy's tank to overflowing as a thankyou for the ride. The snow had practically all gone by then and he took us on a sightseeing tour of the 'Serra da Arrabida' National Park. The scenery was breathtaking as we drove along the coast through the tree lined hills which rose up steeply from the deep blue waters of the Atlantic.

He was excited about showing us somewhere 'special' and he told me to turn off the main road and then pull over at the side of the road on a small grassy verge. We all got out and followed a narrow twisty path which led us down through the trees towards the sea. The path became steps the steeper it got and José told us to count them as we went. We got to around two hundred but then lost count, seduced by the beauty of our surroundings.

We made the final descent down a stone stairway and into the darkness of a huge cave carved from layers of different coloured rock. At the back of the cave stood an ancient, roofed chapel where in times gone by the local fishermen would come to pray. There was a magical eerie silence about the place, broken only by the thump and crash of the waves and the whole scene was lit by the natural light flooding in from two jagged openings.

We spent a long time sitting on the rocks at the cave's entrance mesmerized by the clear blue sea and the crashing waves echoing around the cave behind us. Caine looked down longingly at the water just dying to jump in for a swim. I'm glad he didn't, I've no idea how we'd have got him out again!

Later that evening we drove down to Portinho da Arrabida, past the cave, around the headland and down onto a seafront car park. It literally *was* a seafront car park with just a low concrete kerb along the edge and then a twenty foot drop down into the water below. I found a space and pulled in facing the sea until the tyres bumped gently against the kerb. It's a good job Suzi's brakes were working otherwise we'd have been over the edge!

José knew the owner of the restaurant which was perched on stilts at the far end of the sea wall and we were greeted warmly. It was a cold evening and coffees were brought to our outdoor table. The reflection of a million stars twinkled on the still water as José serenaded us with some Portuguese songs.

As the night grew colder we moved indoors to eat and José insisted I go and get the boys from Billy and bring them to the table. We were doubtful about this but he asked the owner who agreed quite happily.

The boys were delighted, especially Caine who loved to be amongst people and of course he went round to every table saying hello to everybody. Predictably, Nelson ignored everybody and went straight up to our table and sat down quietly right next to his Suzi. Eventually Caine calmed down a bit and came over to us to see if there was any food left for him. Our plates were clean but José had left nearly all of his salad and Caine wanted it.

José didn't believe that he would eat it so Suzi took his plate and handed a piece of tomato to Caine who of course wolfed it down happily. José laughed, he couldn't believe he'd just seen a dog eating tomato and he called the owner over. Other heads were turning too as Caine made the rest of the tomato disappear to a round of applause from his growing audience.

This adulation only spurred him on and now the whole restaurant had stopped eating and everyone was watching and taking pictures of this crazy dog eating tomatoes. Caine wasn't finished yet though and Suzi handed him some cucumber and that was devoured as well, quickly followed by all the lettuce.

Everyone was in hysterics but to us it was all perfectly normal, Caine just loved his fruit and veg. When the plate was empty someone called him over to their table and hand fed him *their* salad. Then someone else did the same until he'd been round the whole place clearing all their plates for them - it seemed no-one ate salad around here!

Eventually, when the show was over and there wasn't a scrap of salad left anywhere he came over to us wagging his tail furiously and flopped down next to Nelson.

Not for long though, he'd spotted someone eating an orange at the next table and in the blink of an eye he was sitting next to them asking for a piece. The orange eater looked over at us questioningly - he won't eat this will he?

Oh yes he will he loves his oranges, go on give him some.

He was handed a piece which of course he ate and then asked for another, which he got. They just couldn't believe it, a dog eating oranges, incredible, the whole place was in uproar. All eyes were on him and even the kitchen staff had all come out to see this mad English dog eating fruit and salad.

The whole mood of the restaurant changed after that with everyone talking and joking with each other across the room. The wine flowed, José sang more songs, more food was ordered and a very merry night was had by all. When we eventually got up to go everyone called to Caine and he had to go round everyone to say good night before he was allowed out of the door - something he was more than happy to do.

When we went to pay our bill the owner insisted there was no charge, he was delighted with all the extra business that Caine had whipped up for him. No no no señor, no money necessary – yes, nice one Caine!!

From there we drove to a beach just in time to see the New Year in, Portuguese style.

Groups of people were gathered around the many fires which were burning all along the shoreline. As midnight approached everyone left the cafés and bars and gathered down on the beach to watch the spectacular fireworks display. After that the brave ones stripped off and ran into the water to take the traditional dip in the Atlantic. The reason for all the fires then became clear as they all huddled around them trying to dry off and get warm again.

We weren't amongst the brave ones and we didn't stay too long after that as José was leaving for Paris early the following day.

After loading his bags into Billy the next morning he took us to the filling station and filled Billy's tank up again despite us insisting there was really no need. Afterwards he asked us if we would take him to meet a friend of his before taking him to the train station.

He directed me to a piece of wasteland behind some old buildings where he said his friend would be. I parked up and we waited, strange place to meet a friend I thought.

A few minutes later a black BMW approached and pulled up right alongside, the passenger got out and José slid the side door open. He then opened up both his holdalls and our eyes widened - they were both full of large blocks of hard black stuff wrapped in polythene. We looked at each other and we both instantly knew what *that* was and it wasn't chocolate!

His 'friend' inspected them all before putting them back, had a quick look over his shoulder and then handed over a carrier bag full of banknotes to José who counted and pocketed it quickly. His 'friend' then grabbed the holdalls and put them in the boot of his car before driving off; hardly a word had been spoken the whole time.

José sat back laughing and with a huge beaming smile on his face he told us how he'd brought sixty kilos of 'Moroccan Black' hashish back with him from Africa. He now had enough money to live on for quite some time.

He could see we weren't very happy with him and still tittering away to himself, he counted out a thick wad of cash from his carrier bag and offered it to us - we politely declined.

'Well that explains why he brought us up here on all those silly little back roads doesn't it,' said Suzi after we'd dropped him off at the station, 'and in the dark as well!'

'It does and no bloody wonder he didn't want to stop at that café where the police car was,' I laughed, 'and remember how he told us he'd come back from Morocco on a friend's boat instead of on the ferry. Well that explains why doesn't it, he'd never have got that little lot through customs would he?'

We didn't go back down to the Algarve the same way, instead we took the main road, the one we would have come up on if I'd had my way. It looked quite new and was beautifully surfaced; a real pleasure to drive on and we reached the Algarve in no time at all.

'Oh my god we would have been right in the shit if we'd have been stopped and searched wouldn't we. They would never have believed it was nothing to do with us would they?' said Suzi, all sorts of horrors running through her mind.

'I wonder what the Portuguese jails are like.' I said thoughtfully.

'Oh shut up Tim that's not funny, we've just carried sixty kilos of hash halfway across the country, that's drug trafficking that is - oh my god we're bloody drug traffickers!'

☺ ☺ ☺ ☺ ☺

Back on the Algarve, we were craving some seclusion and solitude; somewhere well away from all the other campers. I'd seen a reservoir in our atlas which looked fairly isolated and wasn't too far away called Barragem de Beliche.

We still had plenty of water on board and anyway, we were going to be parked next to a reservoir so that shouldn't be a problem. After re-stocking our food cupboards we set off.

Our route would take us through Castro Marim which was somewhere we wanted to visit but before we reached there we came to a crossroads.

Castro Marim was to the right, but left looked more interesting to us and also to Nelson who was sharing Suzi's seat. He looked left and started fidgeting, so left it was. Then after a couple of hundred metres or so I turned right for no particular reason onto a narrow road. It led us up into the hills and down into valleys, past remote homesteads and wandering goatherds until eventually we saw the reservoir.

Our hearts sank as we approached the dam as the first thing we saw was a cluster of French camping cars parked up on the left hand side - we drove on.

There were two German vans parked off to the right as well so we carried on again, driving over the dam itself in the hope it would be quieter over the other side.

No such luck, the Brits occupied this side. There was an old converted bus and two old lorries all painted in the traditional traveller colours of dark green and maroon, surrounded by bikes and toys - we didn't stop there either.

Instead we followed the road around the lake but then it seemed to start taking us away from it. We wanted to be close to the water so I turned left onto the first track we came to; it was quite steep and very bumpy with deep channels in it caused by the rainwater. With a bit of luck nobody would even contemplate driving down a track that bad so there was a good chance we would be the only ones at the end of it - wherever that may be.

I picked my way carefully and Billy lurched and bounced his way slowly down the track until eventually we were back by the lake and right down at water level. The track came to an end right at the water's edge and as luck would have it there was some fairly level ground to park on. I pulled Billy off the track and parked side on to the water, dug holes for his wheels to settle into for levelness, put the roof up and the kettle on.

With the side door facing the water it was like having our very own exclusive lakeside retreat. We laid a blanket on the ground and drank tea as we took in our new surroundings. It was so peaceful; there wasn't a sound to be heard and not a house in sight anywhere. There were no camping cars, no people and no traffic. There was just us, the lake and the hills under a cloudless blue sky - it was heaven.

We weren't keen to leave and somehow we made our food supply last nearly three weeks. The water had run out long ago and we were now drinking the lake water. In the beginning we went to the trouble of boiling it first but that didn't last long. We really didn't want to leave this wonderful place so we stopped boiling it to make the gas last longer, well that and the fact that we just got fed up of doing it! We'd been drinking the water straight from the lake for over two weeks now without any problems.

Sadly though, the time came when we simply had to leave as there was no food left. With heavy hearts we packed everything away, vowing to return as soon as possible. It had rained heavily the previous day and all through the night and the dry dusty ground around Billy had turned to thick gloopy mud - it was probably a good time to go anyway.

We got about twenty metres up the track but then as soon as we hit the slippery slope Billy's wheels started spinning, his tyres struggling for grip. I had to be really careful not to slide sideways or we'd end up in one of those deep ruts and then we'd be stuck good and proper. I made several attempts to get up the track but we simply weren't getting anywhere. I even turned Billy round and tried reversing up in the hope that would make some sort of difference, but it didn't.

I had to admit defeat before Billy got hurt and so I settled him back into his original spot down by the water.

Despite the fact that we were surrounded by all that mud, it was still a beautiful place to be stranded. The main problem was the fact that we had no food, hardly any gas and were miles from any shops.

Well we wouldn't die of thirst that was for sure, but we had to find some food from somewhere and I couldn't imagine there being a shop anywhere around these parts. We had to do something so we set off on foot up the muddy track leaving Billy there all by himself. Looking back down he did look a bit lonely and we hoped he would be ok whilst we were gone.

We reached the tarmac road at the top of the track and then had to decide whether to go left or right.

If we went right, back towards the dam we knew there was no town or village for a very long way. And if we went left we had no idea how far it would be, it could be even further and the atlas didn't show small towns and villages anyway so that was no help.

We were still pondering over this dilemma when we realized the boys had gone off down a dirt track opposite. Nelson was leading the way as usual and just before he went out of sight he sat down and refused to come back. Suzi said 'Looks like Nelly wants us to go that way, he seems to know where he's going and he's usually right isn't he.'

'Usually yeah, but he could just as easily be following the smell of a rabbit.'

I looked to the left, picturing a town just around the corner with a nice big supermercado full of food.

'Well I think we should follow him,' she called, skipping off down the track, 'we've got nothing to lose have we, come on!'

I wasn't so sure about that, but then thinking about it I *was* up against a dog who was *usually* right and a wife who was *always* right!

Well ok we'll go that way then I thought, even though it *is* just a dirt track leading off into the wilderness. I banished all thoughts of my imaginary supermercado and ran after them.

We followed the track as it meandered its way around the open countryside and after a couple of kilometers or so we came to a cluster of small white houses in the middle of nowhere called Sentinela. Some of the houses were in a poor state of repair with sagging roofs, crumbling walls and overgrown gardens while others were immaculate and freshly painted. There were low whitewashed walls around the gardens from behind which, the local dogs eyed us lazily as we passed.

Apart from them we saw no signs of life other than one wrinkly old lady dressed all in black sitting on her doorstep. As we approached she pulled her skirt down to cover her ankles as best she could and mumbled a greeting to us as we passed. There was no sign of a shop anywhere and it only took us a couple of minutes to walk around the whole place, then we were back at the old lady on the step again.

We exchanged greetings with her again and then just as we were passing a little white van rattled its way along the cobbles and stopped next to her. Our luck was in, the driver opened up the back doors and a pao grande fell out and rolled across the cobbles - it was a bread van.

The runaway loaf was quickly retrieved and carelessly chucked back in on top of all the others which were piled up on the floor. They weren't in baskets or on shelves or anything and they weren't even wrapped. They were just tossed in haphazardly onto the worn metal flooring. The old lady bought some papo secos and then left us drooling as she spent the next ten minutes talking to the baker.

When our turn came we bought three pao grandes and six papo secos and luckily he had some used carrier bags for us - then we headed back to Billy.

So we had a good supply of water and we now had bread. We also had at least a year's supply of tea bags so we were going to be living on tea and toast until we could get Billy out again. The ground was already starting to dry out and as long as it didn't rain again for a day or two we'd be able to get out ok - unfortunately for us though, later that night it did rain again.

The gas had finally run out and long hours were spent walking the hillsides collecting wood for the small fire which we had to make every time we needed to make toast or to boil our now smoke - blackened kettle for tea.

The days were warm and sunny again, the nights dark and starry and despite the fact that we were stuck there and living on tea and toast we were loving every minute of it. We took advantage of the good weather to give Billy a good airing. The seat cushions were taken out and put in the sun to dry and to our surprise, tucked underneath one of them we found a wad of banknotes.

We looked at each other – José!

He must have put it there for us to find after we refused to take it from him. I counted it and there was 50,000 escudos altogether which was about £200. Well we couldn't exactly give it back to him now could we and at our current rate of spending that was enough for us to live on for over two months!

We laughed - it would last us a lot longer than that if we couldn't get to any shops to spend it!

We managed to make the bread last for ten days, it was really stale by this time but once toasted it was fine.

There was hardly a sound to be heard, just the odd dog barking each day at around sunset time. We saw no-one the whole time we were there, well that is until the day we became surrounded by men walking about with shotguns. Most of them had camouflage jackets and caps on and they were just blasting away at anything and everything they could find - it was mayhem!

They were walking about aimlessly, going this way and that, shooting in all directions. It seemed like just a matter of time before one of them got themselves shot, but as it turned out it was me and Billy who got shot.

We were cowering inside with the radio on really loud in a futile attempt to block it all out and we had the side door open to give us a view of the lake as a distraction to all the carnage going on around us. Nelson wasn't at all happy - he was sulking because we made him sit inside out of harms way. Caine was even less happy - he was scared of all the loud bangs and he just wanted to go.

Suddenly there was what sounded like gravel landing on Billy and then something stung me on the leg. I looked down; it wasn't gravel but lead shot from one of their guns. It felt like a bee sting and luckily it didn't pierce the skin. I picked it up and rolled it along the table - we looked at each other and declared it was time to leave.

We hastily packed everything away and made a dash for freedom. The track was pretty dry now although it was still a bit sticky and slippery underfoot, but for safety's sake we decided to give it a go anyway.

We set off up the track, skidding and sliding our way up, trying not to slide sideways into the ruts and we made steady progress. It looked like we were going to make it until we turned a corner to find part of the track had been completely washed away by the rain. There was a gully about six feet wide and two foot deep right across the track, we were going nowhere. There was nothing else for it, we would have to try and fill it in ourselves.

We only had one little spade, so Suzi took that and started digging and throwing earth into the hole whilst I gathered big stones and bits of wood, anything I could find really to chuck in the hole. A cup of tea would have been nice at this point but we couldn't be bothered with collecting firewood and lighting a fire so we plodded on. It was hard work and we tired easily, due mainly to the fact that we'd been living on bread and water for the past ten days or so.

With frequent rest breaks we toiled away for hours as world war three raged all around us until eventually we'd filled it in enough to drive over, well that's what we hoped for anyway. We now had a narrow strip of earth across the gap, just wide enough for Billy to go on but it was a bit lower than the original track and we hoped it would be ok.

I got back into Billy as Suzi stood on the far side watching and guiding me, making sure the wheels didn't sink in. If Billy got stuck or fell off the edge we'd be right in the fertilizer.

I inched forward carefully but as soon as his wheels were on the new bit I felt the front go down. This was confirmed by a frantically waving wife so I backed off again. We would just have to build it up some more. I filled the fresh ruts in, drove forward again and this time the wheels didn't sink in.

Then I inched further forward and they sunk in again so I backed off and filled those in. This process was repeated several times until Billy's front wheels had reached the far side. The real test would come when his back end got onto it as that was where his main weight was. The wheels did sink in a bit but we'd done a good construction job and slowly but surely Billy made his way across until we were safely on the other side.

Dripping with sweat and plastered in mud, we danced a little jig and made a final bid for freedom.

On the way back we passed slowly through the tiny hamlet of Botelhas and then found we could go no further as the recent rains had completely washed the tarmac road away.

We didn't fancy trying to fill that one in as well so we quickly turned around and found another way back.

ରୁ ରୁ ରୁ ରୁ ରୁ

At Cabeço one day, a couple of German backpackers came up off the beach and asked if they could have some water. We were just about to eat so we invited them to join us.

Over lunch they told us how they'd taken a year out and were now walking the entire length of the Algarve, stopping for a while to do some work and then moving on again. Their previous week had been spent house minding near Monchique for a Dutch couple whilst they went on holiday.

This gave us an idea and so the next day we put an advert in the Algarve magazine advertising our services as house and animal minders. As luck would have it about a week later a letter arrived from a couple who wanted to visit family in England for two weeks. They were desperately looking for someone to look after their house, two horses, three dogs and a cat.

We rang them straight away and arranged a day to go and see them; they lived not far from Lagos at the other end of the Algarve near a place called Odiaxiere. We found their place quite easily and as we turned off the road a couple of dogs ran down the track and noisily escorted us up to the house, announcing our arrival to anyone within half a mile.

Penny and Ron were a retired couple who'd emigrated about ten years before and renovated the old farmhouse in which they now lived. They loved living on the Algarve but they hadn't been able to visit family in the UK for some time now as they couldn't leave their animals.

'So glad we found you,' said Penny, 'been dying to see the kids and grandkids for ages, let me show you round the place.'

Ron then wandered off to do something else leaving Penny to do all the talking, something it turned out, she was pretty good at.

'Right, well you've already met the dogs, this ones Jem, this ones Maggie and this little runt here is Fido, we love him dearly.'

Fido was a peculiar little thing with a very sad tale to tell. A friend of theirs had been driving along one day when they saw this little dog being thrown out of a car window up ahead of them. It landed in the road and then got run over by the following car which didn't even bother stopping.

Their friend stopped and took him to the vets, who after taking one look at the mess he was in said it would be better and cheaper to have him put down. Instead they, together with Penny and Ron and a few other friends all chipped in to pay for his quite extensive treatment and then he eventually came to live here.

His head was all mangled on the left side and part of his face was missing, exposing some of his teeth. It looked like he was snarling all the time but he wasn't though, he was so gentle and friendly. His left ear had been ripped off and he'd lost an eye, also large patches of his fur were missing which would never grow back. He moved with a very strange gait, due partly to now only having three legs after losing a front one, but mainly because of the fact that his hips had been all smashed up.

Despite all of this he was such a happy little chappy. He loved everyone and got around fine if a little slowly and he could even play with the other dogs.

'Oh you've got dogs,' said Penny seeing the boys watching intently from the front seats, 'let them out, looks like they're dying to meet this rabble.'

I let them out and for the next five minutes the inevitable chaos ensued until everyone had calmed down. Fido took to Caine instantly and the two of them were now busy playing and rolling around in the dust which seemed to please Penny no end. 'How much do you charge, do you charge per week or per day or what?

We had absolutely no idea, well we had a very rough figure in mind but we didn't want to charge too much and scare them off as we really needed the money. We ummed and arred for a bit until she lost patience and told us how much she would be happy to pay for the two weeks. It was more than three times the amount we were going to ask for so we gracefully accepted and shook hands on the deal. Everyone was pleased with the outcome and we all relaxed and drank tea.

'Right then come and meet the horses,' said Penny jumping up and striding out. I got the impression she never sat still for very long judging by Ron's resigned expression. We gulped the last of our tea down and hurried out, catching up with her as she strode purposefully across the yard.

'The black one's called Heston and the grey is Tizzy,' she explained pointing to them standing underneath a makeshift awning in a small paddock of ankle deep dust. There wasn't a blade of grass in sight 'Ok then, time to bring them in for a bite to eat,' she announced.

We put their head collars on and led them into their stables, they were very quiet horses.

'Right,' she said as she opened a door next to the stables, 'the hay's in here and we have to weigh it, it's damned expensive around here.'

The hay was duly weighed, then stuffed into nets which we hung up in the stables and the horses tucked in. I topped up their water buckets as Suzi got a guided tour of the feed store and tack room.

A bit later on we led the horses down the lane to a little paddock where there was some grass and we stood with them whilst they grazed. 'Ok that's long enough,' proclaimed patienceless Penny after a couple of minutes and she marched off across the paddock towards the hedge, 'bring them over here to the bamboo, come along, chop chop!'

We led them over and they tucked into the bamboo, pulling at the long leaves, they loved it - meanwhile Penny had already moved on.

'Right, see this tree here,' she called, 'it's a carob tree, they love these, bring them over here and let them pick a few, come along.'

It was the first time we'd seen carob in its natural state and they looked just like black runner beans but hard, wrinkly and brittle.

The dogs were all having great fun running around in the grass, all except for poor old Fido that is who was having a bit of trouble keeping up. We led the horses back to their paddock and then left after arranging to return in a few weeks time when they would be leaving for the UK.

പ്പ പ്പ പ്പ പ്പ

We were heading back to Monte Gordo but instead, after doing some shopping in Faro we turned off the EN125 and headed for somewhere new - Cabanas.

The road was newly surfaced, with modern white villas and palm trees on either side until it narrowed and became cobbled as we entered the old part of town. Many of the houses were traditionally painted in white with blue or yellow around the windows and doors. The ones that weren't were completely covered with busily patterned tiles.

The road took us right to the waters edge and it was either turn left or right. Nelson was looking left so naturally we went left. We drove slowly along the cobbled waterfront past a long line of low rise shops, bars and restaurants and despite the time of year quite a few of them were open.

The wide expanse of water to our right was the river, 'Ria Formosa' which separates the mainland from the low lying Cabanas island or 'Ilha de cabanas'.

We trundled along happily until the road zig zagged a bit and then we trundled some more. Eventually we found a nice quiet place to park right at the far end of town on a small piece of rough ground which happened to be right next to a water tap - very handy.

We got out and started exploring immediately, following a dusty path for a short way until we reached the high stone walls of what looked like some kind of fort. The walls were about twenty feet high with little domed turrets here and there and we followed an overgrown path around them where we came across a pomegranate tree. It looked like we'd missed the best of them but there were still a few fruits left on the higher branches, we picked a few of the best looking ones and took them back to Billy.

On the way back round we saw some almond trees, they looked a bit neglected but there were still some almonds left right at the top of them. Our arms were already full of pomegranates so we decided we would come back later with a carrier bag and get some.

As the tide was fully in we went for a long walk along the beach until we reached a narrow finger of fine, warm white sand reaching out towards the island at its easternmost end. This was the furthest point we'd reached when we walked from Monte Gordo.

We could swim across to the island from here but instead decided to strip off and soak up the warm sunshine. This narrow little sandbank we were on was only about ten feet wide and with the quiet crystal clear water surrounding us it felt like we were marooned on a tiny desert island.

Next day when the tide was out we took a picnic and walked across to the island. Up and over the sand dunes and down onto a magnificent beach of deserted white sand stretching to the far horizon. We walked along right to the far end, opposite our little 'desert island'.

After a couple of hours it looked like the tide was starting to come in so we decided to head back to Billy. We rounded the point and found that the tide really *was* coming in and it was further in than we thought.

There was no dry land between us and the mainland anymore, we were marooned. There was nothing else for it, we would have to wade back across. The tide was still only halfway in so it shouldn't be too deep and we set off through the shallows with the water getting deeper the further we went, it was now up to our waists.

Caine of course was loving it and he was swimming along happily beside us.

Nelson on the other hand was still back on dry land and kicking up a right fuss, screaming and barking at us and running back and forth at the water's edge. The further we went the worse he got and he absolutely would not enter the water. We waited for him and called him but he wouldn't come so we had to go all the way back for him. I managed to pick him up after a bit of a struggle – something else he didn't like - then we set off once more.

Progress was slow as the sand underfoot was quite soft and I was now heavier than I was before so I was sinking in more. It was a job to stay upright but I was determined not to drop him in the water. We were about halfway across when he started struggling in my arms, he'd had quite enough of this indignity thank you very much, 'I don't need to be carried like a baby, let me go!'

The water was getting deeper now, it was up over my waist and up to Suzi's chest. She was now carrying the bag and having to hold it above her head to keep it dry - she was about as happy as Nelson was at this point! His tail was dragging in the water now which was really pissing him off and on top of that Caine was attacking it which really wasn't helping matters. It was bad enough being carried without having to put up with that and he was trying to tell Caine off which only got him more excited - things were getting out of control.

He was wriggling like a worm and I was getting scratched all over, then there was a clash of heads so I just had to let him go. He hated being in the water but he seemed happier to be in control of his own destiny and he set off resolutely - only in the wrong direction!

No amount of calling would make him turn around so I waded after him and turned him round myself. He didn't appreciate being manhandled at all and gave me an angry growl for my troubles. From then on I stayed behind him to make sure he didn't double back again. All this time Caine was swimming alongside trying to play with him but all he got in response was growling and snapping.

Eventually we made it back to dry land where Caine went absolutely bonkers, running around like a lunatic, rolling in the sand and diving on Nelson.

Nelson wasn't amused though and told him so in no uncertain terms, he'd been through quite a traumatic ordeal and just wanted to be left alone. He had a quick roll in the nice dry sand and then set about cleaning himself.

We thought it might be a good idea the next time we went over to the island if we kept a better eye on the tide, if only for Nelsons sake! We soon got the hang of it and crossed to the island at low tide, making sure we didn't stay too long before heading back.

When the tide was right out many of the locals would go clam fishing, digging for them in the soft muddy sand before the tide came back in. As we walked across we would often see things moving on the sand up ahead of us. They were tiny little crabs and they would scuttle along quickly, darting here and there before disappearing down their tiny holes. Nelson was mesmerized by them and foolishly kept sticking his nose down the holes, he never got bitten though.

We spent a week or so there at Cabanas on our first visit and after that, whenever we stayed there we divided our time between our little desert island and the real one, depending on the state of the tide. It was a nice quiet spot, being on the edge of town but also close enough for us to walk to the shops and bars. The odd camper came and went and the police jeep would patrol regularly but they didn't bother us.

Also, being near the water tap meant we could do our washing but we couldn't really put a washing line up there so we just draped everything all over Billy to dry them

We didn't want to outstay our welcome there so we left before the police did move us on and we spent the next few weeks moving between our regular haunts, just staying a few days at a time.

Most of our time was spent either at Monte Gordo, Cabeço, Manta Rota or Cabanas with our other favourite places being Olhao, Faro and Quarteira.

At Quarteira, there was a sandy track which led from the road on the Eastern side of town and went up into the trees overlooking the beach. It was a really peaceful spot to spend a few days and most of the time we were the only ones there. Even so every night the police would patrol the whole area, driving slowly through the trees in their jeep, shining their headlights everywhere.

We would lie awake watching, just waiting for a loud knock on the door but none came, seems they were quite happy for us to be there as long as we behaved ourselves. There was no water there though so that limited us to four or five days per stay.

Whenever we were at Faro we parked on the far side of the harbour on a large cobbled car park right next to the railway line. It was a popular place for travellers and there would always be quite a few vans parked up.

If it was really busy we'd end up having to park up against the back wall but then we'd only be about ten or fifteen feet away from the line which of course made it quite noisy. As well as the trains it wasn't very far across the water to the airport and we were almost directly underneath the flight path so once we'd done what we wanted in town we tended to move on to somewhere quieter.

One of the main reasons for stopping in Faro though was to buy some wine from the warehouse. It could have been a distillery as well but we never did find out for sure as by the time we'd gone through the sampling ritual, we were in no fit state for sensible conversation.

We happened upon it purely by chance one day as we were exploring the old part of town (Cidade Velha).

Not far from the harbour is the entrance to the old city, a picturesque pillared archway with an ancient clock and bell tower high above it. Perched precariously on top of the adjoining balustrade sit several huge stork's nests, a by now familiar sight around bell towers and other tall buildings all along the Algarve.

We passed through the long stone archway and followed the narrow street which opened out onto a huge cobbled square dominated by the presence of St Mary's Cathedral. Enclosing the square on two sides is the bishop's palace, a long row of majestic white buildings outside which, as if on sentry duty stands a line of mature orange trees.

We left the splendor of the square by a narrow street of run down houses desperately in need of a coat of paint, emerging onto a much smaller square. A pavement café took up half of it whilst the other half was choked up with haphazardly parked cars which barely left enough room for traffic to pass through.

Opposite the café there was a large, plain white(ish) building with two large sliding steel doors painted green. One of the doors was partly open and as we went past the strong sweet smell of a brewery wafted out and invited us to peer into the gloom. It was huge inside and once our eyes adjusted to the darkness we could see several rows of large old barrels disappearing into the dark recesses of the warehouse.

From somewhere in the shadows a voice called out, we were being welcomed in to have a look around.

A little old man made his way over and led us over to the barrels talking away non stop the whole time. There was a price written on each barrel in chalk so it looked like we could probably buy some but it was still quite early and I for one didn't fancy trying any right there and then - the old man had other ideas though.

He picked up a small shot glass from by the first barrel; it didn't look very clean and probably hadn't been washed in years. Then he picked a dead fly out of it and filled it from the squeaky wooden tap before handing it proudly to Suzi. He waited eagerly for her response as she delicately took a sip and then offered it to me.

'No no no,' he insisted, 'it's for you, you must drink all of it Senora,' and of course she was only too happy to oblige.

It obviously met with her approval which pleased him no end. He laughed and put his arm around her and then asked me to take a picture. Suzi handed the sticky glass back to him and he re-filled it before handing it to me. I didn't want to risk offending the nice man by refusing to try it and I knew what to do - I downed it in one. Oh boy it was gorgeous, sweet and strong and it burnt its way down.

'Yes we'll have a bottle of this one, it's delicious.' I said knowing full well that not being used to strong drink like this a second one would be too much, especially this early in the day and on an empty stomach.

'What? oh no no no, you must try this one now,' he said taking the glass and moving on to the next barrel. There was a glass by this barrel too so now we had one each and so the tasting process was repeated. This barrel tasted a bit different to the first one, slightly sweeter than the first if anything and it went down easily, I was getting dizzy already.

The next one however was quite dry and not to my taste but even so I had no trouble getting it down.

The whole time we were doing the tasting he was enthusiastically explaining all about the different grapes and blends and the regions they came from. We understood quite a lot of what he was saying, well at least in the beginning we did but by this time we'd stopped listening to him really. We did try to concentrate but just kept giggling all the time. We were getting out of control.

It pleased him no end to see the fruits of his labour having their desired effect and whenever we liked a particular barrel he'd snatch the glasses off us and give us seconds.

We moved from one barrel to the next, then the next, and the next and the next until we were right down at the far end of the warehouse by which time we were completely pissed and almost in hysterics. It's a good job the old man still had his arm around Suzi most of the time otherwise she would probably have fallen over.

He was beside himself with joy but despite the fact that he hadn't touched a drop he was beginning to slur his words. He probably drinks from morning till night, or maybe it's the fumes getting to him or something, well working in there all day long is bound to have an effect isn't it.

'So which is your favourite then?' I asked Suzi.

'Dunno, can we try the first one again,' she replied pointing back to the far end.

He roared with laughter and we walked back uphill towards the light and the very first barrel we'd tried. That's funny I don't remember the floor sloping before. I really had to concentrate now to try and understand him but it was no good and I gave up trying, the man was clearly an alcoholic.

I was leaning up against the barrel for support as he filled our glasses yet again.

'Do you have a bottle for me to fill?' he slurred as we drained them once more, no wait I think it's my hearing that's slurred, how is that possible?

'Oh wait, I'll just check my pockets,' I said as I rummaged through them, 'no, no bottle sorry,' and for some reason we both found this hilariously funny.

'Not to worry I have one,' he laughed and he relinquished his hold on my hysterical wife to go and look for one.

We waited as he dug out a grubby old plastic water bottle from god knows where, tipped the old water out and then started to fill it. I did wonder for a second or two just how long that old bottle had been kicking around and how many unsavoury characters had been drinking from it. Oh what the hell who cares, just fill it up matey.

I handed him some money and he handed me some change.

I have absolutely no idea how much I gave him or how much *he* gave me. I was just happy in the knowledge that we now had a litre of the stuff to take back to Billy; mind you I reckon we'd drunk almost that much between us already.

He escorted us to the door and we staggered out into the fresh air and dazzlingly bright midday sunshine. He called across to the locals sitting at the pavement café opposite and they all roared with laughter and gave us a nice round of applause. Or was it him they were clapping for nailing some more poor innocent tourists. We both took a bow and then wended our merry way off back down the cobbled street clutching our sticky old bottle with its precious cargo.

We came to know the old man quite well after that as every time we were in Faro we'd pop in for a bottle. Despite the fact that we were regular customers he still insisted on us trying a glassful from practically every barrel. Consequently we were never sober long enough to have a proper conversation with him so we never found out if he actually made the stuff there or not.

One of the pictures I'd taken of him and Suzi together was now in pride of place at the top of his little notice board on the wall by the door.

Olhao was ok too as far as the police were concerned, there was a huge piece of rough ground right by the water and overlooking the fishing harbour. It was another favourite place for travelers and there would always be at least a dozen vans there. Even so there would always be plenty of room to park up without crowding anyone. There was also a handy water tap down by the fishing boats and a huge indoor market in the town.

Every two or three weeks we'd return to Monte Gordo to check for post, stay a few days then move on to Cabeco which is where we seemed to spend the longest. The police would patrol regularly in their jeep and drive around slowly giving everyone the once over before disappearing again. We were on waving terms with them by this time and they seemed quite happy for us to be there as long as we didn't start any more huge bonfires.

ഇ ഇ ഇ ഇ ഇ

Back at Monte Gordo we collected our post and were sitting by Billy reading through letters from home when we were rudely interrupted.

'Alright you two how's it going, where've you been then, no no don't tell me I don't want to know hah hah!'

It was Len, and oddly enough the boy's didn't object to his presence at all which was a bit of a shame – we did though.

'Aha! got some letters I see, family is it? always nice to get post when you're out here. Yeah we got a huge pile of letters ourselves yesterday, got loads of friends back home and all over the world as it goes, still haven't finished reading them all yet.'

I was glazing over already.

'Just off to the shops, then I'm off for a quick drink at Antonio's bar, you fancy coming along Tim?'

'No thanks.'

'Alright be like that then, what's the matter can't take your drink eh?' he laughed to himself, 'oh well never mind, a lot of people can't drink like me, you need to man up a bit mate if you want to compete with me.'

I was staring out to sea at this point, letter still in hand.

'When are you getting yourselves a decent van then eh? when you do, make sure you get one like ours, much better than something like this,' he said giving Billy a disapproving look.

I threw a glance at my yobbo clobberer which was leaning up against the door.

'If I've got time when I get back I'll show you around ours and you can see what a well designed van looks like. Yeah I designed and built it myself.'

'Yes you told us.'

'Not bragging or anything but it's by far the cleverest design I've seen in a van, you'll see what I mean. I can guarantee you'll want one when you see it, I'll let you copy it if you like.'

'Wow really?'

'Yeah it's got a great kitchen for the little lady as well,' he said turning to Suzi, 'you'll love it babe it's got everything you need, right I'm off, can't stop for tea or anything.'

'Oh that's a shame.'

'I'll call and pick you up on the way back and you can see what I mean about the van.'

'Great, can't wait.'

He disappeared leaving us both sitting there still clutching our unfinished letters. Then about an hour later we saw him over on the far side of the car park walking back towards his van.

'Hey where's he going, I thought he was going to come and pick me and my 'little lady' up on the way back.' I said.

'Hahah! yeah what happened to the guided tour.'

'Well I must say that's disappointing.'

'I know, I was really looking forward to seeing the kitchen too,' giggled Suzi.

'Maybe we should go over and ask for a look around.'

'Go on then,' she said.

'I'm not going on my own.'

'Why, you're not scared are you?'

'Yes.'

Later that afternoon as we were walking along the beach the wind picked up and by the time we got back to Billy it was really blowing a hoolie. The first thing we did was bring the roof down before it got damaged any further. It was still being held up by the piece of wood which Caine had reluctantly donated.

Everything was hurriedly put away inside except for our two fold up chairs and the big plastic washing bowl which were shoved underneath. In the short space of time that the side door had been open a surprising amount of sand had been blown in which was now starting to drift up against the sides of the cupboards.

I turned Billy round a bit so that he was facing directly into the wind which meant we weren't being buffeted quite so much and with some luck we wouldn't get blown over.

The rest of that day was then spent cowering inside Billy watching the sand blowing across the car park. At least it wasn't raining as well which was something but it *was* getting colder.

The wind increased as evening approached and we could see what few people there were, struggling to walk along the street, leaning into the wind, getting blown off balance or getting scooted along from behind.

Through the sandstorm we could see Gobadog making his way across the car park, presumably on his way back from the bar. The poor little man was getting blown all over the place, staggering this way and that. Either that or he was really drunk this time. He was trying desperately to stay on his feet but despite the battering he was taking he was sill laughing and talking away to himself as usual.

Some of the vans had gone by this time, probably moved on to the camp site for some shelter. The ones that were still here had all turned into the wind like us, all except for one.

It was a brand new coachbuilt camper and it was still parked side on to the wind. We watched as it rocked alarmingly from side to side. There was a light on so they were at home but why didn't they turn round, maybe they used to live on a boat and were enjoying the motion. Their posh van was getting quite a severe blasting and the sand was already drifting halfway up the wheels.

Despite the storm we were nice and snug inside with our little gas fire on. Billy was rocking gently as a very simple supper was prepared due to us not being able to stand up. Conversation was limited as well because of the noise of the wind and a sleepless night was coming up.

I had to bravely go out into the gale and stuff towels into the air vents at the back again. As soon as I opened the side door though the fire got blown out and the swirling sand came rushing in covering everything again. I got painfully sand blasted the whole time I was out there and then another helping of sand came back in with me. Before I could re-light the fire I had to turn it upside down and give it a good shake to empty all the sand out of it.

The posh camper had gone now and there were four mounds of sand left in the middle of the car park from where their wheels had been.

Just before bed the wind stopped suddenly - in an instant - as though a switch had been flicked, it was that sudden people were falling over in the street!

We breathed a huge sigh of relief and the first thing we did was put the roof back up so that we could stand up again. We all went outside and just stood there looking around; there was a complete, eerie silence about the place. It felt warm again too, looks like we were going to get some sleep after all.

Then about ten minutes later a strange thing happened - another switch was flicked and the wind was back. It was every bit as powerful as it had been except for the fact that it was now coming from completely the opposite direction - it was really weird.

We all dashed back into Billy and I quickly lowered the roof again, ok maybe we won't get much sleep then!

☺ ☺ ☺ ☺ ☺

The rough campers, those like us who chose not to go on camp sites would all have the same problem of where to empty their toilets. I usually found somewhere quiet to bury ours whilst other people would go onto a campsite for one day a week just to empty theirs. However one day on the way to Vila Real de Santo Antonio to do some shopping we discovered how one bloke got around this particular problem.

We were just leaving Monte Gordo and up ahead we could see a posh camper parked at the side of the road and the man was fiddling around with something underneath. There was traffic coming so I couldn't pass them and so they set off again just ahead of us leaving a dark brown trail on the road behind them.

He'd obviously opened the waste tap on the toilet and driven off letting it slowly empty itself along the road as they went. By the time we reached Vila Real it was empty - job done.

We did our regular grocery shopping in 'Paga Pouco', a large supermarket in a scruffy windowless building on the outskirts of town. We'd quickly learned to be very careful about what we bought from there though as some of the produce was a bit iffy to say the least.

On our first visit there we bought some lovely looking figs but later on, when Suzi bit into one she nearly choked and spat it straight out again - it was full of wriggling white maggots. For some reason she has a thing about maggots, they give her the creeps and sleepless nights so having a mouthful of them really freaked her out. It was a long time before we had figs again and even to this day she carefully cuts them open and inspects them before eating one, even if she's just picked it straight from the tree.

One day she picked up a packet of cup cakes in a clear plastic wrapper and there were small flies inside still alive and flapping about - we didn't buy the cakes.

The centre of an orange is not somewhere we expected to find a nest of maggots but unfortunately for Suzi we did, and now all fruit is carefully inspected first and *never* eaten in the dark!

When we'd finished our shopping there, we'd go and park alongside the river where it was nice and quiet and then walk the short distance to the shops.

It was a pleasant spot with palm trees here and there and pavements made up of patterned cobbles. We'd sit on the wall to have our lunch and watch the ferry going back and forth across the river to the distant whitewashed town of Ayamonte in Spain. It was a popular place for campers and there were always a few vans parked here and there.

It was also popular with the local street dogs who knew well enough where they could get some food and there would always be a few of them skulking about. They were quite friendly though and very docile, they just wanted feeding.

A woman from a Dutch camper did feed them regularly. She'd come back from town each day with a couple of loaves of bread and break them up for them to eat. All the local dogs got to know about her and they would be waiting quietly for her return. They were surprisingly well behaved and there was no fighting amongst them considering how hungry they must have been. There would always be one or two though who didn't get a look in and they were chased off by the more dominant ones.

One particular dog knew his place and didn't even bother trying to get any. He just looked on from a distance - he had his own particular technique.

He very bravely ventured up to us as we were sitting on the wall, completely ignoring the boys as they gave him the once over and sat there watching us as we ate. He was a big dog, bigger than our two but skinnier and all brown except for his muzzle which was black and he had big brown eyes and long floppy ears.

Suzi naturally gave him a piece of her sandwich which he accepted graciously, taking it very gently considering he looked like he hadn't eaten for a while. Then he got up and wandered off again.

From then on he became a regular visitor whenever we went there. He'd saunter up to us, accept one piece of bread and then pootle off again.

We watched as he wandered about, going from van to van in the hope of getting something to eat. He'd go up to each van and sit by the door hoping someone would notice him, sometimes they did and sometimes they didn't. Whenever they did he was always happy to take just one offering before strolling off again to the next van.

He became quite a celebrity amongst the campers and someone had named him Antonio, probably the Dutch dog lady. Over the coming weeks he slowly began to put on weight and his coat took on a lovely shine. He looked much healthier than he had when we first saw him and he was much happier too. There was a sparkle in his eyes and a confidence in his walk - it was good to see.

We were walking along the street into town one day when we saw one of those little three wheeler motorbikes coming along the road towards us. It was rattling along on the cobbles with its noisy little engine revving away and a pack of thirty or so dogs running alongside it barking away happily.

The driver wasn't happy though, he was shouting and shooing them away angrily much to the delight of his friends. The dogs took no notice of him at all and just carried on chasing him, loving every second of it. He decided enough was enough and if they wouldn't bugger off then he would just have to out run them.

He gunned the little engine and the bike picked up speed slowly. Far too slowly for the dogs as it turned out as they were still easily keeping up with him.

The tired old two stroke engine was screaming out in protest and it sounded like it was about to explode at any second. The whole scene had become enshrouded in a dense cloud of choking blue smoke and with plastic flapping in the windows, he was now rattling along at what was probably full speed. He was leaning forward inside his little cab in a futile attempt to make it go faster with a determined expression on his face, reddened from all the angry shouting - he was not amused.

The locals were though and they laughed and cheered him on, or maybe they were cheering the dogs on who knows. The bigger dogs were easily keeping up with him, running alongside and barking right in his face. He shouted and kicked out at them repeatedly but the dogs just laughed at him and shouted right back.

The medium sized dogs were following close behind, snapping away at the back tyres and by now the smaller ones were being outpaced and had started to fall behind. They were still in the chase though and were running full pelt along the road, barking frantically and arguing amongst themselves as they went.

Sadly and all too soon the show was over as they all disappeared down the road and around the corner. The last we saw of them through the haze of blue smoke were the smallest dogs still playing catch up.

A few days later we were following a fresh looking dark stain along the road into Vila Real. There were others which were paler and drier but this one was nice and fresh and clearly stood out. As we neared the town we came across a dog lying in the road which looked like it had been hit by a car so I stopped Billy and we got out to see if we could help it.

Our hearts sank as we got closer as the colour and build of the dog became familiar - it was Antonio.

Sadly there was nothing we could do for him as he was already dead; he was still warm though so it must have happened quite recently.

I picked him up and carried him away from the road and for the next hour or so Suzi and the boys sat there quietly watching as I dug a deep hole in the sandy ground and then laid him to rest amongst the trees.

The time had come to go back to Penny and Ron's to house and animal sit, but before we left we went to the post office to pick up some letters we were expecting. This was something which always filled us with dread - going to the post office that is, not getting the letters! There were usually two women serving but as luck would have it, it would always be the same grumpy woman who served us. She should have known us and our names off by heart by this time and we really shouldn't have needed our passports any more but we always did.

As expected, I got the obligatory sigh and slow blink when I asked her for posta restante. With an effort, she reluctantly turned around and without getting off her stool, grabbed a box and dropped it down on the counter. Aww, no hissing stool – I felt a little cheated!

'Passaporte!'

I handed her mine and she studied it carefully, like it was the first time she'd ever seen it. I then watched really closely to make sure she read my name and not my place of birth!

She looked through all the letters and picked out the one that was for me. We both saw one with Suzi's name on but that one was ignored and before we could say anything she'd swung round and returned the box to the shelf behind her. Suzi then handed *her* passport over and asked again for posta restante. Another sigh, this one accompanied by a cold stare followed by another disappointing hissless twist on the stool and the box was brought back to the counter. Her passport was examined intricately and the letter was retrieved.

We then set off along the EN125 which was the main road going all the way along the Algarve before the E1 was built and as we'd discovered the most dangerous road we'd so far driven on.

The Portuguese are normally very placid and laid back but as soon as they get behind the wheel of a car they seem to go completely crazy. We'd be pootling along quietly, minding our own business and enjoying the scenery when suddenly an oncoming car would decide to overtake, seemingly oblivious to the fact that we were coming towards them. They had no intention of backing down and just headed straight for us flashing their headlights, determined to get ahead of the car in front.

I had no choice but to swerve out of the way and luckily there was usually some room but it wasn't exactly a hard shoulder.

As was the case back then with most Portuguese roads they sloped away at the edge and then there was about a two foot wide strip of uneven cobbles running along the outside. It wasn't the best road surface to begin with and once we'd got onto the sloping part near the edge, survival was a bit of a lottery to say the least

Billy hit the cobbles and I had to fight to keep control eventually getting back onto the more level part of the road. Once we'd recovered from the initial shock of our first near miss we were both on the look out for the next one which was never very far away.

We got used to it though and swerving out of the way onto the cobbles soon became second nature, although it was particularly hairy when a lorry did it to us. It seemed like only a matter of time before our luck ran out and we'd have no room to move over or we'd hit a pothole or something.

Funnily enough, there was no horn blowing from anybody and no rude gestures or angry shouts like you'd expect in France or Spain. We could see as they shot past us that the driver would inevitably look relaxed and calm, just driving along casually as if everything was completely normal whilst we were fighting for our lives on the cobbles.

Given the standard of driving it wasn't surprising that seeing crashes on that road was quite commonplace.

We completed our perilous journey without loss of life and arrived safely at Penny and Ron's place the day before they were due to leave for the UK.

As we pulled off the road, their dogs, Jem and Maggie ran down the track to greet us, then escorted us noisily the rest of the way as we drove up to the house. Meanwhile three legged Fido waited patiently at the top, he was overjoyed to see Caine again and the two of them immediately got down to some serious playtime.

Penny and Ron were pleased to see us as well as everything was all booked and if we hadn't turned up as arranged then they wouldn't have been able to go.

I settled Billy into a lovely spot in the shade of a big tree next to the horse's paddock where there was a fine view down the track to the valley beyond. He looked happy enough parked there which was good because that was going to be his home for the next two weeks.

Penny took Suzi off to show her her horsey duties whilst Ron showed me what he wanted *me* to do. After the stables had been cleaned out the straw and muck was to be wheel barrowed around behind the back and carefully piled up in large rectangular stacks.

'Make sure you keep the sides nice and straight like this as you go up, and put all the solids in the middle, this one's finished now,' he said as he forked the last of the straw on the top.

'After a few months the heat inside will compost it nicely and this heap will be reduced to almost nothing, then it'll be ready for the garden.'

I carried on by myself as Ron went off to finish packing. The next barrow was used to start the new one and I carefully laid the straw out as he'd shown me in a large rectangle. When he came back round to see how I was doing he smiled and said.

'Good job Tim, that's exactly how I like it done, thankyou.'

He was happy and it was clearly important to him to have nice tidy stacks. When that job was done he took his strimmer and we went down the track a bit to where a crop of something was growing.

'This is Lucerne, we grow it especially for the horses, they love it and it's good for them too. All you have to do is once a day, cut a strip of about this wide all the way along like this and then take it up to the horses in the wheelbarrow, it's their daily treat.'

As we were passing the house on the way back we passed a stone wall which had fallen down.

'I keep meaning to re-build that dry stone wall but never seem to get round to it, bit of a shame really it would look really nice there with flowers growing along the top of it. Maybe I'll get round to doing it one day who knows.'

We spent the rest of that day familiarizing ourselves with everything and the next day just before they set off Ron said to me,

'One last thing before we go Tim, let me show you the clock.'

We went inside and there was a tall grandfather clock standing proudly against the white wall in the hall.

'It'll need winding up once a day,' he said giving it a loving stroke, 'I'll show you how to do it.'

He opened the front door to reveal two chains dangling down and a large pendulum swinging back and forth with a gentle ticking sound.

'Right, take this one here, and pull down like this, carefully mind you it's a priceless family heirloom, been in my family for generations so please treat her gently, just a few pulls like this once a day should be fine. Whatever you do though don't over-wind it as the rope will come off the pulley and the clock will stop which is believed to be incredibly bad luck and also a sign of impending death in the household. I've been winding it up since I was a child and it's never stopped in all that time.' he said proudly, closing the door gently and giving the glass a delicate rub with his sleeve.

This filled me with dread and I just knew I was going to over wind it, I just knew it.

As we were all standing in the hall having one last chat before they left I stepped back, treading on something which yelped, it was poor old Fido - as if he hadn't suffered enough already. I stepped back again quickly trying to get off him but of course he moved and I trod on him again. This time he screamed pitifully and I staggered backwards at a rate of knots crashing heavily into the grandfather clock which slammed back against the wall.

There was a shriek from Penny and a terrified Fido ran out as fast as his three little legs would carry him as the sound of twanging metal echoed around the hallway. The clock case on top rocked forward and it would have come crashing down on me but Ron was lightning fast, leaping forward to catch it just in time.

Together we settled it back gently into its rightful position and we all held our breaths during the loud silence that followed as Ron tenderly examined it for any damage.

A collective sigh of relief was breathed as we heard it ticking.

'Right come on Ron for pities sake,' said patienceless Penny as she turned to go, 'we've got a plane to catch, leave the bloody clock alone, it'll still be here when we get back.

I wasn't so sure about that and I suppose at that point I should have given him some words of reassurance, telling him that everything would be fine but then I would only have been lying.

With one last loving look back he reluctantly went outside to be confronted by Penny standing in the gateway, hands on hips.

'Ron!'

'Oh yes, one more thing I must show you Tim,'

'Oh bugger you then,' she cried, throwing her hands up in the air and stomping off towards the car, 'I'm bloody well going without you!'

'She can't go without me,' chortled Ron quietly, patting his jacket pocket, '*I've* got the tickets.'

I heard the car door slam shut and the engine start up as we disappeared around the back of the house. We followed a row of prickly pears and then went up a small bank to where a blue pipe came down from the field.

'This is the water supply to the house and every now and again it gets an air lock in it and the water stops. If that happens all you have to do is pull this joint apart here like this, let it cough and splutter for a minute or so until the water flows properly again and then push the pipes back together again like this, it's quite simple.'

There was a distant revving of an engine followed by a long blast on the horn, Ron looked at his watch.

'Plenty of time yet,' he said calmly as we sauntered back, 'well I think that's everything, if you do need to contact us you've got our numbers on Penny's little list.'

I was clutching Penny's 'little list' in my hand, it was actually five A4 pages long (both sides) and covered everything from each individual dog's and horses strict feeding instructions to directions to where we could find the old lady just down the road who sold bread, honey and eggs. There was no menu for the cat who lived in one of the sheds, he supplied his own food and was called 'the cat'.

Ron now had to walk halfway down the track to get to the car as Penny had been inching her way forward impatiently.

He was only halfway into the car when Penny gunned the engine and dropped the clutch, sending a shower of stones clattering up against the underside of the car as the wheels spun wildly on the gravel. Despite all the din we could still hear Penny berating poor old Ron as they raced off down the track. They were almost at the tarmac road by the time Ron was fully in the car with the door shut, just in time for Penny to slam the brakes on and skid to a dusty halt before roaring off into the distance.

☺ ☺ ☺ ☺ ☺

We settled into the routine of life on the Quinta very quickly.

We were given our very own bedroom at the back of the house and it even had an en suite bathroom. We were very excited about that and we both had long hot showers on our first day there.

It was also luxury to use a proper flush toilet for the first time in ages. One that didn't wobble and pinch our bums when we sat on it, and didn't stink or need emptying every couple of days.

Despite all this luxury neither of us felt very comfortable being in there and we both had trouble sleeping. We'd lie awake for hours feeling strangely uncomfortable but it wasn't the bed, it was something else. There was just something about the energies of the room that we weren't comfortable with. Also the bathroom felt unnaturally cold even after our showers which just added to the feeling of uneasiness about our 'quarters'.

Nelson wasn't happy in there either; he was very reluctant to come into the bedroom at all and spent the night out in the hallway, just outside the open door where he could still keep an eye on us. That decided things for us and so despite having the luxury of sleeping in a house and in a real bed, if we were going to get any sleep at all it would be best to sleep in Billy.

So from then on we lived in Billy as usual, only really going into the house to feed the dogs twice a day and to wind up the clock – and use the toilet!

We really enjoyed looking after the horses, mucking out their stables, feeding them and taking them for long walks on the lead rein so they could forage for grass and herbs here and there. I usually took the big one called Heston, he was all black apart from one white sock on a front leg, he was heavily built and towered over me. Luckily he was a gentle giant with impeccable manners and we got on quite well.

Suzi took the smaller grey one called Tizzy, a beautiful Arabian mare and we'd lead them down the track to the small paddock by the road. It was the only place that actually had some grass and then we'd stand around with them for an hour or so whilst they chomped away happily.

After a while Heston lifted his head and walked off towards the hedge taking me with him, heading straight for the large patch of bamboo.

Tizzy thought that seemed like a good idea and followed closely behind and as per Penny's instructions we only let them have five minutes on the bamboo and then moved along again. Well actually it was more like ten minutes but don't tell Penny!

We made our way slowly back along the hedge until we came to the carob tree and I let go of Heston so he could help himself whilst I climbed the tree to pick some for the dogs, he wasn't going to run off anywhere.

After their walk about we let them into their paddock above the house, there was no grass in there whatsoever just dusty soil and a single tree in the middle. There was an old bath by the gate which served as a drinking trough and a small makeshift shelter in the corner in which they stood most of the time trying to avoid the flies.

We felt so sorry for them standing in there all day long that we often took them for long walks up the track behind the house which led out across the open countryside. There wasn't very much for them to eat but they really enjoyed getting out and exploring, as did all the dogs who were having a great time of it.

It was slow progress though as we had to keep stopping every couple of minutes to let poor old Fido catch up with us. It was tiring work for him to go on such a long walk but he insisted on coming with us and he kept up really well most of the time. Eventually though it became too much for him and he just plonked himself down in the middle of the track and watched as we all disappeared out of sight.

I doubled back and peered around the corner to see him still sitting there so I went back for him. He wriggled about apologetically as I approached him, smiling in his grotesque toothy snarly looking way and waving his stumpy front leg about in the air. He looked up at me with his eyes only as his neck wouldn't allow him to lift his head very high.

'I'm so sorry Tim but I simply can't go on, I need a rest, please don't shout at me.'

Of course I didn't shout at him, instead I picked him up. He was beside himself with happiness and he licked my face frantically as I carried him back along the track to the others.

I carried him for a while and then I put him up on Heston's back who wasn't bothered in the slightest. After a couple of minutes of getting used to the motion Fido relaxed on the big broad back, enjoying the view from his new vantage point. After that whenever we all went for a walk he would actually ask to be picked up and put on Heston's back, he loved it.

Suzi's deep love of horses meant she spent a lot of her time in their company, just hanging out with them. She would muck the stables out and then I'd cart it all around the back in the wheelbarrow and fork it out carefully, making sure the sides of the stack went up nice and straight.

For something to do I got stuck into rebuilding the dry stone wall at the front of the house. I'd never done anything like that before so it was a bit of a challenge for me. It was a slow old job and the first thing I did was to take all the loose stones out and put them to one side ready for re-building. By the time I'd done that there wasn't much of the wall left so now I had a big job on my hands, still there was plenty of time to do it.

Over the next few days the wall was painstakingly re-built stone by stone back up to its original height. I then laid a bed of soil along the top for whatever plants and flowers they wanted. It looked pretty good and I was pleased with it for a first time effort.

In the end we actually stayed there for three weeks as Penny phoned up one day and asked if we could stay another week as they wanted some more time with the kids, something we were more than happy to do. As well as the extra money it felt good for us to have a base for a while instead of constantly moving on all the time.

Each day I would carefully and nervously wind the clock up and miraculously at the end of the three weeks it was still going. A good job too as the first thing Ron did when he got out of the car when he got back was to go straight to the clock to make sure it was ok. He was delighted to find it was still going and he'd probably spent the whole time worrying about it - like I had.

They'd had a great time back home with the family but were also glad to be back and to see all their animals nice and happy and well cared for. I got full marks off Ron for my muck heap stacking and they were both thrilled to bits with the new stone wall by the house. They both knew it was something that would probably never have got done.

Of course Penny realized that we'd been sleeping in Billy the whole time and when we told her why, we discovered the reason for our uneasiness.

She told us that before they'd bought the place that particular part of the house was used for slaughtering and butchering animals. Apparently people from all around the local area used to bring their animals to be killed there as well, so given his sensitive nature it was no wonder Nelson refused to go into that bedroom.

Before we left, Penny handed us a lovely big wad of cash and also made a provisional booking with us for the next time they wanted to visit family which was to be in about nine months time - we were thrilled.

As well as that, she also gave us the number of some friends of theirs who would be needing our services in a few months time - more good news.

And so we left with the reassuring prospect of some future income, joy in our hearts and enough cash in our pockets to live on for several months to come.

☺ ☺ ☺ ☺ ☺

Feeling rich after leaving Penny and Ron's we felt able to do some exploring so we turned right on the EN125, filled up with petrol at the nearest filling station and headed west towards Lagos and beyond.

On an impulse we turned off the main road in a small village and took a road which looked as though it might lead us to a beach. After going a short distance the road forked which then meant making a decision as to which one to take. Luckily for us Nelson was sharing the front seat with Suzi, something he always did whenever we took a new road.

'Right then, where are we off to now guys?' he said with his ears pricked up as he squoze his bum further onto the seat, pushing Suzi up against the door. I stopped at the junction as he shuffled and fidgeted in his seat, staring down the right hand fork, ignoring the other one completely. 'Let's go that way!' he chuntered - and so that way it was.

I would probably have gone the other way as that one was tarmac and this one was just a dirt track, but then I had to follow my navigator's instructions didn't I!

It turned out to be a very long and *very* bumpy track which was really quite tedious but at least Nelson was enjoying it. He now had his front feet up on the dashboard as we inched our way along at walking speed in first gear.

'I hope you know where you're going Nelly.'

'Don't worry Timmy just keep going mate, I've got a good feeling about this one!'

I had my doubts but we carried on anyway, trundling along slowly with the hills either side of us growing in height the further along we went. We held our breaths as we rounded each bend hoping to see the sea each time but no chance, just more of the same - the track just went on and on.

We could have turned back I suppose but then going back wasn't really an option was it so we just carried on, and on, and on......

Just as we were actually thinking about giving up we rounded yet another bend in the track when suddenly the hills moved back on one side and we emerged onto a secluded rocky cove with a small sandy beach. It was about two hundred metres or so in length with the deep blue waters of the Atlantic crashing down onto the shore in huge waves which boomed and echoed their way around the steep rocks that rose up on either side. There wasn't a soul around, not even a beach bar - nothing.

We'd officially arrived in paradise, wow thanks Nelson, good call matey - you were right!

I pulled Billy as close to the soft sand as possible, parking with the side door facing the sea. We were in awe and we just sat and studied the idyllic scene for some time before getting out. We kept looking all around, surely there must be someone around here somewhere, there were no vans that was obvious, but surely someone in a tent somewhere?

But no there really was no-one, we had the whole place to ourselves, it was magical, our own private little beach.

We stripped all our clothes off and ran down the sand and straight into the sea, joyously frolicking around in the shallows. Even Nelson ventured in and paddled a bit, we felt like castaways on a deserted island. We then spent the rest of the day lazing around on 'our beach', sunbathing, body surfing the breakers, snorkeling and exploring.

Driftwood was gathered from the waterline and as night time approached we lit a small camp fire on the sand next to Billy. Potatoes were wrapped in foil and placed on the embers to cook slowly and in the meantime we toasted some bread and enjoyed delicious juicy camp fire toast.

The downside to making camp fire toast was that we didn't have a long enough fork to hold the bread with and as a result I'd singed most of the hairs off my hands and wrists in the flames. Protecting my hand by wrapping a tea towel around it worked for about thirty seconds until it caught fire!

A long stick was tried, the theory being that the bread would toast before the stick caught fire - well it didn't and the bread fell into the fire.

I tried taping the fork to another stick as an extension. This worked well for one side of the bread but before the second side was toasted the tape melted, then it caught fire and fell into the flames taking the fork with it!

Hmmm, if only we had a coat hanger then I could make a long fork out of it but we didn't have one so I would just have to keep my eyes open for a piece of stiff wire. In the meantime the bread was propped up against the stones around the fire and eventually they became toast. Well parts of it did anyway, despite being turned there were still some uncooked white bits whilst the bits nearest the flames burned and caught fire.

Well never mind, it was still toast and we were well used to it by this time. We all munched away happily gazing out over the now flat calm sea watching the sun slowly disappear down behind the rocks.

The next time we saw it was when it rose up over the hills behind us as we strolled along the shoreline the next morning. No-one had turned up during the night and we were there all by ourselves again that day, and the next, and the next. We'd been there over a week by the time we needed to go and get some food and water and still we were the only ones there.

It was quite a wrench to leave that wonderful place even for a short time but we simply had to go shopping. Reluctantly we packed everything away and began the long slow journey back along the bumpy track towards civilization with the intention of returning as quickly as possible.

Two hours later we were back on the track again, our cupboards were full of food and our hearts were full of excitement at the thought of returning to 'Smuggler's Cove' as Suzi had named it.

We now had as much water as we could carry, collected from a delightful communal spring we'd come across at the side of the road, several kilos of olives and a huge box full of locally grown fruit and vegetables from a small shop in the nearest village.

On our way to the village we'd spotted what we thought might be some sort of shop - we were getting pretty good at Portuguese shop spotting now.

There was nothing helpful like a sign outside to say it was a shop or anything, it was just a house the same as all the others along the road. The only difference was that this one had a plastic crate outside its open door and a fly screen made of those long brightly coloured plastic strips - all the other houses had their doors closed.

We still weren't entirely convinced it was a shop but as we approached the door the glorious smell of freshly baked bread filled the air. I poked my head through the fly screen and - aha! there was a table full of large 'pao grandes' and a basket full of 'papo secos', perfect.

These loaves looked even bigger than the ones we got at Monte Gordo and we reckoned that if we bought five of them they should last us a good two or three weeks. We planned on staying down at 'Smugglers' for as long as possible this time.

A little old lady dressed all in black appeared from the back room and served us. She had a little trouble believing that we actually wanted five loaves and she made us write the number down on a piece of paper just to make sure.

The loaves were so big that each one filled one of her second hand carrier bags and took up a lot of valuable space in Billy. Still it would be worth it if it meant not having to leave Smugglers for a few weeks. Ok, the bread would be stale by then but at least we could make toast with it.

This time I was a little impatient with the track as I knew what paradise lay at the end of it and at one point I foolishly tried to go a bit faster. I attempted second gear but within about five seconds I realized what a daft idea it was and changed back down to first, resuming our snail's pace once more. Fair enough then - seems like today's lesson will be in patience!

We both held our breaths as we rounded the final bend, hardly daring to look as nightmarish images of a beach full of vans and tents filled our minds. Unbelievably though there was still nobody there and we were both smiling as I followed Billy's tyre tracks and parked him in exactly the same place as before.

Our idyllic lifestyle resumed once more and on one of our many walks across the clifftops, we came across some old wire fencing which had long since fallen down and was just lying in a tangled heap in the undergrowth.

Wire! - toasting fork!

Next time we went that way I took my wire cutters and after untangling it all, cut a good length of the stiffer wire and took it back to Billy. I plaited three lengths of the wire together and after a bit of careful twisting at the end I ended up with a nice long three pronged toasting fork. Excellent, no more singed hairs and perfectly toasted toast!

We'd been there totally on our own for about two weeks without seeing a soul until one night we were woken by the sound of an approaching engine - our hearts sank.

'Oh no is that the police?'

I peered out through the curtains and watched as whoever it was drove around for a bit looking for somewhere to park, eventually opting for a spot a respectable distance away from us.

'No it's just a camper, bloody cheek who said they could park there, this is our beach, I'll have to have words with them in the morning.'

'Outrageous! hey maybe it's Len and Shirl,' giggled Suzi, joking but not really joking.

'Oh god no don't say that, if it is we're moving, anyway I don't think this is their sort of place do you?'

'Hope not.' she replied as we snuggled down again.

When we looked out the next morning we were relieved to see it wasn't them, it was a German couple in a Mercedes van like Len's but it definitely wasn't them and we relaxed.

They were good neighbours and kept themselves to themselves, just giving us the odd friendly wave now and again.

Our food supply was running low again and we were now cutting the mould off the bread before toasting it. We were down to our last loaf but were determined to make it last as long as possible and our water supply was lasting well too. Well we weren't using any for washing clothes because we never wore any so that was helping and we still had about ten litres left which would last us about another week if we were careful.

We managed another five days before the time came for us to leave once more to go and do some shopping. It had been hard to leave the first time but now after having been there for so long it was really tough. I think our worst fear was that by leaving, the magical spell would be broken and when we got back it wouldn't be the same.

We did all our shopping in record time, re-filled with water from the spring which seemed to take ages this time and bought another five loaves of bread from the same bemused bread lady on the main road.

When we got back to 'Smugglers' a couple of hours later nothing had changed, there was still just the one German van there as before. We exchanged greetings with them as once again I followed Billy's tyre tracks back to 'our spot' and the wet patch in the sand left from where the sink drained out.

Over the next couple of weeks more vans began turning up, they seemed to be either Germans or Brits for some reason. There was still plenty of room for everybody though and it was still a beautiful place to live but we were a bit concerned that so many vans would begin to look like a commune and attract the attentions of the police.

We decided to move on before that happened and it was with heavy hearts that we waved goodbye to our beloved Smugglers cove, vowing to return in the not too distant future.

Up Sticks

Up Sticks

Up Sticks

Spring had arrived and we'd been in Portugal for almost six months, it was time to up sticks again and make our way back up to France. Neither of us were very keen to go as we both felt quite settled and had really taken to this beautiful country.

We loved its people, their language and their laid back lifestyle and were both quite sad to leave, although we did take some comfort in the knowledge that we'd hopefully be returning before too long.

We had exciting times ahead of us though as we planned on driving up through Portugal to do some exploring around the Serra da Estrela natural park, the highest mountain range in Portugal. Then after that we'd take a diagonal route across Spain to the south west corner of France to go truck hunting in the Pyrenees.

We knew of three that were for sale but we'd really set our hearts on the one like Pauls and we just hoped it would still be for sale by the time we got there. If we did buy it though we would then have two vehicles which could prove a bit tricky. Typically though, this was something else we hadn't really given very much thought to! What will we do with Billy? Oh well I'm sure we'll think of something, we'll just have to cross that particular bridge when we come to it.

Before that though we'd arranged to meet Mark on Lady Jane some time around the end of April. He would be on his way back down to the free moorings in Santa Margarida, making his way slowly down through the French canal system.

Hopefully he'd be bringing us some tea bags and Marmite!

We'd also heard there was work to be had in the Ardeche region, something to do with peaches we were told. We weren't quite sure what, but we had an address of a peach farm and a date to be there so we'd have to wait and find out what it was all about.

We could do with the work, Penny and Ron's money had lasted us well but that was all gone now and so had Jose's drug money! We had the dates of their next holiday and also those of their friends so we had to make sure we were back in Portugal in good time for them, hopefully with our new wheels.

Ok then time to pack up and hit the road again - thank you so much for your company and see you all in the next book!

♥ The End ♥

(For now!)

Rear cover photo:
Admiring the winter sunset on the steps at Cabeço.
Caine on the top step with Nelson on the lookout for the jogger man!
(Note my yobbo clobberer!)

Printed in Great Britain
by Amazon

68666016R00190